Donald Ray Richards

The German Bestseller in the 20th Century
A complete Bibliography and Analysis
1915–1940

German Studies in America

Edited by Heinrich Meyer

No. 2

Donald Ray Richards

The German Bestseller in the 20th Century
A complete Bibliography and Analysis
1915–1940

Herbert Lang

1968

The German Bestseller in the 20th Century A complete Bibliography and Analysis 1915-1940

by

Donald Ray Richards

Herbert Lang

1968

Printed by Lang Druck Ltd., Berne (Switzerland)

TABLE OF CONTENTS

Heinrich Meyer, Bestseller Research Problems IX

Introduction 1

I. Methods and Results 7
II. Reliability 37
III. Table A 50
IV. Table B 94

Appendix A 254
Bibliography 270

BESTSELLER RESEARCH PROBLEMS

By Heinrich Meyer

If authors are concerned with self-expression, as the lyric poets generally are, they are not likely to be concerned with the public. Yet only when the public is satisfied will it buy a book, spread its fame, and make it into a bestseller. What does the public want? Information, entertainment, escape from the daily drudgery? Perhaps; but what it has most widely endorsed in the past is the art of suspense, which is one of the most rational achievements an artist can attain. The public is quite capable of discovering such art, as is witnessed by the sales of authors like Agatha Christie or Erle Stanley Gardner who have long passed the two hundred million mark. Only Karl May is near this class, though his total sales are perhaps only one tenth of those of the really successful writers. Besides, they are limited largely to central Europe.

What makes a bestseller in Germany? Different from other countries, Germany distinguishes between so-called *Dichter* and mere artists, let alone *Schriftsteller.* Those *Dichter* pattern themselves after the Goethean mould and manage to imbue their works with their own personality, real or imagined, so that every piece of writing, however sloppy, gives at least the impression of being a fragment of a great confession. It may ooze with feeling and sentiment; if properly contrived and seemingly sincere, this will sell, as Ina Seidel has shown. I have analysed her ways in my *Was bleibt* (Stuttgart, 1967) and need not repeat this here. But I must add that I could not recommend her for an American translation when a publishing firm asked my opinion. For she is not an artist in the sense English writers of equal success are. She works on emotions by means of names and other evocative tricks, but such artifices break down in a foreign language: "Echter von Mespelbrun" sounds like a cough and therefore gives the impression of a funny figure, not a secretly beloved idol of all women eager for love from a mysterious, but guaranteed *echter Brunn.*

It would be interesting to discover which of the German bestsellers are in the great tradition of Dumas, Balzac, Poe, Conan Doyle and therefore capable of wide success abroad and which others are only pseudo-poets working on "souls" rather than on artistic sensibility and technical appreciation. But such questions could not even be asked, let alone answered as long as we had no reliable data about bestselling novels. The figures here and there given are incompatible and unreliable, because they lack a uniform basis of information.

Thus Dr. Richards set himself the task to investigate the whole field of recent German fiction and to determine, for a definite period, which books sold in large numbers and how the sales grew within the five-year periods that the bibliographies list. He left out some successful books like Spengler's *Decline of the West* because they were not fiction; and he left out the children's books because their editions are far too varied and would lead outside the area of comparable data. For it was not just the raw facts that Professor Richards wanted, he wanted to lay the foundation for continued research and thus had to treat a uniform material uniformly. Bestsellers, as generally understood, are or, at least until recently, were bestselling novels. He may have occasionally caught a title in his net that should have been thrown out, when a book of songs sounded to him like a novel, but this cannot have happened more than once or twice.

He discovered a great many other matters which will interest bibliographers, librarians, booksellers and students of literature, and which he assembled in his Introduction. There were considerable difficulties to overcome. What period was sufficiently uniform to yield not only interesting, but also reliable data that could be compared? It was the period after 1900, when editions gradually ceased to start with a run of 800 or 1000 and when bestsellers in the modern sense could first become possible. Here, however, all authors that had come into the public domain, like Keller or Meyer, had to be excluded. He made his choice so tactfully that I believe nobody will find anything to object to his choices. But then the main task arose, to make tables for all those authors and their books and to make them workable. The big sheets with which he had started had to be reduced to a size that fit into a typewriter. Through an ingenious system of abbreviations he overcame this difficulty. The only handicap were the two forms of listings, *Auflagen, Ausgaben* and *Thousands.* He gradually evolved a solution for the meaning of the former term as used by some publishers, but where no definite answer was available as to how many thousands constituted an *Auflage,* the progressive number of editions was adequate indication of progressive success, whatever the actual number of copies sold may have been. The ratios, as in all such statistical tables, are not affected, provided the reader distinguishes, like the author, between the number of copies or the number of editions indicated.

The most original contribution of this study, which took Professor Richards the better part of every day and half the night for more than two years, is the arrangement by years. We now can distinguish between a book that rose within the year of publication to nearly a million, like Remarque's first bestseller, and another book that climbed slowly and then more steeply, but steadily, like Thomas Mann's *Buddenbrooks.* It is here, I think, that publishers will find much to analyse and to consider. The studies issuing from Bertelsmann, from some of the professors in literary sociology, especially from Prof. Langenbucher in Munich, point the way. For them an enormous new field is now opened by the uniform treatment of all the material published, which Dr. Richards offers.

Just one example of what may be here considered: Remarque owed his quick success to the greatest promotion then known, hundreds of *Leseexemplare* having been sent to reviewers and *Sortimenter,* whereas Mann's first novel was not pushed by any promotion. But is this all? Did the success not come because the war was far behind in 1929 and had become something one thought about and wanted to know about, but yet one also disliked and did not want to see depicted as heroic and exemplary? This matter needs investigation, since Renn's book also found a ready public; so did Jünger's books and others of their ilk which glorified the soldier and again made heroic antics respectable. Did war books become a substitute for the doings of Old Shatterhand and Winetou? Why the upsurge of war books after the success of Remarque? Were others planning to cash in on the new fashion, had they all been holding their treasured work ready, had only the publishers discovered that there was a market? We do not really know. But we do know that the later books of Remarque succeeded without great promotions and that all of them were translated and became internationally successful.

It is in this area of international success that we are until now almost totally ignorant. It has often been observed that the German public may take up Wilkie Collins now, a hundred years after his books first came out, but it will not read the modern Detective Story and similar highly specialized art forms that succeed best all over the world. O. Phillipps Oppenheim, mediocre as a Detective story writer and not too prominent even as a general mystery writer, seems to be the only one who has appealed to Germans at large, yet the much richer Buchan is barely known to them. But then this raises the general question of literary and intellectual climate and of reading habits of different generations. When a country has many times the number of highschool and university students that Germany has, its reading habits and outlook on life are bound to differ, quite apart from a different attitude toward oneself and others. Most Americans would be repelled by the *Wunschkind* and its manifestly insincere "poetic" feelings, whereas most Germans seem unable to relish literary *art* that is tightly construed as a puzzle, like the Detective story. Germans seem even to enjoy being taken in by words they cannot understand, let us say, a lecture by Heidegger or Gadamer. People who have read Josefine Tey, Ngaio Marsh or Maugham simply would not bite, but walk out.

Everyone acquainted with international publishing is aware of many miscalculations. Everyone who receives Christmas Catalogues from Germany, which seem to have more translated books than German originals, will wonder. Those going over the thick catalogues of *Verlagsneue Exemplare,* no longer derogated as *Ramschlisten,* though this is what they are, must be aware of how many potential fortunes are being lost year in and year out through faulty calculations. When one reads the blurbs and ads of these books, some of which are described as major successes at home, he feels certain that someone slipped up on the facts. Many of those books were no success at home, yet the agents managed to sell them abroad, where they were translated, stocked, sold, and reviewed as if they deserved the greatest respect–but they failed; else they would not be sold at a discount. To be sure, all decisions are made by individuals and thus are not indicative of any universal principle, but it would be rare for similar German books to get translated and then to fail in America or France! But here, too, individuals make decisions, and many of them are quite wrong. For whenever a bestseller turns up, we learn that it had to make the rounds and was rejected more than once by other publishers who had first seen it. On the other hand, we also hear of great awards, advances, promotional activities on behalf of a new title, yet the book flops just the same or does not even come off the ground. Is there then no objective criterion of intrinsic quality that promises success?

I should say that only in the field of specialized art, particularly that of Detective Fiction, is it certain from the outset whether a book is good or not. But when it comes to literature reflecting a personality rather than technical achievement, success becomes almost unpredictable. I may immediately see that the man can write and therefore impels me to read on; I may even be interested in what he has to say, and enjoy additionally the manner in which he says it – this instinct for genuine movement and literary talent is inherent in most seasoned bookmen – but we cannot say whether the public will also take to him personally. Chesterton, who once was so widely read, is no longer popular; he wrote too much like Cicero, I should think; he liked his writing too well, but we are less indulgent of self-love and chattiness than we used to be. Some of us have begun only to irritate "the readers", because new generations have come up with new expectations. Yet apparently they actually read the current experimental output and the tracts of obvious philosophy through which some publishers seem to succeed; but what they get out of these books which we would not, it is hard to tell. This is a problem that can only be solved by questionnaires. But will there be honest answers when people may ponder as to what they "ought to" like? Will they admit that they prefer Bertelsmann to Suhrkamp? What kind of people still read Ganghofer and Karl May and Courths-Mahler? Which people go after Brecht, which after Frisch? Not that Frisch, obviously a commercial writer with an eye to his public, is really that much more modern than Ganghofer or Courths-Mahler, he is even cruder and artistically less skillful, yet he is more modern; thus his appeal may be only that of the mini-skirt. There is no intrinsic merit in being modern, in having the skirt sweep the ground or stop at mid-shanks or mid-thighs, but then we all read the daily paper before we take up the Odes of Horace again. Being of the day is itself a promise of success.

Another problem that the lists of Dr. Richards suggest concerns reviewing. It is wellknown that reviewers tend to foster that book which they can talk about immediately rather than one which they would first have to read carefully. A reviewer worth his salt can write on any book, read or unread, because, if he did not, he could not write a daily column. Nevertheless, there are conscientious reviewers and others. In Germany, reviewing is no longer what it used to be (and generally still is abroad); some review periodicals read like Christmas catalogues cooked up by professional cooks whose income depends on helping sell books and who therefore must use their wiles to *animieren* the reader. Compared with the reviews of the nineteen-twenties, also the tone has changed. Not as though those who write with obvious insincerity when they are paid by the publishers or editors to do so are the same people who write with obvious gusto against every book they have to read, but these two extremes seem to prevail: promotional falsehood and obnoxious hostility. It has been said that reviewers hate authors; but then they must hate themselves as much as those whom they review, for their reviews have often little to do with what a book contains. But even where reviewing is solid and therefore independent of advertisers and publishers, as in most American journals, as in most English journals, and probably elsewhere too, the reviewer is still more likely to pick an unknown book from the stack on his desk, to see what it yields, than to shout with delight: "Ah, yet another Marquand! Wonderful, again a great book by Maugham!" This is the reason why Maugham and Marquand and many other established authors used to complain about being not reviewed at all or so superciliously that it offended. Accomplished and successful writers do never get the attention that struggling unknown talent receives. It is, nevertheless, questionable whether the many review copies sent out to many newspapers bring in enough sales to make up for the cost and whether the whole method of promotional reviewing is not, at least in Germany, due for a thorough review itself. The image of Staackmann, Diederichs, Insel, Kösel, Herder, Müller, Langen etc. was solid enough to sell many books and as sound as that of the Lesering or Bertelsmann now; there was a loyal readership who always looked at the end of the book to find what else the firm had to offer, even, what else the author might have written. Reclam built up his sales by such *in-situ* advertising, as do some American pocket books now. It seems somewhat foolish to have aesthetic standards that will not permit informational advertising in the books themselves, but then there is still the dust cover that can be so used. At any rate, here is another subject crying for research and, if a publisher knows what is good for him or his stockholders, for a change of mind. Too many of the bestsellers in Richards are unknown to most of us, yet they sold. They sold without promotion, it seems; and thus we would like to know how the readers learned about them in the first place. This opens up yet another avenue of investigation: what did, let us say, *Vobach's Frauenzeitung* or the daily papers printing a reputable author (Heinrich Hauser or Hemingway in the *Frankfurter Zeitung)* have to do with the success of the books of these writers? Would Adlersfeld-Ballestrem have been equally successful if her works had only come out as books? This problem applies also to series, Spemann's, Fischer's etc., which through uniform bindings appealed to our collector's instincts. When one liked one Zobeltitz or Ossip Schubin in red cloth, one bought more of them in red cloth! Newspapers, periodicals for special groups, "Bibliotheken" and Collections and their impact on bestsellers needs as thorough an investigation as the types of books that sell to various groups, ages, sexes, publics, countries.

Dr. Richards is, though no doubt a gifted man in many ways and a descendant of one of the leading families of the Latter Day Saints, not so much interested in these commercial aspects as I am. I am thinking especially of the waste of investments on failures, of the poor reviewing in Germany, and of the high prices of small books. If saving could be brought about by new policies, prices could go down and the turn-over up! But I, too, am a scholar in literature, not only in sociology. And I would therefore point out that *Literaturwissenschaft* might also profit from Professor Richards a great deal.

This is a delicate subject, but since my colleagues are acquainted with my critical tongue and typewriter, I may as well risk saying what needs to be said. For it is incontrovertibly true. If we disregard the questionably named and indescribably vague "Literaturwissenschaft", which more often than not is neither *Wissenschaft* nor concerned with *Literatur,* but rather a means to allow a lecturer to talk about that which happens to interest him or which he thinks his audience wants him to talk about, if instead we concern ourselves with *Literaturgeschichte* alone, then a great new revision seems to be needed.

A historian ought, after all, to concern himself with the reality that was. Can he then disregard all the books that obviously were read and keep being read by millions and which are the largest number of books read at any time and reject them as trash, *Trivialliteratur,* subliterary? Even if he just calls them thrillers or "mere entertainment", he is not a true historian. Besides, it is far more difficult to write a really absorbing book than to concoct a clever experimental one; it is far more difficult to tell a good story or to invent a memorable character that stays for a while in the human brains of millions or even of thousands than to fabricate *Kunstgewerbe* in the medium of words, so clever, so original that it can have any passing meaning we want to find there. This fashion will go, for it has come; and everything that is a fashion comes and goes, but the Odyssey has remained and so has Conan Doyle. In other words, what is so wrong about suspense, about entertainment that the critics and professors should always feel impelled to ridicule it? Here is one new area of research that has hardly been tapped in German.

But even for the history itself, the facts of history should perhaps be taken more seriously. What is one to say of the usual surveys that are now offered and that speak more about Expressionism than about Hans Grimm or Ludwig Thoma, who not only were superb craftsmen, but also had and still have a wide public? I am not even adverting to the fact that Hans Grimm was one of the first to point out what we now all over the world have recognized as the major obstacle to peace and order, the lack of living space for the growing populations, I am merely pointing out that *Volk ohne Raum* was read by many more people than any ten of the so called "expressionists" who now are being groomed to become the signature of "their" time. It wasn't their time at all; one hardly paid attention to them; and if a posthumous professor, who then was perhaps not yet born, thinks that people made a great mistake which he has to remedy now, he is not a scholar, but an amateur. People then did read Grimm, not Ehrenstein and Else Lasker-Schüler. There is no need either to reconstruct the entire past in terms of Hitlerism and to reject all those who then thrived and to praise all those who emigrated. Hitler was not even important when *Volk ohne Raum* appeared. Many others lived and enjoyed a public success who cannot simply be *verdrängt* because one feels ill at ease about past politics. Strobl, Meyrinck, Ewers were by no means negligible writers; they knew how to write and even how to finish their books, when Kafka, who tried to write, generally knew only how to start. But why forget the former and play up the latter simply because he later can now be interpreted as a symbol of his race or his time, when this is actually nothing more than re-educating a past which is no longer subject to moralizing and should be studied as it was? Dr. Richards thus could suggest all kinds of new research which cannot be accomplished through thinking, interpreting, and personal moralizing, but which will need in every instance the same careful investigation that is called scholarly and that alone can tell us what reality is and was like. After all, the escape into the vague domain of emotionalism that has crept into so many of the popular disciplines no longer even satisfies the student masses it first seemed to attract. We owe Professor Richards thanks for having given so much of his time to work which opens up so many roads for years to come.

Vanderbilt University Heinrich Meyer

INTRODUCTION

Students of the Sociology of Literature have observed that it is increasingly more difficult to do justice to individual works because the rapidly rising production of printed material makes it physically impossible for any one individual to be thoroughly acquainted with all the works of any one genre of literature, let alone all that appears in print. No one can possibly read all the books published in a particular year. (There were twenty-six thousand titles published as the "deutsche Buchproduktion" of 1964. Of these, twenty-one thousand were first editions and twenty-two per cent of the total was Belletristik. Since 1951 more than two hundred and fifty thousand titles have appeared in German.[1]) Therefore, no one can ascertain the best books of any one year, much less of a decade or a half-century. Such a judgment presupposes a careful reading of all the literature - which now lies outside the realm of possibility. This very situation is the reason for the approach to literature by the establishment of sociological categories, such as reader preferences, printing and reprint statistics, the granting of rights of translation, etc., from which certain conclusions can be drawn, if the sampling rests on a sufficiently broad base. (See my bibliography and particulary the bibliography in Wolfgang

---

[1] Westermanns Monatshefte, 106. Jg., Heft 12 (Dezember, 1965), 124.

Langenbucher's Der aktuelle Unterhaltungsroman.)

There are articles and books which deal with so-called bestsellers, but the authors fail to establish by what criteria their subject is defined, nor do they choose to give the source of their data. The reason is obvious. There are no lists of books on which one can rely for exact information as to publication statistics. Why? Again the reason is clear. Some publishers show only editions (Auflagen), others list thousands, some issue new printings and start the tabulation again, still others give no data whatsoever, and for many novels and shorter works their total success is clouded by the fact that they appeared first in periodicals, reaching millions of people in this form, and may or may not have ever been successful in book-form. One or two examples will serve to illustrate my point. H. G. Rötzer writes of Walter FLEX:

> Flex wählte den Krieg zum Schauplatz seiner Selbstwerdung. Am 16. Oktober 1917 wurde er tödlich verwundet, als er andere retten wollte. Sein bekanntestes Werk ist "Der Wanderer zwischen beiden Welten", 1916 entstanden in memoriam Peter Wurche. Es kam in zwei Jahren zu 39 Auflagen mit 250 000 Exemplaren.[1]

Where does Rötzer get his information? It remains a mystery. If one refers to the publishers' index, the Deutsches Bücherverzeichnis, one finds that this book attained the one hundred and ninety-five thousandth copy in 1920. In writing about "Bestseller, die keiner mehr lesen will," Hanns Arens gives many publication figures without

---

[1]H. G. Rötzer, "Die Antwort der gefallenen Dichter," Rheinischer Merkur, Nr. 47 (20. November 1964), 15.

showing a single source and then makes the following statement:

> Und warum lesen wir heute die Romane von Bernhard Kellermann nicht mehr, zum Beispiel "Ingeborg", "Der Tunnel", "Der Tor", "Das Meer", die alles in allem von 1913 bis 1933 doch Millionenauflagen erlebten?[1]

Again if the Deutsches Bücherverzeichnis is consulted, it is evident that the total number of editions attained by these four books was nowhere near Millionenauflagen. Up to 1935 they (including Der 9. November, Ein Spaziergang in Japan and Yester und Li) totaled eight hundred and sixty-three Auflagen; by 1940 this total had risen to nine hundred and six Auflagen. Arens probably means "thousands" with the term Auflagen, but nevertheless such an hyperbole is unfounded.

Professor Heinrich Meyer, himself a contributor to the field of literary sociology ("Grundlagen der Literatursoziologie," The Age of the World, etc.), suggested that I undertake an independent tabulation of German fiction for a certain period for which bibliographical data are available and thus establish which books were printed (and probably sold) in relatively large numbers. Such a tabulation would serve as a sufficiently broad base for further evaluations, i. e. the readers' taste over a given period of time, etc. While I have personally gathered a considerable number of successful books and plan to work further with them, I could not be comprehensive in my efforts until it had been established which books had been most popular. This, then, has been attempted in the following study.

---

[1]Hanns Arens, "Bestseller, die keiner mehr lesen will," Die Welt der Literatur, Nr. 21 (24. Dezember 1964), 716.

It begins with German books published in 1899 and includes those appearing in 1940. The influence of National Socialism had already made itself felt on the world of books and some interesting disruptions of the success of certain titles occurred. A tabulation similar to this one could be undertaken for the period from 1940 to the present. To give just one example: Volk ohne Raum by Hans GRIMM climbed from four hundred and eighty thousand in 1940 to seven hundred and eight thousand in 1965 (as is found in current advertising of the Klosterhaus-Verlag). However, it would prove to be exceedingly difficult to gather adequate information for the era prior to 1899. Around the turn of this century an edition (or Auflage) was generally equivalent to one thousand copies, but one can find little substantiation for the same relationship earlier in the nineteenth century. This along with the scarcity of data for earlier times undermine the attempt to establish comparative data for periods before the very late 1800's. It was regarded as a striking innovation when the publisher of Conrad Ferdinand MEYER (Haessel in Leipzig) expanded his author's reputation by counting every thousand volumes as an edition (Auflage), thus showing an edition which actually contained five thousand copies as perhaps the seventieth to seventy-fourth editions.[1]

The results of my tabulation are at times quite startling. Some authors, who are rarely if ever mentioned in the common literary histories of today, some of whose very lives seem so obscure

---

[1] Oral communication from Professor Meyer who learned this from Professor Witkop whose works are also published by Haessel.

that it is impossible to locate their dates of birth and death (Margarete HERZBERG, Maria CZYGAN, etc.), were successful as writers - according to the publishers' index. Others were quite popular though they are rarely listed in literary histories (Arthur BRAUSEWETTER, Hans DOMINIK, Paul C. ETTIGHOFER, Max EYTH, etc.). And further, some authors who are often discussed at length as innovators of ideas and styles or protagonists of groups have left but little trace on the wider reading public of their time (Hermann BROCH, Robert MUSIL and Franz KAFKA, for example, who have received recognition primarily since the last world war). This results in the paradox wherein historians of literature mention only in passing or omit entirely books which were widely read, while discussing at length some which had but a small following. This approach is quite arbitrary, for certainly it is neither historical nor sociological in the proper sense. It dwells on the minor variations and innovations that are regarded as essential for the moment, but which will glide into oblivion when new styles are introduced. This arbitrary feature of literary history has often been remarked upon. To overcome such distorted and prejudicial treatment and to do justice to authors who actually were successful, this study has been undertaken. A later investigation will have to determine the reasons behind the success of these books, and of the larger categories into which they fall. Such an investigation lies beyond the scope of this study, and beyond the capacity of a single investigator. It is therefore hoped that the material presented here may also enable others to work further on such projects.

CHAPTER I

METHODS AND RESULTS

At the outset the prime consideration of this work on bestsellers was to establish the limits within which this study would be conducted: (1) the period of time to be covered, and (2) the number of copies or editions which would constitute a bestseller and therefore warrant a book's inclusion.

The period covered is 1915 to 1940. I decided to determine for this period the success of German prose fiction which was first published between 1899 and 1940. Books first appearing prior to 1899, even though they continued to experience great sales after 1915, were omitted for reasons mentioned below.

The exact number of copies which a book must sell in order to be classified a bestseller has never been definitely established, but for this compilation the data are arranged in two tables: (A) a listing in descending order from the highest number of copies determinable for a single book down to those attaining fifty thousand copies within the period 1915 to 1940, and (B) an alphabetical listing of authors and those of their works which reached twenty-one thousand copies or better during the same years.

<u>Christian Gottlob Kayser's vollständiges Bücherlexikon</u> was selected as the source for all data for the years up to 1910 and

its continuation, the Deutsches Bücherverzeichnis, became the main source for the years 1911 to 1940. The former will be referred to as the KBL and the latter as DBV. My original intent was to gather information concerning best-selling German books between the two great wars, 1918 to 1938. However, the DBV appears in volumes including five years (with the exceptions of 1911 to 1914 and 1915 to 1920). Therefore, the limits mentioned above were chosen. The earliest date of publication was established at 1899 to coincide with the complete volume of KBL which covers the years 1899 to 1902.

From Stein's Kulturfahrplan, Lennartz's Deutsche Dichter und Schriftsteller unserer Zeit, the 1924 and 1941-42 editions of the Koehler und Volckmar Barsortimentslagerkatalog and a few other sources mentioned in the bibliography, a preliminary list of eleven hundred and eight-one authors was assembled.

With this preliminary list in hand, more than two years were spent in searching the eighteen thousand five hundred and seventy-one double-columned pages of the DBV for 1915 to 1940; all titles were collected which had attained the twenty-first edition (Auflage) or a printing amounting to at least twenty-one thousand copies. The most recent volumes were read first, i. e. 1936/40 then 1931/35, etc. The data thus gathered were transferred to large columnar pads and then completed. This entailed extensive searching in KBL, both editions of Wilhelm Kosch's Deutsches Literatur-Lexikon, many volumes of Kürschners deutscher Literatur-Kalender, etc. in order to uncover the date of the original publication of each of the compiled works and - in an effort to add to the usefulness of the study and to make possible the adherence to the established limits - the personal dates of each author.

At this point seven hundred and eleven authors were represented and the titles of two thousand and fifty-eight books had been listed. Once more these were carefully checked and the two tables outlined above took final shape. It is noteworthy that eight hundred and sixty-four titles were sufficiently successful to be included in TABLE A, while five hundred and ninety-two authors with two thousand and forty-three of their books are found in TABLE B.

The greatest problem encountered was the determination of the number of copies of a book when the listings in the _DBV_ were in _Auflagen_ or _Ausgaben_. Since the _DBV_ is a publishers' listing, it is therefore often possible to gain an insight into this hitherto unsolved problem by analyzing these entries.

When information of this type is given in the _DBV_ - and it should be kept in mind that there is often no information as to the number of _Auflagen_ or copies printed, it generally appears in one of the following forms (although further abbreviated):

1) 205. _Tausend_ 1939

2) 90.-130. _Tausend_ 1938-40

3) 25. _Auflage_ (159.-171. _Tausend_) 1926

4) 219 000 _Gesamt-Auflage aller Ausgaben_ 1936

5) 153.-172. _Auflage_ 1938

Under 1) we see that the book in question (the _Kriegerlebnis-Tri-_

logie of Walter BLOEM) was printed in its two hundred and five thousandth copy in 1939, while 2) indicates that between the years 1938 and 1940 a certain title by Hans Friedrich BLUNCK (Die grosse Fahrt) attained its ninetieth to one hundred and thirty thousandth copies. Occasionally the entry shows both the Auflagenhöhe and the total number of thousand copies printed - including that edition. Thus in 3) the twenty-fifth Auflage in 1926 is that of Karl MAY'S Durch die Wüste. It was an edition of thirteen thousand copies and the total number of copies printed to that date was one hundred and seventy-one thousand. It is not uncommon - particulary when the Knaur Verlag has begun to publish a book previously printed by another company - to find a listing such as 4) where the total number of copies is shown with the designation Gesamt-Auflage aller Ausgaben (total number of copies in all editions). Ludwig GANGHOFER'S Der Unfried reached two hundred and nineteen thousand copies in 1936. The only difficulty in determining the number of copies in the type of entries already discussed comes in 3) if there follows in later editions of the DBV a listing solely by Auflagenhöhe. For example, if in the 1931/35 DBV Karl MAY'S Durch die Wüste were to show the "28. Auflage" or "31. Auflage", one could only estimate the number of copies by calculating the average number printed for the previous Auflagen. One must not forget that this is only an estimate. Should the popularity of the book have experienced a sudden decline, the Auflage under consideration might contain fewer copies than did the Auflagen printed at the height of the book's success. (The opposite may also be true.) When the data appear in the form illustrated in 5), the question immediately arises: "How many thousand copies did this publisher print in each edition?" It has been vaguely asserted that since the year 1480 the average size of an Auflage is one thousand copies.[1] This may be true for many publishers in the twentieth century, for instance the S. Fischer Verlag, Langen/Müller, etc. However, the list of publishers which follows shows that there are some sizable variations. Moreover, what is true for the works of one author may not apply to the works of another published by the same firm.

For the purposes of this study, however, each Auflage is considered to be one thousand copies, unless there is evidence to the contrary. Reclam Universal-Bibliothek offers one notable example of editions greater than one thousand copies:

> Die niedrigsten Auflagen bei Reclam betragen durchschnittlich 5 000 Exemplare, nur einzelne Bände des Kriegskalenders 1914-18 sind in 3 000 Stücken erschienen.[2]

For more than eighty publishing houses whose listings are often given in Auflagen, information of this type has been obtained and is presented here arranged alphabetically according to the name of the publisher. The illustrative entries from the DBV have been anglicized and simplified for clarity. It is intended that one gain

---

[1]Wolfgang Langenbucher, Der aktuelle Unterhaltungsroman (Bonn: H. Bouvier u. Co. Verlag, 1964), p. 40

[2]Annemarie Meiner, Reclam. Eine Geschichte der Universal-Bibliothek zu ihrem 75jährigen Bestehen (Leipzig: Verlag von Philipp Reclam Jun., 1942), p. 215.

an idea as to the publishing habits of these companies, but in many instances the supporting data are so thin that it would be unwise to assume an established trend. However, one thing is certain: many publishers do maintain some general limits in the size of their Auflagen, whether it be one thousand to five or ten to twenty-five thousand copies, etc.

F. P. BACHEM, G. m. b. H. (Köln): In 1875 Ferdinande Freiin von BRACKEL published Die Tochter des Kunstreiters and the listings of this work indicate that one Auflage is synonymous with one thousand copies: 43-66 thousand 1918-19, 67-77th Auflage 1921-24, 88-97th Auflage 1930, 98-102nd Auflage 1932, 103-106 thousand 1936. For this publisher there are many more such examples, but one more is sufficient to establish my point: Isabelle KAISER'S Die Friedensucherin (1908) is listed as follows: 9-11 thousand 1917 and 12-16 thousand 1919 (Bachem), 17-22nd Auflage 1921 (Cotta), 23-27th Auflage 1936 (Bachem).

FRIEDRICH BAHN (Schwerin): The 1921/25 DBV shows the 6-7th Auflagen (8 and 9 thousand) 1921 and 1923 for Die Persönlichkeit Jesu by Dietrich VORWERK. This one example is not adequate to establish a precedent, but it does show these two editions to be one thousand copies each.

C. H. BECK'SCHE VERLAGSBUCHHANDLUNG (Köln): Vom grossen Abendmahl by Walter FLEX indicates the following: 10th Auflage (20-22 thousand) 1918, 39-40th Auflage (84-87 thousand) 1920. Here the thirty-ninth and fortieth editions contain two thousand copies each, while the tenth Auflage was three thousand. In 1920 the same author's Wallensteins Antlitz in its ninth Auflage included the twenty-seven to thirty thousandth copies, four thousand in one Auflage. Considered with his Der Wanderer zwischen zwei Welten - 1-3rd Auflage (1-10 thousand) 1917 and 54-59th Auflage (176-195 thousand) 1920 - this proves that editions vary from two to three to four thousand copies each. However, August SPERL'S Die Fahrt nach der alten Urkunde shows that some editions also contained the conventional one thousand copies: 17-18th Auflage (19-20 thousand) 1917, 27-28th Auflage (30-31 thousand) 1925.

BERGSTADTVERLAG (Breslau): Nanni Gschaftlhuber by Anna Hilaria von ECKEL points quite clearly to one thousand copies per Auflage: 1-6th Auflage 1919, 16-25 thousand 1925, 22-27th Auflage 1928, 28-32nd Auflage 1931, 36-43 thousand 1936. Further Paul KELLER'S Die Heimat: 62-81st Auflage 1920, 152-161st Auflage 1924, 162-169th Auflage 1927, 200-207 thousand 1935.

LUDOLF BEUST (Leipzig): The 1921 edition of Arthur DINTER'S Die Sünde wider das Blut shows that this particular Auflage was twenty—five thousand copies: 15th Auflage (146-170 thousand). The average Auflage, however, contained approximately ten thousand three hundred copies.

ADOLF BONZ & CO. (Stuttgart): Ludwig GANGHOFER'S Almer und Jägerleut indicates that between one and two thousand copies make up each Auflage: 7th Auflage (9-10 thousand) 1915, 11 and 12 thousand 1920, 9-10th Auflage (13-15 thousand) 1921, 15th Auflage (16-17 thousand) 1923. Though his Tarantella - 17-21st Auflage (55-59 thousand) 1920 - includes one thousand copies per Auflage, the average for the preceding editions is three thousand three hundred and seventy-five. His Oberland presents quite a different picture: 7th edition (78 thousand) 1920. Previous editions average nearly thirteen thousand copies each.

BREITKOPF & HÄRTEL (Leipzig): Auflage and Tausend are used synonymously in the entry of Ein Kampf um Rom by Felix DAHN: 113-125th Auflage 1920, 152-180th Auflage 1924, 181-240 thousand 1930, 341-390 thousand 1932, 616-645 thousand 1940.

WILHELM BORNGRÄBER VERLAG (Berlin): The eighth Auflage of Der geniale Mensch by Hermann TÜRCK contained eight thousand copies (13-20 thousand 1917). The previous seven editions averaged only seventeen hundred each.

BRUNNEN-VERLAG KARL WINCKLER, G. m. b. H. (Berlin): For Elisabeth FRANKE'S Das grosse stille Leuchten we find the 12th Auflage (26-30 thousand) 1924. This edition was of five thousand copies, but the previous Auflagen averaged just slightly more than two thousand each.

BUCHHANDLUNG GUSTAV FOCK, G. m. b. H. (Leipzig): The first and second editions of Gustav Adolf ERDMANN'S S. M. S. "Emden" und sein Kommandant averaged fifteen thousand copies each, while the third *Auflage* included twenty thousand: 1-30 thousand 1915, 3rd *Auflage* (31-50 thousand) 1916. The same is shown by Gustav FALKE'S *Viel Feind, viel Ehr'*: 1-2nd *Auflage* (1-30 thousand) 1915, 3rd *Auflage* (31-50 thousand) 1916.

BRUNO CASSIRER (Berlin): Here *Auflage* seems to mean simply one thousand copies. Christian MORGENSTERN *Galgenlieder. Nebst dem "Ginggang"*: 24th *Auflage* 1916, 56-84th *Auflage* 1921-23, 94-99 and 100 thousand 1928.

J. G. COTTA'SCHE BUCHHANDLUNG NACHFOLGER (Stuttgart und Berlin): Even though almost twenty examples could be given to illustrate that one *Auflage* is usually equal to one thousand copies, the following three are enough. *Der Pojaz* by Karl Emil FRANZOS: 6-8th *Auflage* 1907, 13-17th *Auflage* 1920, 18-22 thousand 1923, 23-25 thousand 1928. Rudolf STRATZ *Der weisse Tod*: 24-25th *Auflage* 1916, 31-40th *Auflage* 1920, 40-60 thousand 1922, 61-66 thousand 1928. Hermann SUDERMANN *Litauische Geschichten*: 2-25th *Auflage* 1917, 26-60th *Auflage* 1918, 61-70 thousand 1922, 71-75 thousand 1928. However, this is not always the case, as is shown by *Lebrecht Hühnchen* by Heinrich SEIDEL: 12-14th *Auflage* (16-75 thousand) 1916-18, 112-131 thousand 1920. The first eleven *Auflagen* amounted to a total of only fifteen thousand copies but the next three editions averaged twenty thousand each.

DEUTSCHE LANDBUCHHANDLUNG, G. m. b. H. (Berlin): Though sometimes listed in thousands, the designation *Auflage* is used and does not always mean one thousand copies, as is the case with Grete Lenz, ein Berliner Mädchen by Heinrich SOHNREY: 7th Auflage 1911, 12th Auflage 1920, 13th Auflage 1925, 17th thousand 1934. His Die hinter den Bergen indicates five thousand per Auflage: 14th Auflage (35-39 thousand) 1927. Nevertheless, the previous editions averaged between two and three thousand copies. The first twenty editions of SOHNREY'S Der Bruderhof totaled twenty-nine thousand and then: 21st Auflage (30-35 thousand) 1919, 36-40 thousand 1925, editions of five thousand copies. The following entry for his Friedesinchens Lebenslauf indicates an edition of ten thousand: 46th Auflage (61-70 thousand) 1918. One more example is given to show that this variance also exists for the works of other authors. Swaantje SWANTENIUS Hermann Löns und die Swaantje: 6-105 thousand 1921-25, 19th Auflage 1927, 123-125 thousand 1936. It appears obvious that the nineteenth Auflage is more than one thousand copies.

DEUTSCHER VERLAG (Hamburg): Vom Hofe, welcher unterging by Hermann BURTE offers the only example for this firm: 2nd Auflage (11-20 thousand) 1922, 6th Auflage 1936 (Diesterweg) and 14th Auflage 1939, also published by Diesterweg. The second edition contained ten thousand copies.

DEUTSCHES DRUCK- UND VERLAGSHAUS (Berlin): The large number of examples available yields no exact number of copies per Auflage, but these do tell us that one might expect between fourteen and thirty thousand. Hedwig COURTHS-MAHLER Die Bettelprinzess: 3-5th

Auflage (21-70 thousand) 1915, 1916, 6-7th *Auflage* (71-110 thousand) 1917, 10th *Auflage* (151-180 thousand) 1919. Two works by Maria CZYGAN are cited: *Deutsche Mädel* - 1st *Auflage* (1-20 thousand) 1917, 2nd *Auflage* (21-40 thousand) 1918 - and *Sigrid* - 1st *Auflage* 1916, 2nd *Auflage* (21-40 thousand) 1917. Three novels by Margarete HERZBERG: *Die Intrigantin* - 1-3rd *Auflage* (1-70 thousand) 1919, *Baroness Kläre* - 1-5th *Auflage* (1-70 thousand) 1915-17, *Lillis Vergeltung* - 1-2nd *Auflage* (1-40 thousand) 1916-17. Elisabeth KRICKEBERG'S *Siddys Ehekontrakt*: 1-2nd *Auflage* (1-60 thousand) 1917-1919. Three stories by Hedda von SCHMID. *Die fünf Seemöwen*: 1st *Auflage* (1-30 thousand) 1918. *Ein Steppenkind*: 1-10 thousand 1915, 3rd *Auflage* (21-30 thousand) 1916. Lola STEIN'S *Der gute Kamerad*: 1st *Auflage* (1-30 thousand) 1918. Finally Anny WOTHE'S *Zauber-Runen*: 1-4th *Auflage* (1-70 thousand) 1919.

DEUTSCHE VERLAGS-ANSTALT (Stuttgart): Most evidence points to the equal relationship of one *Auflage* being one thousand copies. This is particularly clear in three of Ludwig FINCKH'S works. *Die Reise nach Tripstrill*: 31-35th *Auflage* 1920, 36-45 thousand 1922. *Der Rosendoktor*: 85-94th *Auflage* 1920, 95-136 thousand 1921-25. *Der Bodenseher*: 33-37th *Auflage* 1920, 38-45 thousand 1921-22. Auguste SUPPER'S *Der Herrensohn*: 1-6th *Auflage* 1916, 20-22nd *Auflage* 1920, 23 and 24 thousand 1924, 25th thousand 1928. The popular *Kriegsnovellen* by Detlev von LILIENCRON are another example: 213-214th *Auflage* 1924, 220-229 thousand 1928-29, 230-231 thousand 1934. Eight other titles by Clara VIEBIG besides her *Absolvo te*: 1-17th *Auflage*

1907, 20th *Auflage* 1919, 24-26th *Auflage* 1922, 27-28 thousand 1928. The novels *Die Geschichte der Anna Waser* by Frau Maria WASER, *Das Hanneken* by Johanna WOLFF and Hermine VILLINGER'S *Die Rebächle* further illustrate this point. (One should also refer to SCHUSTER & LOEFFLER.) Amid so much evidence of this type, there is one entry which clearly shows a considerable divergence: *Lori Graff* by Hans von HOFFENSTHAL - 44th *Auflage* (54-61 thousand) 1920-25 - indicates an edition of eight thousand copies. Also Heinrich MEYER'S novel *Konrad Bäumlers weiter Weg* (1938) appeared in an edition of five thousand copies.[1] This points to initial printings of more than one thousand which would necessitate later adjustments by the publisher - if the correspondence between *Auflage* and thousands of copies mentioned above were to be maintained.

EUGEN DIEDERICHS VERLAG (Jena): Entries for this firm are usually listed in thousands, but Wilhelm VERSHOFEN'S *Der Fenriswolf* shows 3rd *Auflage* (6-8 thousand) 1922. The first two editions averaged two thousand five hundred and the third *Auflage* contained three thousand copies.

MORITZ DIESTERWEG (Frankfurt a. M.): The first two editions of Adolf SCHMITTHENNER'S *Vergessene Kinder* included five thousand copies each, while the 1930 printing contained three thousand: 1st and 2nd *Auflage* (1-10 thousand) 1924-25, 20-22 thousand 1930.

---

[1] Oral communication from Professor Heinrich Meyer.

DÜRR & WEBER, G. m. b. H. (Leipzig): Deutsche Literaturgeschichte in einer Stunde by KLABUND: 1-10 thousand 1920, 2nd Auflage (20-30 thousand) 1922. Both of these editions were ten thousand copies each.

ALEXANDER DUNCKER VERLAG (Weimar): One Auflage equals here one thousand copies. Horst Wolfram GEISSLER'S Der ewige Hochreiter: 1st Auflage 1917, 12-15th Auflage 1920, 16-20 thousand 1929.

H. ENDERLEIN (Dresden): The second Auflage of the mystery novel Der Ndjaro by Otto EICKE contained fifteen thousand copies: 2nd Auflage (11-25 thousand) 1924.

ENSSLIN & LAIBLINS VERLAGSHANDLUNG (Reutlingen): There are several very successful authors missing in the tables which follow, no doubt, because this firm ceased to list any consecutive tabulations of editions or number of copies after 1925. Instead the designation neue Auflage is used. I have listed Ebba Hüsing by Willrath DREESEN under 68,000+ in TABLE A and indicated in TABLE B that there was a "new edition" in 1921, but for the neue Auflage by ENSSLIN & LAIBLIN I have found no key as to the actual number of copies it contained. From this example it is clear that some of the data given in this study are unfortunately incomplete. Nevertheless, there is one example where a single edition by this company totaled ten thousand copies: Viktor MENZEL'S Schwurbrüder: 4th Auflage (41-50 thousand) 1925.

FACKELREITER-VERLAG, G. m. b. H. (Bergedorf): Die Forschungsreise des Afrikaners L. M. ins innerste Deutschland... by Hans PAASCHE yields the figure eight thousand three hundred thirty-three copies for the fourth, fifth and sixth Auflagen: 1st Auflage 1921, 4-6th Auflage (26-50 thousand) 1923-25, 7th Auflage 1929. The first three editions also averaged the same amount.

S. FISCHER, A.-G. (Berlin): Usually each Auflage - and all but a very few of this firm's listings are in Auflagen - is equivalent to one thousand copies, though in the first two decades of this century there is some deviation. Der Weg ins Freie by Arthur SCHNITZLER, first published by S. Fischer, was continued in 1920 by the Sieben-Stäbe-Verlag without interrupting the count: 29-33rd Auflage 1918, 39-45th Auflage 1922-24, 83-86th Auflage 1928-29, 87-136 thousand of all editions 1929 (Sieben-Stäbe-Verlag). Hermann BAHR'S Die Hexe Drut: 5th Auflage 1914 (S. Fischer), 6-55 thousand 1929 (Sieben-Stäbe-Verlag). Zwei Menschen by Richard DEHMEL: 28-29 thousand of all editions 1917, 64-79 thousand of all editions 1922-25, 80-83rd Auflagen aller Ausgaben 1927. Bernhard KELLERMANN Der Tunnel: 121-145 thousand 1917, 208-238th Auflage 1922-24, 249-253rd Auflage 1928, 339-343rd Auflage 1935, 96-100 thousand of the unabridged special edition (354-358th Auflagen aller Ausgaben) 1940. Several of Thomas MANN'S works indicate this point also. Der Tod in Venedig: 44-68th Auflage 1922-25, 69-80 thousand 1930. Der kleine Herr Friedemann und andere Novellen: 81-96 thousand 1921-25, 97-107th Auflage 1927, 1930. Königliche Hoheit: 99-148th Auflagen aller Ausgaben (1-50 thousand of the unabridged special edition) 1932. Buddenbrooks:

1,086-1,165th _Auflage_ of all editions (901-980 thousand of the unabridged special edition 1932) 1931-32. It is evident that the fifth _Auflage_ of Peter ALTENBERG'S _Wie ich es sehe_ consisted of two thousand copies, but one cannot ascertain the size of editions sixteen through twenty: 4th _Auflage_ 1904, 5th _Auflage_ (6-7 thousand) 1910, 8-9 thousand 1914, 16-18th _Auflage_ 1922, 19th and 20th _Auflagen_ 1928. The sixth _Auflage_ of _Maria_ by Peter NANSEN included two thousand copies: 4-5th _Auflage_ 1899, 6th _Auflage_ (10-11 thousand) 1905, 7th _Auflage_ 1908, 18-19 thousand 1917, 28th _Auflage_ 1920, 36-38th _Auflagen_ 1928.

E. FLEISCHEL & CO. (Berlin): The indication is that one _Auflage_ equals one thousand, since the first seventeen editions of a certain book by this firm were considered seventeen thousand by the Deutsche Verlags-Anstalt which continued the publication after 1922: Clara VIEBIG _Absolvo te_: 1-17th _Auflage_ 1907 (Fleischel), 20th _Auflage_ 1919, 24-26th _Auflage_ 1922, 27-28 thousand 1928 (Deutsche Verlags-Anstalt).

PAUL FRANKE VERLAG (Berlin): From the listings of Kurt MARTENS' _Literatur-Geschichte unserer Zeit_ we see that one _Auflage_ could be one thousand and that the first eleven editions contained fewer than two thousand copies each: 11th _Auflage_ 1928, 16-25 thousand 1933.

FRANCKHSCHE VERLAGSHANDLUNG (Stuttgart): From the four examples cited here it is evident that _Auflage_ and one thousand are synonymous. Fritz STEUBEN Der fliegende Pfeil: 1-4th Auflage 1930, 5-15th Auflage 1931-35, 16th Auflage 1935, 17-41 thousand 1936-39, 42-46 thousand 1940. His Der rote Sturm: 1-11th Auflage 1931-35, 12th Auflage 1935, 13-35 thousand 1936-40, 36-37 thousand 1940. Tecumseh, der Berglöwe: 1-8th Auflage 1932-35, 9th Auflage 1935, 10-24 thousand 1936-40, 25-29 thousand 1940. Erhart WITTEK Durchbruch anno achtzehn: 1-15th Auflage 1933-35, 16th Auflage 1935, 17-44th Auflage 1936-40, 45-49 thousand 1940.

FURCHE-VERLAG, G. m. b. H. (Berlin): Of the following novels by Elisabeth van RANDENBORGH, the first cited here clearly indicates that one Auflage is equal to one thousand copies, but the second clouds this view and the third destroys it. Neu ward mein Tagewerk: 1-9th Auflage 1933-35, 10th Auflage 1935, 11-30 thousand 1936, 31-35 thousand 1937. Die harte Herrlichkeit: 1-4th Auflage 1935, 5th Auflage 1935, 7th Auflage 1936, 16-20 thousand 1936, 30-32 thousand 1940. Amries Vermächtnis: 1-4th Auflage 1935, "6. Aufl.; 11.-20. Tsd. 1936-37", 21-24 thousand 1940.

WILHELM GOLDMANN VERLAG (Leipzig): One Auflage is the same as one thousand copies in the entry of Reinhold EICHACKER'S Die Fahrt ins Nichts: 1-10 thousand 1924, 11-13th Auflage 1929.

GREINER & PFEIFFER (Stuttgart): Even though the ninth edition includes ten thousand copies, the previous eight average only two thousand three hundred and seventy-five each. Karl SCHWERIN Wilde Rosen und Eichenbrüche: 9th Auflage (20-29 thousand) 1920.

FR. WILHELM GRUNOW (Leipzig): It would seem that each *Auflage* amounted to slightly more than two thousand copies. Fritz ANDERS (Max Allihn) *Skizzen aus dem Volksleben*: 4th *Auflage* (7-9 thousand) 1907, 6th *Auflage* (12-13 thousand) 1911.

GRÜTLI-BUCHHANDLUNG DES MONTANA-VERLAGS, A.-G. (Zürich): The sixth *Auflage* of MUNDUS' *Die Sonnenstadt...* contains ten thousand copies, but the previous five editions were only six thousand on the average: 3-4th *Auflage* 1923, 6th *Auflage* (31-40 thousand) 1923.

D. GUNDERT VERLAG (Stuttgart): While most of the more recent data are in thousands, earlier there are some such as the 4th *Auflage* (13-16 thousand) 1915 for Agnes SAPPER'S *Das kleine Dummerle und andere Erzählungen*, and for *Warme Herzen* by Anna SCHIEBER: 3rd *Auflage* (9-13 thousand) 1919, 14-25 thousand 1925, 1928. These printings thus show editions of four to five thousand copies.

GUIDO HACKEBEIL, A.-G. (Berlin): The first and second editions of Hanna FORSTER'S *Die Privatsekretärin* amounted to twenty-five thousand copies each: 1st and 2nd *Auflagen* (1-50 thousand) 1921, 1924.

ALFRED HAHNS VERLAG (Leipzig): From Fritz KOCH-GOTHA'S *Die Häschen-Schule* one gains an example of four thousand copies in an edition: 1-15th *Auflage* (1-60 thousand) 1924-25, 16-27th *Auflage*

1926-28, 51-55th *Auflage* 1935, 63-66th *Auflage* 1940. If this book had continued to be published at the same rate as the first fifteen editions then the sixty-sixth *Auflage* would have included the two hundred and sixty-four thousandth copy.

ERICH HECHT (München): The twenty-fifth *Auflage* of *Die Herzensflickerin* by Hans SCHROTT-FIECHTL would indicate that each edition included four thousand copies. But if the entry for the 1919 printing merely covered one *Auflage*, one would have an edition of five thousand: 21-25 thousand 1919, 25th *Auflage* (100 thousand) 1924.

HANS HEDWIGS NACHFOLGER, CURT RONNIGER (Leipzig): The fourth Auflage of the anonymously appearing *Vom Dämon der Unzucht gepackt* contained ten thousand copies: 4th *Auflage* (31-40 thousand) 1920.

CARL HENSCHEL VERLAG (Berlin): The following *Kriminal-Romane* indicate that each *Auflage* is equal to one thousand copies. Margarethe KOSSAK *Die Erbtante*: 15-30th *Auflage* 1919, 42-46 thousand 1925. Gabriele von SCHLIPPENBACH *Subotins Erbe*: 16-30th *Auflage* 1919, 42-46 thousand 1925. Dietrich THEDEN *Menschenhasser*: 16-30th *Auflage* 1919, 42-46 thousand 1925. Theo von BLANKENSEE *Gelöste Rätsel*: 16-30th *Auflage* 1919, 42-46 thousand 1925.

HERDER & CO. VERLAGSHANDLUNG, G. m. b. H. (Freiburg i. Br.): It is evident that Herder & Co. published editions varying from approximately fifteen hundred to two thousand five hundred copies.

Peter DÖRFLER _Als Mutter noch lebte_: 6-11th _Auflage_ (11-20 thousand) 1917-18, 15-20th _Auflage_ (26-36 thousand) 1920, 21-25th _Auflage_ (37-46 thousand) 1922, 47-69 thousand 1930, 83-86 thousand 1940. These editions contained sixteen hundred and sixty-six to two thousand copies. Bernhard ARENS _Der Sohn des Mufti_: 6-7th _Auflage_ (13-16 thousand) 1920, 8-10th _Auflage_ (17-22 thousand) 1923. Here each is two thousand copies. Alfons GEYSER _Sidya, der treue Sohn_: 11-12th _Auflage_ (22-26 thousand) 1920. Twenty-five hundred copies were in this edition. The works of Anton HUONDER, Karl KÄLIN and Joseph SPILLMANN offer numerous examples of editions of two thousand and twenty-five hundred copies. Note that the size of editions varies even for the same book.

HINSTORFFSCHE VERLAGSBUCHHANDLUNG (Wismar i. M.): Here the number of copies per _Auflage_ varies from two to five thousand, as is shown by the following two novels by Nathanael JÜNGER, _J. C. Rathmann und Sohn_: 3rd _Auflage_ (11-13 thousand) 1918, 5th _Auflage_ (19-23 thousand) 1922, 24-26 thousand 1937, and _Hof Bokels Ende_: 5th _Auflage_ (12-13 thousand) 1918, 7th _Auflage_ (19-23 thousand) 1921.

OTTO JANKE (Leipzig): Hans WERDER'S _Tiefer als der Tag gedacht_ illustrates that each _Auflage_ might equal one thousand, even though this example is far from conclusive: 31-35 thousand 1921, 50th _Auflage_ 1925.

VERLAGSANSTALT HERMANN KLEMM (Berlin-Grunewald): The single entry of this type shows that here, at least, the edition was of six thousand copies. Wilhelm RAABE Der Hungerpastor: 46th Auflage (91-96 thousand) 1916.

ALEXANDER KÖHLER (Dresden): While the average number of copies per Auflage seems to be five thousand, the listing for 1921/25 figures to be fifteen thousand copies. Hermann Martin POPERT Helmut Harringa: 34th Auflage (166-170 thousand) 1917, 37-38th Auflage (181-190 thousand) 1918, 45-48th Auflage (251-310 thousand) 1921-25, 49th Auflage 1930.

J. KÖSEL & F. PUSTET (Kempten): From Peter DÖRFLER'S Der Weltkrieg im schwäbischen Himmelreich we find the first six editions being slightly more than two thousand copies, while the following entry - the fourteenth Auflage - points to the usual one Auflage being one thousand. For Die Fugger und ihre Zeit by Franz von SEEBURG the ninth edition was five thousand copies: 9th Auflage (31-35 thousand) 1927, 36-40 thousand 1933.

G. KOEZLE (Chemnitz): The term Auflage seems to mean one thousand copies. Käthe PAPKE Wettergasse 18: 1-3rd Auflage 1918-19, 5-6th Auflage 1920, 13-14th Auflage 1927, 1928, 15th Auflage 1931, 19-22 thousand 1937.

CARL KRABBE VERLAG (Stuttgart): Even though two editions were labeled the seventh, the amount of five thousand copies per Auflage is consistent. Ernst von WOLZOGEN Die Gloriahose: 6th Auflage (51-55 thousand) 1916, 7th Auflage (56-60 thousand) 1919, 7th Auflage (61-65 thousand) 1922, 66-70 thousand 1932.

LANGEN-MÜLLER (München): This company usually lists the number of copies in thousands. Where this is not the case, each Auflage seems to represent one thousand as is shown by Emil STRAUSS' Freund Hein: 32-36th Auflage 1935, 37-41 thousand 1936, and Die dreizehn Bücher der deutschen Seele by Wilhelm SCHÄFER: 33-37 thousand 1929, 43-82nd Auflage 1934-35, 83-90 thousand 1935.

LANGEWIESCHE-BRANDT (Ebenhausen bei München): The first example cited below indicates editions of eighteen thousand three hundred and thirty-three copies each. The second example gives us no exact data, but it could be interpreted to mean that the three hundred and twenty-six thousandth copy was the last of the thirty-ninth Auflage and therefore the preceding editions averaged approximately eight and one third thousand copies each: Wilhelm LANGEWIESCHE Jugend und Heimat: 1-3rd Auflagen (1-55 thousand) 1918 and Will VESPER Die Ernte der deutschen Lyrik: 310-326 thousand 1936-39, 40th Auflage 1940.

PAUL LIST VERLAG (Leipzig): Again one must assume that the count of editions is carried on continuously by several companies. If so, the following entry indicates that one Auflage equals one thousand. Carl HAUPTMANN Einhart der Lächler: 30-35 thousand 1922 (Kurt Wolff), 36-38 thousand 1928 (Horen Verlag), 100th Auflage der Gesamt-Auflage 1933 (List).

R. LÖWIT-VERLAG (Leipzig): The eleventh edition of Hugo BETTAUER'S Die Stadt ohne Juden was an edition of five thousand:

11th Auflage (51-55 thousand) 1924.

MEIEN-VERLAG (Oberhof): The size of each edition varies considerably here. For two novels by Gertrud PRELLWITZ this variation lies between five and ten thousand copies. Drude: 3rd Auflage (10-20 thousand) 1921. Vorfrühling: 5th Auflage (41-45 thousand) 1924.

E. S. MITTLER & SOHN (Berlin): The editions of this firm also exhibit various sizes. The fifth and sixth editions of In Stahlgewittern by Ernst JÜNGER totaled six thousand together: 5th and 6th Auflagen (13-18 thousand) 1924, and for his Das Wäldchen 125 each edition contained only one thousand copies: 2-5th Auflage (13-16 thousand) 1926-30.

MORAWE & SCHEFFELT VERLAG (Berlin): There were eight thousand copies in the twenty-fifth edition of Liesbet DILL'S Lo's Ehe: 25th Auflage (13-20 thousand) 1918.

EMIL MÜLLER (Barmen): From the works of Käthe DORN we see that each Auflage probably contained one thousand copies. Das weisse Kleid: 1-4th Auflage 1910, 7-24th Auflage 1911-12, 100th Auflage 1920, 148 thousand 1925. Leuchten müssen wir is listed in thousands only, while Die schönsten Hände is given only in Auflagen.

GEORG MÜLLER VERLAG, A.-G. (München): Auflage and thousand appear to be synonymous. Hans Heinz EWERS Die Besessenen: 3rd Auflage 1909, 8th Auflage 1912, 29th Auflage 1918, 35-39 thousand 1922,

40-44 thousand 1925.

NORDLAND VERLAG (Magdeburg): It is impossible to give exact figures for this firm, but in the listing below editions one through nine each averaged more than eight thousand and three hundred copies: Wulf SÖRENSEN Die Stimme der Ahnen: 1-18 thousand 1933-34, 24-34 thousand 1935, 61-75 thousand 1936, 10th Auflage 1939.

GEBRÜDER PAETEL (Berlin-Steglitz): There appears to be one thousand copies in each Auflage, but again several publishers are involved. Wilhelm JENSEN'S Karin von Schwedin: 32nd Auflage 1916, Jubiläums-Ausgabe 50th edition 1921, 49th and 53-57th Auflagen 1925 (all published by Gebrüder Paetel), 58-62 thousand 1928 and 63-92 thousand 1935 (Koehler & Amelang), 93-132 thousand 1936-39 and 133-158 thousand 1940 (Hase & Koehler). Briefe, die ihn nicht erreichten by Elisabeth von HEYKING offers an interesting evidence: 96th Auflage 1920, 101st and 102nd Auflagen in 1925. Wilhelm Kosch[1] gives the figure ninety-eight thousand in 1921 which substantiates the above conclusion - if one can depend on his data.[2]

PHAIDON VERLAG, DR. HOROVITZ (Wien): In Borgia by KLABUND each Auflage contained one thousand copies: 1-40th Auflage 1928-29, 46-95 thousand 1931.

---

[1]Wilhelm Kosch, Deutsches Literatur-Lexikon (Halle/Saale: Max Niemeyer Verlag, 1928), I, 920.

[2]Dr. Gerhard Lüdtke (ed.), Kürschners deutscher Literatur-Kalender auf das Jahr 1925 (Berlin: Walter de Gruyter & Co., 1925), 342.

Here the 100th Auflage is cited but no date is given.

QUELLE & MEYER VERLAGSBUCHHANDLUNG (Leipzig): Since in this case we can only draw our conclusions from entries where both the Auflagenhöhe and the number of thousand copies are given, it follows that slightly more than three thousand six hundred to five thousand copies were printed per edition. August HINRICHS Die Hartjes: 1-2nd Auflage (1-10 thousand) 1924-25, 11-14 thousand 1928, 15-19 thousand 1935. Gustav SCHRÖER Die Flucht aus dem Alltag: 1-3rd Auflage (1-11 thousand) 1924-25, 12-14 thousand 1928, 15-30 thousand 1930, 31-40 thousand 1932.

QUICKBORN-VERLAG (Hamburg): In the one example here, each Auflage equals eleven thousand copies: Paul WRIEDE Hamburger Volkshumor in Redensarten: 1-5th Auflage (1-55 thousand) 1924-25.

PHILIPP RECLAM JUN. (Leipzig): It has already been shown that the editions of the Universal-Bibliothek contained five thousand copies (see page 11), but for Reclams Moderne Romane it seems that each Auflage included only one thousand. Euphemia von ADLERSFELD-BALLESTREM Pension Malepartus: 25-27th Auflage 1926-29, 30-32nd Auflage 1931-35, 33rd Auflage 1935, 34th Auflage 1936, 35-40 thousand 1936. Heinrich HAUSER Brackwasser: 1-14th Auflage 1928-30, 15th Auflage 1931, 17-21 thousand of all editions 1935.

DIETRICH REIMER, A.-G. (Berlin): Here each Auflage is one thousand copies. Paul EIPPER Menschkinder: 40th Auflage 1929, 44-53rd Auflage (i. e. 1-10 thousand of the Neuausgabe) 1935.

ERICH REISS VERLAG (Berlin): Here one Auflage also equals one thousand. Fritz von UNRUH Der Opfergang: 2-10th Auflage 1919, 11-20 thousand 1925.

CARL REISSNER (Dresden): There would seem to be one thousand copies in each edition. Karl TROTSCHE (see Karl SCHWERIN) Söhne der Scholle: 13-15th thousand 1918, 22nd Auflage 1921, 26-36th Auflage 1933.

EUGEN SALZER (Heilbronn): Auflage indicates thousand in this example. William WOLFENBERGER Unseres Herrgotts Rebberg: 2nd Auflage 1916, 3-5 thousand 1920.

CARL SCHÜNEMANN VERLAG (Bremen): The information given for Georg DROSTE'S Ottjen Alldag un sien Kaperstreiche is illustrative of several of the difficulties encountered in interpreting the type of data gathered for this study: 8th Auflage (13-18 thousand) 1920, 13-23 thousand 1921-24, 24-26 thousand 1926, 1-5 thousand of the new printing 1937. Why do the listings for 1920 and 1921-24 both cover the thirteen to eighteen thousandth copies? As I see it, there are two possible explanations: (1) the printing which began in 1920 was continued to the twenty-three thousandth copy in 1924 and the entire printing was considered one Auflage, and thus the repetition of data in the later entry, or (2) there was a Neuausgabe between 1920 and 1924 which had attained the twelve thousand mark and which was not reported (or listed) in the DBV. The fact that all editions were not reported to the publishers of the DBV is evident from the gaps which exist in the listings given from one time period to the next (see CHAPTER II). In the above example one should notice that for the new printing in 1937 a new count of total copies was begun.

SCHUSTER & LOEFFLER (Berlin): Once again the continuity of the count of a book published consecutively by several publishers is important, since Waldemar BONSELS' Himmelsvolk was published from 1923 by the Deutsche Verlags-Anstalt: 295th Auflage 1921, 370-400th Auflage 1923, 421-425 thousand 1931, 441-445 thousand 1940. The lack of data between two hundred and ninety-five thousand and three hundred and seventy thousand is indeed large enough to allow room for doubt. However, the rapid increase in the popularity of this book would tend to clarify this point and justify the conclusion that each Auflage means just one thousand copies.

DR. SELLE-EYSLER, A.-G. (Berlin): There exists a rather large variation in the size of editions here. Each Auflage equals one thousand copies for RODA RODA'S Der Schnaps, der Rauchtabak und die verfluchte Liebe: 30th Auflage 1930, 35-37th Auflage 1924, 38-47 thousand 1938 (P. Franke Verlag). For the following two works by Heinrich ZILLE each edition varies between seventy-five hundred and ten thousand copies: Kinder der Strasse: 43-48 thousand 1918, 11-14th Auflage (55-84 thousand) 1920-25, 14th vermehrte Auflage (91-99 thousand) 1925. Mein Milljöh: 33-38 thousand 1918, 7-10th Auflage (45-74 thousand) 1920-25, 11th Auflage (81-90 thousand) 1925.

B. SIEGMUND & CO. (Berlin): The third edition of Artur

BREHMER'S *Die kühne Fahrt des "Deutschland"* contained ten thousand copies, the first and second *Auflagen* being equally as large: 3rd *Auflage* (21-30 thousand) 1917.

JOSEF SINGER VERLAG, A.-G. (Berlin): The first nine editions of *Die Verführten* by Hans HYAN averaged two thousand copies each: 9th *Auflage* 1919, 19-28 thousand 1920. One is not in a position to say whether the ten thousand copies published (or listed) in 1920 comprised one or five editions.

J. G. SPEIDEL'SCHE VERLAGSBUCHHANDLUNG NACHFOLGER (Wien & Leipzig): The terms *Auflage* and thousand are used synonymously. Mirko JELUSICH *Der Soldat*: 1-30 thousand 1939, 31-40th *Auflage* 1940.

GERHARD STALLING, A.-G. (Oldenburg i. O.): Gustav SCHALK'S *Nordgermanische Götter- und Heldensagen* indicates that each *Auflage* varies between five and ten thousand copies: 7th *Auflage* (31-35 thousand) 1925, 8th *Auflage* (36-45 thousand) 1930.

PAUL STEEGEMANN (Berlin): My example here, the thirty-ninth edition of *Die Dinte wider das Blut* by Artur SÜNDER, is an edition of fifty-nine thousand copies: 39th *Auflage* (640-693 thousand) 1921-22.

UNION DEUTSCHE VERLAGSGESELLSCHAFT (Stuttgart): Each edition appears to contain one thousand copies. Franz TRELLER *Der Sohn des Gaucho*: 38-40th *Auflage* 1928, 42nd *Auflage* 1931, 44 thousand 1936, 48-51 thousand of all editions 1939. This is also clearly evident in his Der Letzte von "Admiral": 32-37th Auflage 1921-23, 42-45th Auflagen 1927, 47 thousand 1936, new printing 52-55 thousand of all editions 1939. Max FELDE Der Arrapahu: 23-26th Auflage 1921-25, 28th Auflage 1927, 30-34 thousand 1939. Jakob SCHAFFNER Der Dechant von Gottesbüren: 1-10 thousand 1917 (S. Fischer), 22nd Auflage 1925 (Union), 25 thousand 1933 (Deutsche Verlags-Anstalt). Maximilian KERN Selbst der Mann: 12-14 thousand 1913, 15th Auflage 1916, 29th Auflage 1920, 38th Auflage 1922, 48th Auflage 1926, 53rd Auflage 1931.

VERITAS VERLAG (Bonn): Each edition is one thousand copies or slightly fewer. Hans ESCHELBACH Ihm nach: 1-3rd Auflage 1911-14, 5th Auflage 1915, 15th Auflage 1920, 14-20 thousand 1930, and Sonnensehnsucht: 10th Auflage 1918, 22-24 thousand 1936.

VERLAG DER SCHULBRÜDER (Kirnach-Villingen): Here are Auflagen ranging from ten thousand to more than nineteen thousand copies each, as is seen in these two works by Kassian KARG: Das kleine Geheimnis - 1-6th Auflage (1-115 thousand) 1924 - Einführung ins innerliche Leben - 1-5th Auflage (1-50 thousand) 1922-25.

VERLAG ROTE HILFE (Berlin): Erich MÜHSAM'S Gerechtigkeit für Max Hoelz! included twenty thousand copies in the third edition: 3rd Auflage (26-45 thousand) 1926.

VERLAGSBUCHHANDLUNG "STYRIA" (Graz): The fourth edition of Peter ROSEGGER'S Steirische Geschichten contained five thousand copies, but the previous three editions averaged six thousand six hundred and sixty-six copies each: 4th Auflage (21-25 thousand) 1921. The third edition of Arthur ACHLEITNER'S Auf einsamer Höh! was five thousand, while its fourth edition contained eleven thousand copies - or perhaps fifteen thousand: 3rd Auflage (8-12 thousand) 1905, (13-23 thousand) 1905, 4th Auflage (18-27 thousand) 1905.

GUSTAV WEISE VERLAG, G. m. b. H. (Stuttgart): One thousand copies equals one Auflage. Franz TRELLER Das Kind der Prärie: 2nd Auflage 1913, 10-20 thousand 1929, 30 thousand 1932. Since there are no listings between those given above, it might be concluded that the first ten thousand copies were printed in the first and second editions.

GEORG WESTERMANN (Braunschweig): Here the first two editions of Heinrich SCHARRELMANN'S Berni im Seebade contained ten thousand copies: 1-10 thousand 1918, 11-20 thousand 1921, 3rd Auflage 1922, 43-52 thousand 1930.

H. A. WIECHMANN (München): Although the data are limited and far from adequate, each Auflage seems to be one thousand copies. Max JUNGNICKEL Ins Blaue hinein: 1st Auflage 1917, 11th Auflage 1918, 21-25 thousand 1932.

KURT WOLFF VERLAG, A.-G. (München): Each Auflage appears to indicate one thousand. Arnold ZWEIG Die Novellen um Claudia: 12-18 thousand 1917 and 64-73rd Auflagen 1922 (K. Wolff), 85-110 thousand 1930 (G. Kiepenheuer).

JULIUS ZWISSLER VERLAG (Wolfenbüttel): This firm seems to

follow the conventional pattern of one thousand copies per *Auflage*. Thusnelda von SALDERN *Das Margaretenbuch*: 18-20th *Auflagen* 1900-03, 23rd *Auflage* 1907, 36th *Auflage* 1919, 41-45 thousand (G. Kallmeyer), 45-50 thousand 1938 and 51-54 thousand 1934 (F. Bahn).

CHAPTER II

RELIABILITY

In a presentation of this type, where a large quantity of data is rendered, it is essential to discuss the dependability of the sources. The reliability of the data itself, of the dates used and of the completeness of the whole must be established.

From the material presented in the preceding chapter, it is clear that publication data were not always reported by the publishers themselves to the editors of the DBV. As another example we find that Rosa BARTH'S Was Peterli als Bergführer erlebte simply shows no listing in the DBV for the years 1931/35: 1-12 thousand 1927, 13-18 thousand 1930, 30-35 thousand 1936. Obviously eleven thousand copies were printed between the listings of the 1926/30 and the 1936/40 DBV. Hence one must assume that no information was available to the publishers of the DBV for the period 1930 to 1936.

The information which I have compiled here is only as accurate as the publisher intended it to be. If he were paying royalties on editions of five thousand copies and were publishing six thousand in each, the figures in the DBV would of course indicate the former, and there would be no way to determine the actual number of copies printed. In at least one instance the publisher was requested to withhold information concerning the number of copies which had been printed. "Auf Wunsch der Verfasserin [Hedwig COURTHS-MAHLER] verweigert der Verlag die Bekanntgabe der Auflagenhöhen."[1] Nevertheless, this compilation of data is the most complete and comprehensive of its kind ever to be assembled from one definite source such as the Deutsches Bücherverzeichnis.

In TABLE A and TABLE B one will encounter the abbreviation for circa (c.) which means "approximately" and which implies that the given figure is the result of some calculation. The editions of the same work published by various publishing houses were merely added together in order to obtain an approximation of the total number of copies printed, or Auflagen of known quantity were used to project the size of later Auflagen which are thus based on the average size of preceding editions.

There are other sources from which one might obtain the type of information collected for this paper. Several publishers (such as G. Grote, E. Diederichs, etc.) place advertisements at the end of their books and give there the current number of editions or copies printed of books published by them, while some give this information on the title page - at least for the book concerned. Some periodicals (such as Die neue Rundschau) carry advertisements which often show similar data. Kürschners deutscher Literatur-Kalender often gives publication figures, though one can never be sure of the year for which this is intended. The 1928 edition of Wilhelm Kosch's Deutsches Literatur-Lexikon also lists data which seem to originate with Kürschner. For more recent authors and their works

---

[1] Kosch, 1928, Spalte 233.

one might consult Franz Lennartz' Deutsche Dichter und Schriftsteller unserer Zeit, but again we have no information as to his source material. Of these possible sources, only the first - the actual listings published by the publisher himself either in books from his own press or in periodicals as advertisement - was considered reliable enough to be cited in this study, in which case these were used to verify the data which had been originally obtained in the DBV. For instance, I obtained a copy of Richard SKOWRONNEK'S Morgenrot which had been published in 1916 by Verlag Ullstein & Co. The title page shows "19.-25. Tausend" but no such information appears in the DBV (which lists "11.-18. Tsd. 1916"). It is true that Kürschner shows data for books not listed in my tables and for years when the DBV gives no information, but this was never used (with the exception of BLOEM, as is mentioned below) since one can never be sure of his sources. As an example let me refer to Richard SKOWRONNEK'S Die schwere Not for which the only figure given in the DBV is the date 1916. In the 1930 volume of Kürschner (Spalte 1184) we find the indication that five hundred thousand copies had been reached in 1918. His Morgenrot (mentioned above) is said to have attained one hundred thousand in 1918 (Spalten 1184-1185). Even if these figures derive from the author himself, we could only depend on their accuracy if the author had taken them from his publisher's accounts. Certainly an author who had published many titles and experienced considerable success could not be expected to remember the exact number of copies attained by each of his works or even the years in which they first appeared. In TABLE A there are only four instances where material of this type was used. An advertising flier printed by S. Fischer Verlag in October 1936 to announce the publication of Thomas MANN'S Joseph in Ägypten provides the figures for his Buddenbrooks and Der Zauberberg. The figures for his other works agreed with the last listings in the DBV (and it should be noted that Thomas MANN is conspicuously missing from the 1936/40 DBV). Wilhelm LANGEWIESCHE is the source of the other two exceptions, for he reports in Der deutsche Buchhandel der Gegenwart in Selbstdarstellungen the information which I have cited for his Jugend und Heimat and Wolfs. Geschichten um ein Bürgerhaus, 1. und 2. Buch.[1] The same applies for TABLE B concerning Thomas MANN and Wilhelm LANGEWIESCHE, and here several figures were taken from Kürschner for the novels of Walter BLOEM, but these data for BLOEM were not included in TABLE A for reasons mentioned above.

All authors who died before 1900 as well as those whose books all appeared before that date were eliminated from this study. Even though TABLE B includes all the works of an author - if that author continued to publish successfully after 1900 - TABLE A contains only those works which appeared in 1899 and later. Thus it goes without saying that several dates assume significance, namely the date of the first publication of a book and the personal dates of the authors, i. e. date of birth and death.

The prime source for the date of the first publication is of course the DBV. Almost all these dates for books appearing between

---

[1]Dr. Gerhard Menz (ed.), Der deutsche Buchhandel der Gegenwart in Selbstdarstellungen (Leipzig: Verlag von Felix Meiner, 1925), p. 110.

1915 and 1940 come from this source, as do some dates for books published earlier. For example, one sees that Johanna KLEMM'S Waldasyl was first released in 1913: 1-12 thousand 1913. Several other sources (already mentioned in CHAPTER I) were also consulted and would not need to be mentioned further except for the fact that two of the main contributors to this phase of my study (the 1928 and 1949 editions of the Deutsches Literatur-Lexikon by Wilhelm Kosch and Kürschners deutscher Literatur-Kalender) are sometimes grossly in error. These inaccuracies are of several types: (1) incorrect personal dates, (2) incorrect dates of the first publication of a book and (3) incorrect listing of titles. Since Kosch gives only a selected - not comprehensive - listing of works, he cannot be accused of omission.

Wilhelm Kosch (1949, page 217) gives 1897 as the birth date of Bruno BREHM, but Kürschner (1937/38, Spalte 89) shows 1892 (as does Franz Lennartz, 1959, page 109). Since the data published by Dr. Lüdtke in Kürschner originate from questionaires answered by the writers themselves, the earlier date would seem more reliable and has therefore been used in this study.

The date of the first appearance of the Bismarck-Trilogie by Emil LUDWIG is 1922 according to Kosch (1949, page 1586). He also lists a title Bismarck with the date 1926. Kürschner (1932, Spalte 873) also shows Bismarck 1926. If the DBV is consulted, three distinct Bismarcks appear. First, Bismarck. Ein psychologischer Versuch: 3rd and 4th Auflage 1912, 6th Auflage 1913, which has two hundred and seventy-six pages and was published by the S. Fischer Verlag, which also printed a new expanded three hundred and thirteen page edition: 8th and 9th Auflagen 1917. This was continued in 1921 by Cotta: 10th-12th Auflagen, and a note states that a neue Bearbeitung appeared in 1926 published by Rowohlt Verlag. Second, a three-part drama entitled Bismarck. Trilogie eines Kämpfers appeared in the years 1922 (part three: Die Entlassung) and 1924 (part one: Volk und Krone and part two: 1870) and contained a total of two hundred and sixty-three pages. Third, the DBV for the years 1926/30 lists a Bismarck. Geschichte eines Kämpfers: 1-44 thousand 1926 and 1927 which was published by P. Zsolnay. This work contained seven hundred pages and was obviously not the drama-trilogy first published in 1922 and 1924, which was also listed in this DBV in an edition of 1927. The last Bismarck cited from the DBV seems to be the source of the entry in Kürschner and the second entry in Kosch, who uses the date of appearance of the third part of the trilogy for the entire drama.

Henriette Jacoby, a novel by Georg HERMANN, offers my second example. Kosch (1928, Spalte 141) gives 1915 as the date of first publication and states that the 95th Auflage had been reached in 1925. His 1949 edition (under Georg H. BORCHARDT on page 200) again shows 1915 and includes no further data. For this novel the KBL of 1907/10 contains the following entry: 1-18th Auflage 1908. A date seven years before that found in Kosch's Deutsches Literatur-Lexikon! To further substantiate the fact that this book appeared before the date found in Kosch, I present the entry from the DBV for 1915/20:

31st _Auflage_ 1914.

Still a third example is found under _Wanderschuhe_ by Anna SCHIEBER. Kosch (1949, page 2459) writes that it appeared in 1919. _KBL_ for 1907/10, however, shows: 1-5 thousand 1911. An error of eight years for Kosch! _Warme Herzen und andere Geschichten_ by the same writer was first published in 1924 according to Kosch (1949, page 2459), while the _DBV_ for 1915/20 shows the 3rd _Auflage_ (9-13 thousand) 1919. Thus this book was in its third edition five years before Kosch writes that it came into existence.

For _Mehr Liebe. Betrachtungen_ by Arthur BRAUSEWETTER, Kosch (1949, page 215) shows 1925 as the date of its first publication (_Kürschner_ for 1932 simply gives no date), while the following is found in the _DBV_ for 1915/20: 1st _Auflage_ 1919, 11-20 thousand 1920, 100 thousand 1925. Thus BRAUSEWETTER'S book is supposed to have appeared six years later than it actually did. Kosch (1949, page 215) also gives the year 1925 as the date for BRAUSEWETTER'S _Die grosse Liebe_ (again the 1932 _Kürschner_ has no date). Two entries from the _DBV_ clarify this point: 21-22nd _Auflage_ 1920, 25-30th _Auflage_ 1921-24. Thirty editions had already been printed by Philipp Reclam Jun. Verlag before the date given in Kosch's book.

Both the 1928 (_Spalte_ 3228) and the 1949 (page 3560) editions by Kosch give the date 1925 for the first publication of Stefan ZWEIG'S _Die Augen des ewigen Bruders. Eine Legende_. The 1932 _Kürschner_ lists the same date. From the _DBV_ for 1921-25 we see that there was an edition of this work published by Insel Verlag in 1922, three years earlier.

There are numerous examples where the difference between the dates shown in Kosch and those in the DBV is only one or two years. Where the date in the DBV was known, it was preferred. Kürschner also tends to list dates which are one year earlier or later than those in the DBV, and my conclusion is that Kürschner was the source from which Kosch gained much of his information.

An example of the third type of error is found in Kosch's 1949 edition (page 3090) under the name Hellmuth UNGER. The year 1929 is given as the date of the first publication of his novel entitled Helfer der Menschheit, while later in the list of his works the novel Max Koch is said to have appeared in 1936. If one checks through the DBV it is clear from a note that these two titles refer to one and the same novel: 1-3rd Auflage 1929-30 (under the title Helfer der Menschheit, 4th Auflage 1936 - now Max Koch), 7-75 thousand 1938-39, 76-100 thousand 1940. Kosch was misled by the change in title and listed two separate novels.

To the above-mentioned examples of the inaccuracies in the various volumes of Kürschners deutscher Literatur-Kalender may be added several more. The first is the listing of Helmut LORENZ' Die versunkene Flotte, a novel supposedly published for the first time in 1935 (Kürschner, 1937/38, Spalte 472). (This author is not found in the book by Kosch.) The following data are found in the DBV: 1-19 thousand 1926-29, 20-30 thousand 1935. Therefore, it had already attained its thirty thousandth copy and had been on the market for nine years by the year it appeared in print - according to Kürschner.

Further one finds that Lorenz Lammerdien (likewise not included in Kosch's Lexikon) by Emil STRAUSS was an Erzählung which appeared in 1933 (Kürschner, 1937/38, Spalte 786), while the various volumes of the DBV show: Lorenz Lammerdien. Erstes Kapitel eines unvollendeten Romans. Dezbr. 1899, having forty-eight pages, published in 1917 by the S. Fischer Verlag for the Donnerstags-Gesellschaft of Berlin, 1-10 thousand 1933 (Langen-Müller), 11-15 thousand 1935, 21-30 thousand 1940. The copy of this story in the Joint University Library in Nashville, Tennessee was published in 1933 by Alfred Langen and Georg Müller, contains fifty-seven small pages and bears the full title: Lorenz Lammerdien. Eine angefangene Erzählung. This is a clear indication that it is no more a complete novel than was the 1917 edition of the Donnerstags-Gesellschaft, but that Kürschner either did not have access to this information or chose to ignore it. It is interesting to note that Franz Lennartz (1959, page 740) also uses the year 1933 for this story.

Thus, for the dates of first publication as they are found in my study - especially for those appearing before 1915, there might be a variance of from one to several years from the date of the actual appearance, in accordance with the accuracy of my sources.

Finally, the completeness of the whole study must be discussed. Due to the very nature of this work, the possibility exists that one or several titles might have been inadvertently omitted during the tedium of the gathering process. However, if one fails to find an author or a particular title in my tables, the reason will in all probability be the result of insufficient data in the DBV,

i. e. no figures concerning the Auflagenhöhe.

This compilation of data offers a firm base from which additional studies can be launched. One area which definitely needs to be examined in some detail - and which has not been taken into consideration for this paper - is the effect on the reading public and upon the success of different books first published in journals. The data found in my study could then be further supplemented by such a survey, for many of these novels and stories appeared first in newspapers or other periodicals.

Another area of considerable importance not treated here is the part played by Leihbibliotheken which abound in Germany. For many readers these provided access to the most popular literature of the day. Therefore, the titles of those books loaned most often by such "lending libraries" should receive special attention.

Still another study could be conducted concerning the many Roman-Reihen which were printed - usually without data as to the total number of copies. One recognizes, for instance, the names Roman für Alle, Der Roman für Sie, Der neue, spannende Roman, Wiener Roman, Goldmanns Romanbibliothek, Ensslins neue Romane, Romane des Feierabends, Romane des Herzens, Der Roman-Erzähler, Roman-Perlen, Paetels Roman-Reihe, Romansammlung aus Vergangenheit und Gegenwart, Fischers Romanschatz, Engelhorn Bibliothek, Kronen Bücher, List Bücherei, Ullstein Bücher, etc. The success of an author could sometimes be gauged by the number of his novels printed in such series and also by the number of publishers who chose to include him.

There are only a few representatives of the Kriminal-Roman

listed in the following tables (e. g. Adolf STARK, Dietrich THEDEN, etc.). This is due primarily to the lack of information furnished by the publishers of reading matter of this type, which experienced an ever increasing popularity during this period - as is evidenced by the large number of titles printed. No "western" novels appear for the same reason - with the exceptions of Karl MAY. However, there are several Indianer-Geschichten (see Joseph SPILLMANN, Anton HUONDER).

The ever-popular fairy tale has been excluded, because it generally had an origin before the earliest limit of this study, but also because prose fiction intended principally for the young was not included (for example Margarete THIELE, Frau Frida SCHANZ, Henny KOCH, etc.). There is such a mass of this type of literature, that it simply could not be contained here - even though the sociological implications which arise from the reading matter devoured by the young people may not be overlooked. In this connection one might question the inclusion of a few authors such as Heinrich SCHARRELMANN, but it was felt that where a work was not labeled specifically for the young it could be taken up. Several writers of children's stories (such as Agnes SAPPER, Anna SCHIEBER, etc.) also wrote for the adult reading public. Where such was the case, an attempt has been made to include the latter and omit the children's books. With this in mind, one does not question the absence of writers like Margarete OERTZEN (though generally her works would not have been included due to a lack of sufficient data in the DBV).

Sagen, including Germanic *Heldensagen* such as those by Leopold WEBER, have also been excluded because of the general and ancient nature of this source.

I have chosen to include a rather large number of what one might designate "war tales" or *Kriegserlebnisse*, most of which became extremely popular during and shortly after World War I (Artur BREHMER, Gustav Adolf ERDMANN, Anton FENDRICH, Friedrich FREI, Heino von HEIMBURG, Robert NEUBAU, Max IMMELMANN, Reinhard ROEHLE, K. A. NERGER, Rolf SOMMER, etc.), several of which appeared during the Great War and experienced a rebirth during the Third Reich (Edgar Freiherr von SPIEGEL, Robert MORAHT), a few which were first published in the twenties (Burggraf Nikolaus zu DOHNA-SCHLODIEN, Felix Graf von LUCKNER, Johannes SPIESS) and those which arose during the Third Reich (Paul Heinrich KUNTZE, Albert SEMSROTT, Ernst UDET, Johannes WERNER, etc.). The reason for their inclusion lies not only in their popularity, but also in the fact that one cannot know to what extent these books are fact or fiction. Several works designated as *Lebenserinnerungen* and *Tagebücher* are likewise present (Max FELDE - *Jagderlebnisse*, Gorch FOCK - *Tagebuchblätter*, Karl HAGENBECK - *Erinnerungen*, etc.). There are also a few biographies which I would call "fictionalized" which have found inclusion (Emil LUDWIG). There was some difficulty in determining just what was fiction. Some very successful writers are not included because it was felt that their works were not fiction but more on the order of *Lebensbücher*, particularly Heinrich LHOTZKY.

Several authors (such as Hilde von SELKOW and Adolf WALDMANN) have been omitted because their works were printed in quantities less than fifty thousand and because it was impossible to establish either the personal dates of the author or the date of the first appearance of the book.

Some titles appeared for the first time and attained the twenty-one thousand copies necessary to be included in my TABLE B between 1899 and 1914 but were not listed again in any of the _DBV_ volumes between 1915 and 1940. Therefore, they were completely eliminated (e. g. Erdmann GRAESER, _Lotte Glimmer_, a novel which reached its twenty-first _Auflage_ in 1913, etc.).

As has already been brought out several times, there exists a rather sizeable gap in data after the National Socialists assumed the reins of government in Germany. This is particularly evident by the omission of important figures from the listings of the _DBV_ for the years 1936/40 (such as Thomas and Heinrich MANN, Jakob WASSERMANN, Stefan and Arnold ZWEIG). This fact, so obvious for names such as these, must also hold true for numerous lesser figures whose writings, however popular, were undesirable to the government and simply suppressed.

It should be reiterated that authors publishing prose fiction before 1899 were not included, whether or not they enjoyed numerous reprints in the twentieth century. This is itself an extensive area open to further research.

CHAPTER III

TABLE A

This is a presentation in descending order of popularity of more than eight hundred and fifty titles which have three factors in common: (1) all were printed in a total of at least fifty thousand copies, (2) all were published for the first time between 1899 and 1940, and (3) all were successful to the degree given here between the years 1915 and 1940.

The value of this table lies in the ease with which it enables one to ascertain the very best-selling books at a glance. It also allows one to visualize quickly several books enjoying approximately the same degree of popularity. As a word of caution it must be mentioned that TABLE B should be consulted before arriving at the latter type judgment, since only there one can immediately see the number of years required to reach the pinacle shown in TABLE A. Naturally, two books, one appearing in 1900 (Ludwig GANGHOFER'S Der Dorfapostel) and the other first printed in 1915 (Hellmuth von MÜCKE'S Ayesha), have not experienced the same rate of sales - even though they both show three hundred and thirty-two thousand copies in TABLE A. GANGHOFER'S book had reached this figure in 1933, thirty-three years after its publication, while Ayesha required only thirteen years for the printing of the same number of copies (1915 to 1927).

The following examples will clarify the use of this table. Max BROD'S Tycho Brahes Weg zu Gott was published in 1916. By 1930 more than seventy-seven thousand copies had been printed. The plus sign (+) indicates at least one edition which was printed without any data and which has therefore contributed nothing to the total. (This same indication is used in TABLE B.) Consulting TABLE B we find that this edition was printed in 1931 and would certainly add to the total of seventy-seven thousand already reached in 1930. This title appears in TABLE A like this:

BROD, Max: Tycho Brahes Weg zu Gott 1916 77,000+ 1930

The year 1910 saw the appearance of Konrad Pilater by Jakob SCHAFFNER. By adding the editions of the several publishers I arrived at the approximation of seventy-four thousand in 1929, but there was also a Neuausgabe in 1929 which must remain unaccounted for.

SCHAFFNER, Jakob: Konrad Pilater 1910 c 74,000+ 1929

In both tables I have used abbreviations wherever expedient and have refrained from placing periods after them. Many had to be in German for the sake of consistency, since most words for which they stand are German. Only where the English abbreviation was very well-known and shorter did I deviate from this principle (ed. instead of Hrsg. for editor, i. e. instead of d. h., etc.) The underlining of titles has likewise been omitted. The abbreviations found in my tables follow with the plurals shown in the parentheses:

ABBREVIATIONS	GERMAN	ENGLISH
A(n)	Auflage(n)	edition
Ag(n)	Ausgabe(n)	printing, issuance, edition
Anek(n)	Anekdote(n)	anecdote
Anst	Anstalt	establishment
Aufz(n)	Aufzeichnung(en)	notes, memoranda
ausgew	ausgewählt	selected, chosen
Bd(e)	Band(¨e)	volume
c	ungefähr, etwa, zirka	approximately, circa
d	definite article	the
dass	dasselbe	the same
Det	Detektiv-	detective
dt	deutsch	German
Dtg	Dichtung	work of fiction, poetic work
Dtld	Deutschland	Germany
e	indefinite article	a, an
ed	Herausgeber	editor
Erin(n)	Erinnerung(en)	reminiscences, memoirs
Erl(e)	Erlebnis(se)	experiences
Erz(n)	Erzählung(en)	story
Evang	Evangelisch	Protestant
Frhr	Freiherr	baron
ges	gesammelt	collected
Gesch(n)	Geschichte(n)	story

Grot(n)	Groteske(n)	grotesque
hist	historisch	historical
Hrsp(e)	Hörspiel(e)	radio play
Hum	Humoreske(n)	humoresque
hum	humoristisch	humorous
ie	d. h., eigentlich	that is, actually
ill	illustriert	illustrated
isländ	isländisch	Icelandic
kl	klein	small, little
Krg-Ab	Kriegsabenteuer	war adventures
Krim	Kriminal-	mystery, detective, crime
Leg(n)	Legende(n)	legend
Mär(n)	Märchen	fairy tale
nA	neue Auflage	new edition
nAg	neue Ausgabe	new printing
nd	kein Datum	no date
née	geborene	used to indicate the maiden name
nF	neue Folge	new series, new issuance
ni	keine Informationen	no information, no data
Nov(n)	Novelle(n)	---
od	oder	or
Plau(n)	Plauderei(en)	casual essays
Ps	Pseudonym	pseudonym

R(e)	Roman(e)	novel
Rom(n)	Romanze(n)	romance
Rsbr(e)	Reisebericht(e)	book of travels
russ	russisch	Russian
s	siehe, vergleiche	see, refer to
S-A	Sonder-Auflage	special edition
S-Ag	Sonder-Ausgabe	special printing
Sat(n)	Satire(n)	satire
Schil(n)	Schilderung(en)	descriptions, tales
Schl	Schlesische	Silesian
Sk(n)	Skizze(n)	sketch
T	Tausend	thousand
Tageb	Tagebuch	daily journal, diary
Tl	Teil	part
Tr	Tragödie	tragedy
Tril	Trilogie	trilogy
u	und	and
u a	und andere	and other
utop-	utopisch	utopian
v	von	from, of
V	Verlag	publisher, publishing house, firm
z	zu	to
zw	zwischen	between

TABLE A

ABOVE 500 THOUSAND

MANN, Thomas: Buddenbrooks 1901	1,305,000	1936
HEIN, Alfred: Kurts Maler. E Lieblings-R 1922	999,000	1922
REMARQUE, E. M.: Im Westen nichts Neues 1929	900,000+	1929
BONSELS, W.: D Biene Maja u ihre Abenteuer 1912	790,000+	1940
SÜNDER, Artur: D Dinte wider das Blut after 1917	693,000	1922
FLEX, Walter: D Wanderer zw zwei Welten 1917	682,000	1940
VOSS, R.: Zwei Menschen 1911	620,000+	1929
HERZOG, R.: Die Wiskottens 1905	615,000	1939
PLÜSCHOW, Gunther: D Abenteuer d Fliegers v Tsingtau... 1916	610,000	1927
LÖNS, Hermann: Der Wehrwolf 1910	565,000+	1939
BÖHME, Margarethe: Tageb einer Verlorenen... 1905	563,000+	1931
WILAMOWITZ-MOELLENDORFF, F. v: Carin Göring 1933	550,000	1940
KELLER, Paul: Waldwinter 1902	518,000	1938
SCHENZINGER, K. A.: Anilin 1936	505,000	1940

401 THOUSAND TO 500 THOUSAND

RILKE, R. M.: D Weise v Liebe u Tod d Cornets Christoph Rilke 1899	500,000+	1934
ROSE, Felicitas: Heideschulmeister Uwe Karsten 1909	500,000	1937
MOLO, W. v: Fridericus Tril 1918	485,000	1936
HERZOG, R.: D Stoltenkamps u ihre Frauen 1917	483,000	1941
GRIMM, Hans: Volk ohne Raum 1928	480,000	1940

TABLE A (con't.)

HEER, J. C.: Der Wetterwart 1905	c 477,000	1940
SCHLEICH, K. L.: Besonnte Vergangenheit 1921	469,000	1940
FRENSSEN, G.: Jörn Uhl 1901	463,000	1939
KULL, Franz: Fünf Jahre Fremdenlegionär... 1921	450,000	1923
BONSELS, W.: Himmelsvolk 1915	445,000	1940
LÖNS, H.: Das zweite Gesicht 1912	435,000	1938
RICHTHOFEN, M. Frhr v: D rote Kampfflieger 1917	420,000	1938
COURTHS-MAHLER, Hedwig: Gib mich frei! 1912	402,000+	1919
COURTHS-MAHLER, H.: Was Gott zusammenfügt... 1913	402,000	1919
HEER, J. C.: Der König der Bernina 1900	402,000	1940

301 THOUSAND TO 400 THOUSAND

SAPPER, Agnes: Die Familie Pfäffling 1906	400,000	1940
HERZOG, R.: Die vom Niederrhein 1903	395,000	1940
LUCKNER, Felix Graf v: Seeteufel. Abenteuer... 1921	392,000	1938
HERZOG, R.: Das grosse Heimweh 1914	389,000	1940
ROSEGGER, Peter: Als ich noch der Waldbauernbub war. Band I 1902	384,000	1933
KELLER, Paul: Ferien vom Ich 1915	371,000	1935
BINDING, R. G.: Der Opfergang 1912	360,000	1933
GILLHOFF, J.: Jürnjakob Swehn, der Amerikafahrer 1917	360,000	1940
LÖNS, H.: Mümmelmann. Ein Tierbuch	360,000	1935
SPIEGEL, Edgar Frhr v und z Peckelsheim: Kriegstagebuch U 202 1916	360,000	1938

TABLE A (con't.)

KELLERMANN, Bernhard: Der Tunnel 1913	358,000	1940
BONSELS, W.: Indienfahrt 1916	350,000	1930
COURTHS-MAHLER, H.: Des Anderen Ehre 1912	349,000+	1919
LEHNE, Fr.: Ein Frühlingstraum 1906	345,000	1940
COURTHS-MAHLER, H.: Kathes Ehe 1914	342,000	1919
HERZOG, R.: Die Burgkinder 1911	339,000	1938
GANGHOFER, L.: Der Dorfapostel 1900	332,000	1933
MÜCKE, Hellmuth v: Ayesha 1915	332,000	1927
ETTIGHOFER, P. C.: Verdun, d grosse Gericht 1936	330,000	1940
BEUMELBURG, Werner: Sperrfeuer um Dtld 1929	328,000	1940
KELLER, P.: Der Sohn der Hagar 1907	328,000	1931
COURTHS-MAHLER, H.: Die Testamentsklausel 1915	325,000	1919
KRÖGER, Theodor: Das vergessene Dorf 1934	325,000	1939
GANGHOFER, L.: Der hohe Schein 1904	324,000	1935
HERZOG, R.: Das Lebenslied 1904	321,000	1936
HEER, J. C.: Laubgewind 1908	320,000+	1940
POPERT, H. M.: Helmut Harringa 1910	c 315,000	1930
SEIDEL, Ina: Das Wunschkind 1930	310,000	1940

201 THOUSAND TO 300 THOUSAND

ETTIGHOFER, P. C.: Nacht über Sibirien 1937	300,000	1940
ROSEGGER, P.: Als ich noch der Waldbauernbub war. Band II 1902	300,000	1931
SEELIGER, E. G.: Peter Voss d Millionendieb... 1913	300,000+	1935

TABLE A (con't.)

ZWEIG, Stefan: Sternstunden d Menschheit... 1927	300,000	1931
EYTH, Max: Hinter Pflug u Schraubstock... 1899	298,000+	1937
GANGHOFER, L.: Die Trutze v Trutzberg 1915	298,000	1937
COURTHS-MAHLER, H.: Lena Warnstetten 1916	295,000	1919
HERZOG, R.: Hanseaten 1909	294,000	1936
WASSERMANN, Jakob: Das Gänsemännchen 1915	291,000	1931
FLAISCHLEN, Cäsar: Heimat und Welt... 1916	284,000	1934
BLOEM, Walter: Kommödiantinnen 1914	280,000	1936
SPECKMANN, Diedrich: Heidjers Heimkehr 1904	274,000	1940
BEYERLEIN, F. A.: Jena oder Sedan? 1903	270,000	1926
ETTIGHOFER, P. C.: Eine Armee meutert... 1937	266,000	1940
GANGHOFER, L.: Das Gotteslehen 1899	266,000	1934
HERZOG, R.: Die Buben der Frau Opterberg 1921	265,000	1940
SCHMÖCKEL, Hermann: Martin Luther. Lebensbild 1916	265,000	1938
SELL, Sophie Charlotte v: Weggenossen 1911	262,000	1940
DINTER, Arthur: Die Sünde wider das Blut 1917	260,000	1934
MANN, Heinrich: D Kaiserreich, 1. Bd: D Untertan 1911	260,000	1931
ROSEGGER, P.: Als ich noch der Waldbauernbub war. Band III 1902	260,000	1931
FRENSSEN, G.: Peters Moors Fahrt nach Südwest... 1906	253,000	1936
HERZOG, R.: Der Graf von Gleichen 1901	250,000	1940
PAASCHE, Hans: Fremdenlegionär Kirsch... 1910	250,000	1918
SCHMÖCKEL, H.: Hindenburg. Ein Lebensbild 1915	249,000	1937
HOUBEN, H. H.: D Ruf d Nordens. Abenteuer... 1928	245,000	1940

TABLE A (con't.)

SCHENZINGER, K. A.: Der Hitlerjunge Quex 1932	244,000	1940
ETTIGHOFER, P. C.: Gespenster am toten Mann 1931	240,000	1940
THOMA, Ludwig: Lausbubengeschichten. Aus meiner Jugendzeit 1935	240,000	1940
FRENSSEN, G.: Hilligenlei 1905	239,000	1940
EWERS, H. H.: Alraune. Gesch e lebenden Wesens 1911	238,000+	1922
BARTSCH, Rudolf: Schwammerl 1912	236,000	1932
GOOTE, Thor: Wir fahren den Tod 1930	235,000	1940
ZAHN, Ernst: Lukas Hochstrassers Haus 1907	235,000	1940
ZERKAULEN, Heinrich: Anna und Sigrid 1931	234,000	1940
COURTHS-MAHLER, H.: Die Bettelprinzess 1914	c 230,000	1924
DWINGER, E. E.: Die letzten Reiter 1935	230,000	1940
GRIMM, Hans: D Zug d Hauptmanns v Erckert 1932	230,000	1940
WINCKLER, Josef: Der tolle Bomberg 1924	230,000+	1940
DWINGER, E. E.: Zwischen Weiss und Rot... 1930	225,000	1940
MUSCHLER, R. C.: Die Unbekannte 1934	220,000	1936
FOCK, Gorch: Seefahrt ist not 1913	218,000	1936
GANGHOFER, L.: Der Mann im Salz 1906	213,000	1932
STEHR, Hermann: Der Heiligenhof 1918	213,000	1940
COURTHS-MAHLER, H.: Die Assmanns 1917	210,000+	1919
SAPPER, Agnes: Werden u Wachsen. Erle 1910	210,000	1937
SCHRÖER, Gustav: Heimat wider Heimat 1929	210,000	1940
SPÖRL, Heinrich: Man kann ruhig darüber sprechen 1937	210,000	1939
JANSEN, Werner: Robert d Teufel (D irdische Unsterblichkeit) 1924	208,000	1940

TABLE A (con't.)

SPECKMANN, Diedrich: Heidehof Lohe 1906	208,000	1932
KELLER, Paul: Die Heimat 1904	207,000	1935
WOTHE, Anny: Aus dämmernden Nächten 1914	207,000	1919
BLOEM, Walter: Kriegserlebnis-Trilogie 1916 (three volumes in one)	205,000	1939
GANGHOFER, L.: Das Schweigen im Walde 1899	205,000+	1929
SIMPSON, Margot v: Fürst Woronzeff 1930	204,000+	1934

151 THOUSAND TO 200 THOUSAND

BEREND, Alice: D Bräutigame d Babette Bomberling 1914	200,000	1930
DWINGER, E. E.: D Armee hinter Stacheldraht... 1929	200,000	1940
EWERS, H. H.: Horst Wessel. E dt Schicksal 1932	200,000	1934
KYBER, Manfred: Unter Tieren 1912	200,000	1938
LUDWIG, Emil: Wilhelm der Zweite 1926	200,000	1929
NOLDEN, Arnold: Auf Schiffen, Schienen... 1930	200,000	1938
ROSE, Felicitas: Der Mutterhof 1918	200,000	1939
ROTHACKER, Gottfried: D Dorf an der Grenze 1936	200,000	1940
KRETZER, Max: Der Mann ohne Gewissen 1905	195,000	1929
MAY, Karl: Unter Geiern 1914	195,000	1938
VESPER, Will: Tristan und Isolde 1911	195,000	1940
FINCKH, Ludwig: Rapunzel 1909	194,000	1940
KELLER, Paul: Hubertus 1918	192,000	1931
MEYRINK, Gustav: Der Golem 1915	191,000	1931

TABLE A (con't.)

BODENREUTH, F.: Alle Wasser Böhmens fliessen nach Deutschland 1937	190,000	1940
ERNST, Otto: Asmus Sempers Jugendland 1905	190,000	1932
WIECHERT, Ernst: Hirtennovellen 1935	190,000+	1940
HERZOG, R.: Der Abenteuerer 1907	189,000	1928
LUDWIG, E.: Napoleon 1925	189,000	1931
SCHRÖER, Gustav: Um Mannesehre 1932	185,000	1940
VOSS, Richard: Der heilige Hass 1915	184,000+	1927
KELLERMANN, Bernhard: Yester und Li 1904	183,000	1937
BUSSE, Karl: Trittchen. Aus d Aufzn e Verwundeten 1939	180,000	1940
SCHIEBER, Anna: ...und hätte die Liebe nicht 1912	180,000	1936
SCHUMACHER, H. V.: Liebe u Leben d Lady Hamilton 1910	179,000	1929
HERZOG, R.: Kameraden 1922	178,000	1932
SPÖRL, Heinrich: Die Feuerzangenbowle 1933	173,000	1940
GANGHOFER, L.: Waldrausch 1908	172,000	1933
HAUPTMANN, Gerhart: Der Ketzer von Soana 1918	172,000	1938
KAMPE, Otto: Ein Korb voll Kirschen 1914	172,000	1934
GRABEIN, Paul: Die vom Rauen Grund 1914	c 171,000	1940
BEUMELBURG, W.: Die Gruppe Bosemüller 1930	170,000	1939
DOMINIK, H.: Ein Stern fiel vom Himmel 1934	170,000	1940
FRENSSEN, Gustav: Der Glaube der Nordmark 1936	170,000	1940
HINDENBURG, Paul v: Aus meinem Leben 1920	170,000	1933
MAY, Karl: Halbblut u a Erzn 1916	170,000	1940
SCHÄFER, Wilhelm: Die 13 Bücher d dt Seele 1922	170,000	1940

TABLE A (con't.)

STRAUSS, Emil: Der Schleier 1920	170,000+	1940
ZWEIG, S.: Die Augen des ewigen Bruders 1922	170,000	1933
ZWEIG, S.: Brennendes Geheimnis 1931	170,000	1933
LIENHARD, Friedrich: Oberlin 1910	169,000	1935
DOMINIK, Hans: Land aus Feuer und Wasser 1939	167,000	1940
KAMPE, Otto: Robinson 1913	165,000	1937
LEHNE, Fr.: Die geborene Krause 1915	c 165,000+	1922
SCHUMACHER, H. V.: Lord Nelsons letzte Liebe 1911	165,000	1929
FEDERER, Heinrich: Berge und Menschen 1911	163,000	1936
BISCHOFF, Charitas: Amalie Dietrich. E Leben 1909	161,000	1940
VOLCK, Herbert: D Wölfe. E dt Flucht durch Siberien 1918	161,000	1940
BERENS-TOTENOHL, Josefa: Der Femhof 1934	160,000	1940
SPIEGEL, E. Frhr v u z: Oberheizer Zenne, d letzte Mann d "Wiesbaden" 1917	160,000	1938
HAGENBECK, Karl: Von Tieren und Menschen 1908	159,000+	1940
HERMANN, Georg: Jettchen Gebert 1906	159,000	1931
JELUSICH, Mirko: Cromwell 1934	158,000	1940
HERZOG, R.: Wieland der Schmied 1924	155,000	1931
RENN, Ludwig: Krieg. Erlebnisbericht 1928	155,000	1931
FINCKH, Ludwig: Der Rosendoktor 1906	154,000	1940
BONSELS, W.: Menschenwege... 1918	153,000	1922
KÜLPE, Frances: Mutterschaft 1907	153,000	1940
SCHIEBER, Anna: Alle guten Geister... 1905	153,000	1938
FEDERER, Heinrich: Pilatus 1912	152,000	1935

TABLE A (con't.)

LETTOW-VORBECK, Paul: Heia Safari! 1920	151,000	1940

126 THOUSAND TO 150 THOUSAND

DOHNA-SCHLODIEN, N. z: D "Möwe" zweite Fahrt 1917	150,000	1917
DOMINIK, H.: Die Macht der Drei 1922	150,000	1940
DWINGER, E. E.: Der Tod in Polen. D volksdeutsche Passion 1940	150,000	1940
FEUCHTWANGER, Lion: D hässliche Herzogin Margarete Maultasch 1923	150,000+	1930
HUCH, Friedrich: Pitt u Fox, d Lebenswege d Brüder Sintrup 1909	150,000	1927
KUNTZE, Paul H.: D Volksbuch unserer Kolonien 1938	150,000	1940
LANGSDORFF, Werner: U-Boote am Feind... 1937	150,000	1940
UDET, Ernst: Mein Fliegerleben 1935	150,000	1938
ZWEIG, S.: Amok. Novellen e Leidenschaft 1922	150,000	1931
HESSE, Hermann: Unterm Rad 1905	149,000	1930
JANSEN, Werner: Das Buch Treue 1916	149,000	1940
DORN, Käthe: Das weisse Kleid 1910	148,000	1925
MANN, Thomas: Königliche Hoheit 1909	148,000	1932
HANDEL-MAZZETTI, E. Gräfin v: Jesse und Maria 1906	147,000	1936
PRELLWITZ, Gertrud: Vom Wunder des Lebens 1909	147,000	1926
BAUM, Vicki: Der Eingang zur Bühne 1920	146,000	1931
GREINZ, Rudolf: Allerseelen 1910	146,000	1940
BONSELS, W.: Das Anjekind 1913	145,000	1940
FENDRICH, Anton: Wir. Ein Hindenburgbuch 1917	145,000	1917
KNITTEL, John: Via Mala 1934	143,000+	1940

TABLE A (con't.)

BEREND, Alice: Frau Hempels Tochter 1913	142,000	1928
BEUMELBURG, W.: Mit 17 Jahren vor Verdun 1931	142,000	1940
KELLER, Paul: Das letzte Märchen 1905	142,000	1931
BAUM, Vicki: Hell in Frauensee 1927	141,000	1931
GANGHOFER, L.: Das neue Wesen 1902	141,000	1928
KELLER, Paul: Die Insel der Einsamen 1913	141,000	1931
ZAHN, Ernst: Frau Sixta 1926	141,000	1940
BLOEM, Walter: Das eiserne Jahr 1911	140,000+	1914
BURTE, Hermann: Vom Hofe, welcher unterging 1912	c 140,000	1939
GANGHOFER, L.: Hochlandszauber 1931	140,000	1935
JOHST, Hanns: Mutter ohne Tod. D Begegnung 1933	140,000	1940
KRÖGER, Theodor: Heimat am Don 1937	140,000	1938
RILKE, R. M.: Briefe an einen jungen Dichter 1929	140,000	1932
STEGUWEIT, Heinz: Der Jüngling im Feuerofen 1932	140,000	1940
FLEX, Walter: Vom grossen Abendmahl 1915	139,000	1940
HERZOG, R.: Jungbrunnen 1918	139,000	1935
FEDERER, H.: D letzte Stündlein d Papstes 1914	138,000	1938
HESSE, Hermann: Knulp 1915	137,000	1940
SCHNITZLER, Arthur: Der Weg ins Freie 1908	136,000	1929
BEUMELBURG, Werner: Donaumont 1923	135,000	1940
MANN, Thomas: Der Zauberberg 1925	135,000	1936
MAY, Karl: Winnetous Erben 1910	135,000	1939
THOMA, Ludwig: Jozef Filsers gesammelter Briefwexel Teil I 1912	135,000	1940

TABLE A (con't.)

BUSSE, Hermann Eris: Heiner und Barbara 1936	134,000	1940
GANGHOFER, Ludwig: Der Ochsenkrieg 1914	134,000	1934
SCHRECKENBACH, Paul: D König v Rothenburg 1911	134,000	1935
FEDERER, Heinrich: E Nacht in den Abruzzen 1916	c 132,000	1927
GRAF, Kurt: Das fidele Kurt-Graf-Buch 1921	c 132,000	1940
NEUMANN, Alfred: Der Teufel 1926	132,000	1932
GJELLERUP, Karl: Der Pilger Kamanita 1906	131,000	1928
KELLERMANN, Bernhard: Ingeborg 1906	131,000+	1936
BLUNCK, Hans Friedrich: Die grosse Fahrt 1935	130,000	1940
ESCHELBACH, Hans: Die beiden Merks 1903	130,000	1930
LÖNS, Hermann: Mein braunes Buch. Haidbilder 1907	130,000	1923
NEEFF, Adolf: Kleines Sternbüchlein c 1916	130,000	1940
WEHNER, Josef Magnus: Sieben vor Verdun 1930	130,000	1940
BEREND, Alice: D Reise d Herrn Sebastian Wenzel 1912	129,000	1926
DOMINIK, Hans: Der Wettflug der Nationen 1934	128,000	1940
ROSEGGER, Peter: Erdsegen 1900	126,000	1940

101 THOUSAND TO 125 THOUSAND

BERENS-TOTENOHL, Josefa: Frau Magdlene 1935	125,000	1940
DAUTHENDEY, Max: D acht Gesichter am Biwasee 1911	125,000	1940
FISCHER-GRAZ, Wilhelm: Das Licht im Elendhaus 1903	125,000	1926
GÜNTHER, Agnes: Die Heilige und ihr Narr 1913	125,000	1940
PHILIPPI, Felix: Jugendliebe 1917	125,000	1925
SWANTENIUS, Swaantje: Hermann Löns u d Swaantje 1921	125,000	1936

TABLE A (con't.)

WOLZOGEN, Ernst v: Das dritte Geschlecht 1899	125,000	1916
HERMANN, Georg: Henriette Jacoby 1908	124,000	1932
HESSE, Hermann: Peter Camenzind 1903	124,000	1930
ERNST, Otto: Appelschnut 1907	123,000	1940
BESTE, Konrad: D vergnügliche Leben d Doktorin Böhmfink 1934	122,000	1940
FLAISCHLEN, Cäsar: Jost Seyfried 1905	122,000	1927
HANDEL-MAZZETTI, E. Gräfin v: Meinrad Helmpergers denkwürdiges Jahr 1900	122,000	1938
JANSEN, Werner: Geier um Marienburg 1925	121,000	1940
SONNLEITNER, A. T.: D Höhlenkinder im heimlichen Grund 1918	121,000	1940
BLOEM, Walter: Volk wider Volk 1912	120,000+	1914
JANSEN, Werner: Das Buch Liebe 1918	120,000	1940
KLABUND: Bracke. Eulenspiegel-Roman 1918	120,000+	1932
LUDWIG, Emil: Juli 14. 1929	120,000	1929
SCHENZINGER, K. A.: Metall 1939	120,000	1939
SEIDEL, Ina: Lennacker, d Buch e Heimkehr 1938	120,000	1940
THOMA, Ludwig: Lausbubengeschichten 1905	120,000	1933
VESPER, Will: Das harte Geschlecht 1931	120,000	1940
VIEBIG, Clara: Am Totenmaar. Margrets Wallfahrt. Das Miseräbelchen. Der Osterquell 1901	120,000	1928
WIECHERT, Ernst: Der Todeskandidat. La Ferme Morte. Der Vater 1934	120,000	1939
BOREE, Karl F.: Wartalun. E Schlossgesch 1911	119,000+	1925
KELLER, Paul: Die alte Krone 1909	119,000+	1934
KELLER, Paul: In fremden Spiegeln 1920	118,000	1931

TABLE A (con't.)

ROSNER, Karl Peter: Der König. Weg u Wende 1921	118,000	1930
HANDEL-MAZZETTI, E. Gräfin v: D arme Margret 1910	117,000	1930
MOSZKOWSKI, Alexander: D unsterbliche Kiste 1907	116,000	1922
WERNER, Johannes: Franziska v Altenhausen 1927	c 116,000	1938
BONSELS, W.: Eros u d Evangelien... 1920	115,000	1925
FALLADA, Hans: Kleiner Mann, was nun? 1932	115,000	1935
HERZOG, R.: Es gibt ein Glück 1910	115,000	1932
MANN, Heinrich: Im Schlaraffenland 1910	115,000	1929
SPECKMANN, D.: Das goldene Tor 1907	115,000	1934
SUDERMANN, Hermann: Das hohe Lied 1908	115,000	1939
THOMA, Ludwig: Tante Frieda. Neue Lausbubengeschn 1907	115,000	1940
WIECHERT, Ernst: Die Majorin 1934	115,000	1938
FRENSSEN, Gustav: Klaus Hinrich Baas 1909	114,000	1923
LUCKNER, Felix Graf v: Seeteufel erobert Amerika 1928	114,000	1937
BREHM, Bruno v: Apis und Este 1931	113,000	1940
ERNST, Otto: Semper der Jüngling 1908	113,000	1930
EYTH, Max v: Der Schneider von Ulm 1906	113,000+	1935
STRATZ, Rudolf: Schloss Vogelöd 1921	113,000	1929
BLOEM, Walter: Der krasse Fuchs 1906	112,000+	1922
HEER, J. C.: Tobias Heider 1922	112,000	1940
WASSERMANN, Jakob: Der Fall Mauritius 1928	112,000	1935
WITTEK, Erhart: Männer. E Buch d Stolzes 1936	112,000	1940
WOTHE, Anny: D Garten d Vergessenheit 1915	112,000+	1919

TABLE A (con't.)

MAY, Karl: Im Reiche d silbernen Löwen, III 1902	111,000	1939
ZAHN, Ernst: Das zweite Leben 1918	111,000	1927
DWINGER, E. E.: Auf halbem Wege 1939	110,000	1940
DWINGER, E. E.: Wir rufen Deutschland. Heimkehr und Vermächtnis 1932	110,000	1939
GANGHOFER, L.: Gewitter im Mai 1904	110,000+	1927
HARDT, Ernst: An den Toren des Lebens 1912	110,000	1928
HAUSMANN, Manfred: Lampioon. Abenteuer e Wanderers 1928	110,000	1939
KOLBENHEYER, E. G.: D Begegnung auf d Riesengebirge 1933	110,000	1940
KRAZE, Friede H.: D magischen Wälder... 1933	110,000	1939
LICHTENBERGER, Franz: Reinecke Fuchs 1911	110,000	1936
LÖNS, Hermann: Mein grünes Buch. Jagdschilderungen 1901	110,000+	1925
NEEFF, Adolf: Kurzweil c 1916	110,000	1940
NIESE, Charlotte: Um die Weihnachtszeit u a Erzn 1905	110,000	1930
OSTWALD, Hans: Das Zillebuch 1929	110,000	1929
SAPPER, Agnes: D kleine Dummerle u a Erzn 1904	110,000	1938
SAPPER, Agnes: Frieder. D Gesch v kl Dummerle 1920	110,000	1930
SKOLASTER, Hermann: Schwester Beata 1938	110,000	1940
WIECHERT, Ernst: Wälder u Menschen. E Jugend 1936	110,000	1938
ZWEIG, Arnold: D Novellen um Claudia 1912	110,000	1930
MÜLLER-PARTENKIRCHEN, Fritz: Kramer & Friemann 1920	109,000+	1940
DIEHL, Ludwig: Suso 1921	108,000	1940
MAY, Karl: Im Reiche d silbernen Löwen, IV 1902	107,000	1939

TABLE A (con't.)

WASSERMANN, Jakob: Christian Wahnschaffe 1919	107,000	1933
ZABEL, Eugen: D Roman einer Kaiserin. Katharine II. von Russland 1911	107,000+	1940
SPECKMANN, D.: Die Heidklause 1919	106,000	1928
ZAHN, Ernst: Herrgottsfäden 1901	106,000	1936
BAUM, Vicki: Student chem Helene Willfüer 1929	105,000	1932
HESSE, Hermann: Weg nach innen 1931	105,000	1940
LIENHARD, Friedrich: Thüringer Tagebuch 1903	105,000	1935
Der Marsch nach Hause. Heitere Geschichten 1903	105,000	1927
WIECHERT, Ernst: D Magd d Jürgen Doskocil 1932	105,000+	1939
SALOMON, Ernst v: Die Geächteten 1930	104,000	1939
FRENSSEN, Gustav: Die Brüder 1917	103,000	1922
GANGHOFER, L.: Das grosse Jagen 1918	103,000	1929
HESSE, Hermann: Schön ist die Jugend 1916	103,000	1937
HOFFMANN, Hans: Spätglück. Sturmwolken 1901	103,000	1928
STRATZ, Rudolf: D deutsche Wunder 1916	103,000	1930
DOMINIK, Hans: Atomgewicht 500 1935	102,000	1940
FIGDOR, Karl: Die Herrin der Welt 1919	102,000	1920
HEYKING, Elisbeth v: Briefe, d ihn nicht erreichten 1903	102,000+	1925
KRIEGER, Arnold: Mann ohne Volk 1934	102,000+	1939
STRATZ, Rudolf: Seine englische Frau 1913	101,000	1928

76 THOUSAND TO 100 THOUSAND

BINDING, R. G.: Unsterblichkeit 1921	100,000	1935

TABLE A (con't.)

BRAUSEWETTER, Arthur: Mehr Liebe 1919	100,000	1925
DOHNA-SCHLODIEN, Burgraf N. z: S. M. S. "Möwe" 1915	100,000	1916
DOMINIK, Hans: Atlantis 1925	100,000	1940
DWINGER, E. E.: Zug nach Siberien 1933	100,000	1940
ETTIGHOFER, P. C.: Sturm 1918. Sieben Tage deutscher Schicksal 1938	100,000	1939
ETTIGHOFER, P. C.: V d Teufelsinsel zum Leben 1932	100,000	1940
FINCKENSTEIN, Ottfried Graf: Die Mutter 1938	100,000	1940
GLAESER, Ernst: Jahrgang 1902 1928	100,000	1931
HARBOU, Thea v: Der Krieg und die Frauen 1913	100,000	1919
HAUPTMANN, Carl: Einhart der Lächler 1907	100,000	1933
HEIMBURG, Heino v: U-Boot gegen U-Boot 1917	100,000	1917
HEINZE-HOFERICHTER, Mara: Friedel Starmatz 1928	100,000	1936
KAHLENBERG, Hans v: Nixchen... 1899	100,000	1925?
KENNICOTT, M. B.: Das Herz ist wach... 1934	100,000+	1940
KOLBENHEYER, E. G.: Meister Joachim Pausenwang 1910	100,000	1940
LANGENSCHEIDT, Paul: Arme, kleine Eva 1907	100,000	1930
MOLO, Walter v: Der Schiller-Roman 1918	100,000+	1935
NERGER, K. A.: S. M. S. "Wolf" u "Wölfchen" 1919	100,000	1919
PRESBER, Rudolf: Mein Bruder Benjamin 1919	100,000	1937
ROSE, Felicitas: Der Tisch der Rasmussen 1920	100,000	1939
ROSEN, Erwin: Orgesch 1921	100,000	1921
SCHNITZLER, Arthur: Reigen. Zehn Dialoge 1900	100,000+	1923
SCHROTT-FIECHTL, Hans: Die Herzensflickerin 1912	100,000	1924
SKOWRONNEK, Richard: Die Sporck'schen Jäger 1912	100,000+	1929

TABLE A (con't.)

STEGUWEIT, Heinz: Heilige Unrast 1936	100,000	1940
STRAUSS UND TORNEY, Lulu v: Bauernstolz 1901	100,000+	1938
THOMA, Ludwig: Altaich 1918	100,000	1940
UNGER, Hellmuth: Robert Koch (Helfer d Menschheit) 1929	100,000	1940
VOIGT-DIEDERICHS, Helene: Auf Marienhoff 1925	100,000	1940
WINCKLER, Josef: Pumpernickel. Menschen u Geschn um Haus Nyland 1926	100,000	1933
BRAUN, Otto: Aus nachgelassenen Schriften eines Früh-vollendeten 1920	99,000	1922
GRABEIN, Paul: Ursula Drenck 1908	c 99,000	1935
MANN, Thomas: Tonio Kröger 1914	99,000+	1935
SPECKMANN, Diedrich: Herzensheilige 1909	99,000	1936
ZILLE, Heinrich: Das H. Zille-Werk, 3 Bde, 1. Bd: Kinder d Strasse 1908	99,000	1925
BREHM, Bruno v: Weder Kaiser noch König... 1933	98,000	1940
HERZOG, Rudolf: Horridoh Lützow 1932	98,000+	1940
KELLER, Paul: Stille Strassen 1912	98,000	1932
SVENSSON, Jon: Nonni 1913	c 98,000	1939
STEHR, Hermann: Peter Brindeisener 1924	98,000	1940
FRENSSEN, Gustav: Der Pastor von Poggsee 1921	97,000	1935
MÜLLER-HENNIG, Erika: Wolgakinder 1934	97,000	1940
WEBER, Alexander Otto: Mixed Pickles 1904	97,000	1924
JELUSICH, Mirko: Caesar 1929	96,000	1940
KELLER, Paul: Die fünf Waldstädte 1910	96,000	1932
KELLERMANN, Bernhard: Das Meer 1910	96,000	1929

TABLE A (con't.)

ROSE, Felicitas: Das Lyzeum in Birkholz 1917	96,000	1937
SONNLEITNER, A. Th.: Die Höhlenkinder im Pfahlbau 1919	96,000	1940
BRAUSEWETTER, Arthur: Wer die Heimat liebt wie du 1916	95,000	1931
DOMINIK, Hans: Himmelskraft 1937	95,000	1940
GÜNTHER, Agnes: Von d Hexe, die e Heilige war 1913	c 95,000	1931
HEER, Jakob Christoph: Nick Tappoli 1920	95,000	1932
HUCH, Ricarda: Lebenslauf d heiligen Wonnebald Pück 1905	95,000	1931
KLABUND: Borgia 1928	95,000	1931
LÖNS, Hermann: Isegrimms Irrgang 1916	95,000	1938
LÖNS, Hermann: Der zweckmässige Meyer 1911	95,000	1937
MECHOW, Karl Benno v: Vorsommer 1934	95,000	1940
MEYRINK, Gustav: Das grüne Gesicht 1916	95,000	1921
NEEFF, Adolf: Vom alten Fritz c 1916	95,000	1939
PAUL, Adolf: Die Tänzerin Barberina 1915	95,000	1938
SCHIEBER, Anna: Amaryllis u a Geschn 1914	95,000	1933
SCHRÖER, Gustav: Der Heiland vom Binsenhofe 1918	95,000	1937
WOTHE, Anny: Die Vogesenwacht 1915	95,000	1919
FRANK, Leonhard: Der Bürger 1924	94,000	1929
HUNNIUS, Monika: Meine Weihnachten 1922	94,000	1939
BRANDT, Rolf: Albert Leo Schlageter... 1926	93,000	1940
DOMINIK, Hans: Die Spur des Dschingis-Khan 1923	93,000	1939
ZAHN, Ernst: Vier Erzn aus Helden d Alltags 1907	93,000	1934
BINDING, Rudolf Georg: Sankt Georgs Stellvertreter 1934	92,000	1940

TABLE A (con't.)

MAY, Karl: Am Jenseits 1899	92,000	1931
ROSEGGER, Peter: Alpensommer 1909	92,000	1933
BARTSCH, R.H.: D Geschichte von d Hannerl u ihren Liebhabern 1913	91,000	1934
BARTSCH, R. H.: Zwölf aus der Steiermark 1908	91,000+	1933
FRENSSEN, Gustav: Der Untergang d Anna Hollmann 1911	91,000+	1937
LAAR, Clemens: D Kampf um die Dardanellen 1936	91,000	1940
THOMA, Ludwig: Jozef Filsers gesammelter Briefwexel Tl II 1912	91,000	1940
WEBER, Alexander Otto: Ohne Maulkorb 1904	91,000	1924
BINDING, R. G.: Moselfahrt aus Liebeskummer 1932	90,000	1924
BONSELS, W.: Ave vita. Leben, ich grüsse Dich 1905	90,000+	1922
DOMINIK, Hans: Das stählerne Geheimnis 1934	90,000	1940
FENDRICH, Anton: Mit d Auto an d Front 1915	90,000	1917
FORSTER, Hanna: Die Privatsekretärin 1916	90,000	1924
GILLHOFF, Johannes: Jürnjakob Swehn, der Amerikafahrer Auswahl 1917	90,000	1940
KOLBENHEYER, E. G.: Karlsbader Novelle 1934	90,000	1940
KRICKEBERG, Elisabeth: Siddys Ehekontrakt 1917	c 90,000	1923
LIENHARD, Friedrich: Der Spielmann 1913	90,000	1922
MEYRINK, Gustav: Walpurgisnacht 1917	90,000	1920
PAUST, Otto: Volk im Feuer 1935	90,000+	1940
PLÜSCHOW, Gunther: Segelfahrt ins Wunderland... 1926	90,000	1939
REDWITZ, Marie v: Der Liebe Dornenpfad 1918	90,000	1919
RILKE, R. M.: Briefe an eine junge Frau 1930	90,000	1933
Die Teufelsmauer. Heitere Geschn... 1904	90,000	1927

TABLE A (con't.)

THIESS, Frank: Die Verdammten 1930	90,000	1930
THOMA, Ludwig: D lustige Geschichtenbüchlein 1936	90,000	1940
TUCHOLSKY, Kurt: Rheinsberg 1912	90,000	1928
WINNIG, August: Heimkehr 1935	90,000+	1940
ZILLE, Heinrich: Das H.-Zille-Werk, 3 Bde, 2. Bd: Mein Milljöh 1914	90,000	1925
ZWEIG, Stefan: Verwirrung der Gefühle 1926	90,000	1931
STEHR, Hermann: Drei Nächte 1909	89,000+	1935
HEER, Jakob Christoph: Joggeli 1902	88,000	1937
HESSE, Hermann: Demian 1919	88,000	1937
BONSELS, W.: Mario. E Leben im Walde 1939	87,000	1940
GANGHOFER, Ludwig: Hubertusland 1912	87,000	1929
JANSEN, Werner: Das Buch Leidenschaft 1920	87,000	1940
SCHRECKENBACH, Paul: D böse Baron v Krosigk 1907	87,000	1940
WOTHE, Anny: Zauber-Runen 1919	c 87,000	1922
DÖRFLER, Peter: Als Mutter noch lebte 1912	86,000	1940
ROSEGGER, Peter: Die Abelsberger Chronik 1907	86,000	1933
SPECKMANN, Diedrich: Neu-Lohe 1920	86,000	1939
BINDING, Rudolf Georg: Legenden der Zeit 1909	85,000	1940
DOMINIK, Hans: Lebensstrahlen 1938	85,000	1940
GANGHOFER, Ludwig: Damian Zagg 1906	85,000	1929
GREINZ, Rudolf: Der Garten Gottes 1919	85,000	1940
HAARBECK, Lina: Geschichten aus d Rauhen Hause 1936	85,000	1940
KELLER, Paul: Seminartheater u a Geschn 1916	85,000+	1932
SPECKMANN, Diedrich: Geschwister Rosenbrock 1912	85,000	1939

TABLE A (con't.)

WINNIG, August: Der weite Weg 1932	85,000	1940
BONSELS, W.: Der tiefste Traum 1911	84,000+	1926
DORN, Käthe: Die schönsten Hände 1911	84,000	1925
LANGENSCHEIDT, Paul: Ich habe dich lieb! 1909	84,000	1930
SCHLEICH, Karl Ludwig: Es läuten die Glocken 1912	84,000+	1930
SONNLEITNER, A. Th.: D Höhlenkinder im Steinhaus 1920	84,000	1940
ZAHN, Ernst: Die Clari-Marie 1904	84,000	1939
ZAHN, Ernst: Helden des Alltags 1905	84,000	1939
ZAHN, Ernst: Lotte Esslingers Wille und Weg 1919	84,000	1926
BARTSCH, Rudolf Hans: Vom sterbenden Rokoko 1909	83,000+	1934
BARTSCH, Rudolf Hans: Frau Utta u d Jäger 1914	83,000	1932
DEHMEL, Richard: Zwei Menschen 1903	83,000	1927
GANGHOFER, Ludwig: Die Jäger 1905	83,000	1929
HANDEL-MAZZETTI, E. Gräfin v: D dt Held 1920	83,000	1936
HAUPTMANN, Gerhart: D Narr in Christo Emanuel Quint 1910	83,000	1928
HERZOG, Rudolf: Der alten Sehnsucht Lied 1906	83,000	1935
ZAHN, Ernst: Nacht 1917	83,000	1926
BINDING, R. G.: Keuschheitslegende 1919	82,000	1934
CAROSSA, Hans: Der Arzt Gion 1931	82,000	1940
KRÜGER, Hermann Anders: Gottfried Kämpfer 1904	82,000	1930
MAY, Karl: Ardistan und Dschinnistan 1909	82,000	1928
SAPPER, Agnes: Frau Pauline Brater. Lebensbild e dt Frau 1908	82,000	1929
SCHRÖER, Gustav: Der Schelm von Bruckau 1938	82,000	1940

TABLE A (con't.)

WASSERMANN, Jakob: Der niegeküsste Mund 1903	82,000	1928
BUSSE, Hermann Eris: Bauernadel 1933	81,000	1938
STRAUSS, Emil: Der Engelwirt 1900	81,000	1940
SUDERMANN, Hermann: Litauische Geschichten 1917	81,000	1940
FEUCHTWANGER, Lion: Jud Süss 1917	80,000+	1929
FLEX, Walter: Wallensteins Antlitz 1918	80,000	1940
GRIMM, Hans: Der Ölsucher von Duala 1918	80,000+	1940
KELLER, Paul: Altenroda 1921	80,000	1932
KRÖGER, Timm: Im Nebel (from Leute eigener Art) 1906	80,000	1926
LÖNS, Hermann: D Tal der Lieder u a Schiln ?	80,000	1925
MANN, Thomas: Der Tod in Venedig 1913	80,000	1930
PANY, Lenore: Gegen den Strom 1916	80,000	1919
ROSEGGER, Peter: D Adlerwirt v Kirchbrunn 1907	80,000+	1920
SCHÄFER, Wilhelm: Die Anekdoten 1935	80,000+	1940
SCHNITZLER, Arthur: Frau Berta Garlan 1901	80,000+	1925
SOMMER, Rolf: Fliegerhauptmann Oswald Boelcke 1916	80,000	1918
STILGEBAUER, Eduard: Götz Krafft. D Gesch e Jugend in 4 Bänden, Bd I: Mit tausend Masten 1904	80,000	1930
VOSS, Richard: D Erlösung. D wunderbare Gesch e wundersamen Menschen 1918	80,000	1925
ZAHN, Ernst: Einsamkeit 1909	80,000	1939
BERNDORFF, Hans Rudolf: Spionage 1929	79,000	1934
KNEIP, Jakob: Hampit der Jäger 1927	79,000	1939
OBERLÄNDER, Adolf: Heiteres und Ernstes 1917	79,000	1923
ROSE, Felicitas: D graue Alltag u sein Licht 1922	79,000	1937

TABLE A (con't.)

BIERBAUM, Otto Julius: Prinz Kuckuck... 1907	c 78,000+	1922
BREHM, Bruno v: Das war das Ende 1932	78,000	1940
HEER, Jakob Christoph: Felix Notvest 1901	78,000	1935
JELUSICH, Mirko: Der Löwe 1936	78,000	1940
KINAU, Rudolf: Blinkfüer. Helle u düstere Biller 1918	78,000	1934
ROSEGGER, Peter: I. N. R. I. 1905	78,000	1931
BEUMELBURG, Werner: Deutschland in Ketten... 1931	77,000	1940
BROD, Max: Tycho Brahes Weg zu Gott 1916	77,000+	1930
JELUSICH, Mirko: Hannibal 1934	77,000	1940
LOBSIEN, Wilhelm: Klaus Stötebeker 1927	77,000	1939
UTSCH, Rudolf: Herrin und Knecht 1936	77,000	1940
HEUBNER, Rudolf: D heilige Geist, Tl I: Jakob Siemering & Co. 1917	c 76,000	1934
SCHRECKENBACH, Paul: Um die Wartburg 1913	76,000	1933

50 THOUSAND TO 75 THOUSAND

FRANK, Leonhard: Der Mensch ist gut 1919	75,000	1935
GOOTE, Thor: Wir tragen das Leben 1932	75,000	1939
HAUPTMANN, Gerhart: Die Insel der grossen Mutter... 1925	75,000+	1925
HAUSMANN, Manfred: Abel mit d Mundharmonika 1932	75,000	1940
HUCH, Friedrich: Geschwister 1903	75,000	1927
KUNTZE, Paul Heinrich: Volk und Seefahrt 1939	75,000	1940
LANGEWIESCHE, W.: Jugend und Heimat 1916	75,000	1925

TABLE A (con't.)

MANN, Thomas: Das Wunderkind 1903	75,000	1927
PHILIPPI, Felix: Cornelie Arendt 1915	75,000	1925
REMARQUE, E. M.: Der Weg zurück 1931	75,000	1931
SCHIEBER, Anna: Annegret 1922	75,000	1937
SÖRENSEN, Wulf: Die Stimme der Ahnen 1933	75,000+	1936
SVENSSON, Jon: Nonni u Manni 1914	75,000+	1927
WAGGERL, Karl Heinrich: Das Wiesenbuch 1932	75,000	1934
BURTE, Hermann: Wiltfeber, der ewige Deutsche 1912	74,000+	1940
HANDEL-MAZZETTI, E. Gräfin v: Jungfrau u Märtyrin 1914	74,000	1927
LANGENSCHEIDT, Paul: Du bist mein! 1910	74,000	1928
MALTZAHN, Elisabeth: Das heilige Nein 1912	74,000	1936
MAY, Karl: Trapper Geierschnabel 1923	74,000	1939
SCHAFFNER, Jakob: Konrad Pilater 1910	c 74,000+	1929
SCHOLZ, Wilhelm v: Die Pflicht 1926	74,000	1940
STRATZ, Rudolf: Du Schwert an meiner Linken 1912	74,000	1928
FOCK, Gorch: Hein Godenwind, de Admirol v Moskitonien 1912	73,000	1940
GONTARD-SCHUCK, Margarete: Seelenverkäufer... 1914	73,000	1920
LÖNS, Hermann: Aus Forst u Flur. Tiernovellen ?	73,000	1935
NIESE, Charlotte: Das Lagerkind 1914	73,000+	1940
ROSEGGER, Peter: Sonnenschein 1901	73,000	1933
EURINGER, Richard: Fliegerschule. 4. Buch d Mannschaft 1929	72,000	1940
LANGENSCHEIDT, Paul: Blondes Gift 1911	72,000	1930
MAY, Karl: Und Friede auf Erden 1904	72,000	1939

TABLE A (con't.)

SVENSSON, Jon: Sonnentage 1914	c 72,000	1939
ZAHN, Ernst: Jonas Truttmann 1921	72,000	1930
BROCKDORFF, Gertr. Baronin v: Die letzte Zarin. Alexandra Federowna 1917	71,000+	1940
GLUTH, Oskar: Der verhexte Spitzweg 1928	71,000	1940
HERZOG, Rudolf: Die Welt in Gold 1913	71,000+	1932
HEUBNER, Rudolf: Der heilige Geist, Tl II: Jakob Siemerings Erben 1918	c 71,000	1934
KARRASCH, Alfred: Parteigenosse Schmiedecke 1934	71,000	1940
KELLER, Paul: Grünlein. E dt Kriegsgesch... 1915	71,000	1927
LANDSBERGER, Arthur: Lu, die Kokette 1914	71,000+	1928
PAPKE, Käthe: Das Forsthaus... 1920	c 71,000	1940
ROSE, Felicitas: Die Eiks von Eichen 1908	71,000	1937
ROSEGGER, Peter: Nixnutzig Volk... 1906	71,000	1933
BLOEM, Walter: Gottesferne 1920	70,000	1932
BLUNCK, Hans F.: König Geiserich 1936	70,000	1939
BORCHART, Elsbeth: Des Weibes Waffen 1916	70,000	1919
DOMINIK, Hans: Der Brand d Cheopspyramide 1926	70,000	1940
DWINGER, E. E.: Das namenlose Heer (from <u>Die Armee hinter Stacheldraht...</u>) 1935	70,000	1940
FREI, Friedrich: Unser Fliegerheld Immelmann... c 1916	70,000	1916
HERZBERG, Margarete: Die Intrigantin 1919	70,000	1919
HERZBERG, Margarete: Baroness Kläre 1915	70,000	1917
HERZOG, Rudolf: D Fähnlein d Versprengten 1926	70,000	1926
HOCH, Christa: Soldatentöchter. Offiziergeschn 1912	70,000	1919

TABLE A (con't.)

HÖCKER, Paul Oskar: Kleine Mama 1910	70,000	1937
JENSEN, Wilhelm: Über die Heide 1907	70,000	1921
KYBER, Manfred: Neue Tiergeschichten (Unter Tieren, Bd II) 1926	70,000	1935
LANGSDORFF, Werner: Flieger am Feind... 1934	70,000	1940
MIEGEL, Agnes: D Fahrt d sieben Ordensbrüder 1933	70,000	1939
NEUBAU, Robert: Kriegsgefangen - über England entflohen c 1916	70,000	1916
OBERKOFLER, Joseph Georg: Der Bannwald 1939	70,000	1940
SCHMIDT, Franz v: Ich heisse Viktor Mors... 1937	70,000	1938
SCHRECKENBACH, Wolfgang: Die Stedinger. D Heldenlied e Bauernvolkes 1936	70,000	1940
SCHRÖER, Gustav: Die Flucht aus dem Alltag 1924	70,000	1940
STEGUWEIT, Heinz: Frohes Leben 1934	70,000	1940
VIESÈR, Dolores: Das Singerlein 1928	70,000	1939
HANDEL-MAZZETTI, E. Gräfin v: Unter dem Richter von Steyr 1912	69,000	1927
SPECK, Wilhelm: Der Joggeli 1907	69,000	1924
DREESEN, Willrath: Ebba Hüsing 1909	68,000+	1919
ECKMANN, Heinrich: Eira u der Gefangene 1935	68,000	1940
FENDRICH, Anton: An Bord. Kriegserle... 1916	68,000	1917
FOCK, Gorch: Sterne überm Meer 1917	68,000	1940
KEYSERLING, Eduard v: Beate und Mareile 1903	68,000+	1925
LETTOW-VORBECK, Paul: Meine Erinnerungen aus Ostafrika 1920	68,000	1938
SCHIROKAUER, Alfred: Ferdinand Lassalle... 1912	68,000	1930
SCHRECKENBACH, Paul: Die letzten Rudelsburger 1913	68,000	1933

TABLE A (con't.)

SLEZAK, Leo: Meine sämtlichen Werke 1922	68,000+	1940
WISPLER, Leo: Spiel im Sommerwind 1937	68,000	1940
DURIAN, Wolf: Kai aus der Kiste 1927	67,000+	1937
ERNST, Otto: Semper der Mann 1917	67,000	1938
HEER, Jakob Christoph: Der lange Balthasar 1915	67,000	1929
SCHARRELMANN, Heinrich: Berni, I. E kl Junge, was er sah... 1916	67,000+	1929
SCHRECKENBACH, Paul: Der getreue Kleist 1910	67,000	1933
WEBER, Alexander Otto: Satyr lacht -- 1904	67,000+	1924
ZAHN, Ernst: Firnwind 1906	67,000	1930
BEUMELBURG, Werner: D König u d Kaiserin. Friedrich d Grosse u Maria Theresia 1937	66,000	1940
SEELIGER, Ewald Gerhard: Bark Fortuna oder Mandus Frixens erste Reise 1909	66,000	1930
STRATZ, Rudolf: Alt-Heidelberg, du Feine... 1902	66,000	1932
STRATZ, Rudolf: Für dich 1909	66,000	1930
STRATZ, Rudolf: Herzblut 1909	66,000	1928
ZAHN, Ernst: D Liebe des Severin Imboden 1916	66,000	1933
BIERBAUM, Otto Julius: Zäpfel Kerns Abenteuer 1905	65,000	1940
BOREE, Karl F.: Dor und der September 1931	65,000	1934
CAROSSA, Hans: Geheimnisse des reifen Lebens 1936	65,000	1940
DOMINIK, Hans: Befehl aus dem Dunkel 1933	65,000	1940
DOMINIK, Hans: Kautschuk 1930	65,000	1940
ERNST, Paul: Erdachte Gespräche. E Auswahl 1921	65,000+	1939
FRENSSEN, Gustav: Dummhans 1929	65,000+	1940

TABLE A (con't.)

HANDEL-MAZZETTI, E. Gräfin v: D Geheimnis d Königs 1913	65,000	1927
HOFFENSTHAL, Hans: Lori Graff 1909	65,000	1930
MANN, Heinrich: D Kaiserreich, 3. Bd: Die Armen 1912	65,000	1931
MAY, Karl: Der sterbende Kaiser 1923	65,000	1939
OEHRLEIN, Ernst: D Rose v Sankt Pauli (Jan Feltens Liebesabenteuer) c 1918	65,000	1932
PLEYER, Wilhelm: Die Brüder Tommahans 1937	65,000	1940
REUTER, Gabriele: Ellen von der Weiden 1900	65,000	1929
THIESS, Frank: Frauenraub 1927	65,000	1933
WERFEL, Franz: Barbara oder die Frommigkeit 1929	65,000+	1930
WERFEL, Franz: Verdi. Roman der Oper 1924	65,000	1928
ZAUNERT, Paul: Von Riesen u Zwergen u Waldgeistern 1937	65,000	1940
ZILLICH, Heinrich: Der Urlaub 1933	65,000	1940
FOCK, Gorch: Schullengrieper u Tungenknieper... 1911	64,000	1940
FOCK, Gorch: Nordsee 1916	64,000	1926
HESSE, Hermann: Narziss und Goldmund 1930	64,000	1940
PRESBER, Rudolf: Von Leutchen, die ich liebgewann 1905	64,000	1927
ROSE, Felicitas: Erlenkamp Erben 1924	64,000	1932
STILGEBAUER, Eduard: Götz Krafft. D Gesch e Jugend in 4 Bänden, Bd II: Im Strom der Welt 1904	64,000	1930
WIECHERT, Ernst: Das heilige Jahr 1936	64,000	1940
ADLERFELD-BALLESTREM, E. v: Trix 1903	63,000	1937
DOMINIK, Hans: John Workmann, d Zeitungsboy... 1921	63,000+	1938

TABLE A (con't.)

FINCKH, Ludwig: Die Reise nach Tripstrill 1911	63,000	1939
HERZOG, Rudolf: Kornelius Vanderwelts Gefährtin 1928	63,000	1938
JANSEN, Werner: Heinrich der Löwe 1923	63,000	1940
ROMBACH, Otto: Adrian, der Tulpendieb 1936	63,000	1940
ZAHN, Ernst: Albin Indergand 1900	63,000	1928
BEHRENS-LITZMANN, Anna: Herbstgewitter 1915	62,000	1919
KURZ, Isolde: Vanadis. Schicksalsweg e Frau 1931	62,000+	1937
LUX, Joseph August: Grillparzers Liebesroman. Die Schwestern Fröhlich 1912	62,000	1930
PONTEN, Joseph: Der babylonische Turm 1918	62,000	1932
RODA RODA, Alexander: Die verfolgte Unschuld 1914	62,000	1918
STRAUSS, Emil: Kreuzungen 1904	62,000	1925
MÜLLER-GUTTENBRUNN, Adam: D grosse Schwabenzug 1913	61,000	1940
PONTEN, Joseph: Der Meister 1919	c 61,000+	1940
ROSE, Felicitas: Meerkönigs Haus 1917	61,000	1937
SCHNITZLER, Arthur: D griechische Tänzerin u a Novn 1904	61,000	1921
STEGEMANN, Hermann: Der Kampf um den Rhein 1924	61,000	1935
BARTSCH, Rudolf Hans: Das deutsche Leid 1912	60,000	1929
BEUMELBURG, Werner: Kampf um Spanien... 1939	60,000	1940
Mieze Biebenbachs Erlebnisse. Erinn e Kellnerin ?	60,000	1919
BONSELS, W.: Mario und die Tiere 1927	60,000	1940
BONSELS, W.: Mario u d Tiere (with pictures) 1928	60,000	1940
BONSELS, W.: Blut 1909	60,000	1926
BRÜES, Otto: Das Gauklerzelt 1939	60,000	1940

TABLE A (con't.)

BÜRGEL, Bruno H.: Der Stern von Afrika 1921	60,000	1937
DILL, Liesbet: Die Spionin 1917	60,000	1928
DOMINIK, Hans: D Erbe d Uraniden 1928	60,000	1939
DOMINIK, Hans: Vistra, d weisse Gold Dtlds 1936	60,000	1937
FEDERER, Heinrich: Patria 1916	60,000+	1924
FRANCK, Hans: Der Regenbogen. 7 mal 7 Geschn 1927	60,000	1936
HAAS, Rudolf: Matthias Triebl 1915	60,000	1934
HEER, Jakob Christoph: Heinrichs Romfahrt 1918	60,000	1918
HÖCKER, Paul Oskar: D reizendste Frau - ausser Johanna 1935	60,000	1940
HUCH, Felix: Der junge Beethoven 1927	60,000	1940
JÜNGER, Ernst: In Stahlgewittern 1920	c 60,000	1940
KLABUND: Pjotr 1923	60,000+	1932
KOLBENHEYER, E. G.: Paracelsus, Tl I: D Kindheit d Paracelsus 1917	60,000	1940
LANGEWIESCHE, W.: Wolfs. Geschn um e Bürgerhaus 1. Buch: Im Schatten Napoleons 1919	60,000	1925
2. Buch: Vor Bismarcks Aufgang 1919	60,000	1925
LÖNS, Hermann: Das Lönsbuch ?	60,000+	1925
MAY, Karl: Vom Rhein zur Mopimi 1923	60,000	1940
MAY, Karl: Benito Juarez 1923	60,000	1939
MIEGEL, Agnes: Unter hellem Himmel 1936	60,000	1940
MUSCHLER, Reinhold Conrad: Bianca Maria 1924	60,000	1931
NEEFF, Adolf: Anekdoten von Bismarck 1917	60,000	1940
PHILIPPI, Felix: Das Schwalbennest 1919	60,000	1925

TABLE A (con't.)

REDWITZ, Marie v: Meeresrauschen u Herzensstürme 1918	60,000	1919
RILKE, R. M.: Auguste Rodin 1903	60,000	1934
ROSEGGER, Peter: Weltgift 1903	60,000+	1933
ROSEN, Erwin: D dt Lausbub in Amerika, Tl I 1911	60,000+	1926
SCHNITZLER, Arthur: Fräulein Else 1924	60,000	1928
SCHRÖER, Gustav: Das Land Not 1928	60,000	1933
SPÖRL, Heinrich: Wenn wir alle Engel wären 1936	60,000	1939
STEIN, Lola: Der gute Kamerad 1918	c 60,000	1923
STRAUSS, Emil: Lebenstanz 1940	60,000	1940
WILDENBRUCH, Ernst v: Neid 1900	60,000	1939
WOTHE, Anny: Drei graue Reiter 1919	60,000+	1919
EWERS, Hans Heinz: Das Grauen 1907	59,000	1922
FEDERER, Heinrich: In Franzens Poetenstube 1918	59,000	1930
GEORGY, Ernst: Jugendstürme 1900	59,000	1921
KELLER, Paul: Von Hause. E Päckchen Humor... 1917	59,000	1929
LUX, Joseph August: Lola Montez 1912	59,000	1930
SCHMITTHENNER, Adolf: Das deutsche Herz 1908	59,000	1939
BEREND, Alice: Spreemann & Co. 1916	58,000	1933
BUSCHBECKER, Karl Matthias: Wie unser Gesetz es befahl 1936	58,000	1939
HÖCKER, Paul Oskar: Zwischen Hochzeit u Heirat (Die junge Exzellenz) 1914	58,000	1937
HUNNIUS, Monika: Mein Onkel Hermann 1922	58,000	1940
LAND, Hans: Stadtsanwalt Jordan 1915	58,000	1930
LAND, Hans: Stürme 1922	c 58,000	1922

TABLE A (con't.)

LÖNS, Hermann: Kraut u Lot 1911	58,000	1922
MAY, Karl Schloss Rodriganda 1923	58,000	1940
NECKE, Max: Weihnachtsgeschichten 1909	58,000	1932
PAASCHE, Hans: D Forschungsreise d Afrikaners L. M. ins innerste Deutschland 1921	c 58,000	1929
SPECKMANN, Diedrich: Erich Heydenreichs Dorf 1913	58,000	1922
STOCKHAUSEN, Juliane: D Soldaten der Kaiserin 1924	58,000	1932
TRENKER, Luis: Der verlorene Sohn 1934	58,000+	1938
WAGGERL, Karl Heinrich: Brot 1930	58,000	1940
WIECHERT, Ernst: Der Kinderkreuzzug 1935	58,000	1939
ZAHN, Ernst: Die Frauen von Tannò 1911	58,000+	1925
BARTSCH, Rudolf Hans: Seine Jüdin oder Jakob Böhmes Schusterkugel 1921	57,000	1922
FLEX, Walter: D Kanzler Klaus v Bismarck 1914	57,000	1937
GANGHOFER, Ludwig: Das Kind u d Million 1919	57,000	1926
HUNNIUS, Monika: Mein Weg zur Kunst 1925	57,000	1935
IMMELMANN, Max: Immelmann, d Adler v Lille 1934	57,000	1940
ROSE, Felicitas: Pastor Verden 1912	57,000	1940
ROSEGGER, Peter: Die Försterbuben 1908	57,000	1933
SCHRECKENBACH, Paul: Die von Wintzingerode 1905	57,000	1933
SCHRECKENBACH, Paul: Der deutsche Herzog 1915	57,000	1934
VIEBIG, Clara: Einer Mutter Sohn 1906	57,000	1929
WASSERMANN, Jakob: Etzel Andergast 1931	57,000	1934
BAUM, Vicki: Menschen im Hotel 1929	56,000	1931
BOY-ED, Ida: Ein königlicher Kaufmann 1910	56,000	1926

TABLE A (con't.)

BUSCH, Fritz Otto: Flieger gegen England 1939	56,000	1940
BUSCH, Fritz Otto: U-Boote gegen England 1939	56,000	1940
FEDERER, Heinrich: Gebt mir meine Wildnis wieder 1918	56,000	1929
FLEX, Walter: Wolf Eschenlohr 1919	56,000	1931
HANDEL-MAZZETTI, E. Gräfin v: Brüderlein u Schwesterlein 1913	56,000	1927
LUDWIG, Emil: Bismarck. Gesch e Kämpfers 1911	c 56,000+	1927
MÜLLER-PARTENKIRCHEN, Fritz: Die Firma 1935	56,000	1940
ROSENHAYN, Paul: Elf Abenteuer des Joe Jenkins 1916	56,000	1927
SCHRECKENBACH, Paul: Michael Meyenburg ?	56,000	1933
SEMSROTT, Albert: Der Durchbruch der "Möwe" 1928	56,000+	1940
ZAHN, Ernst: Die da kommen und gehen 1908	56,000+	1923
BAHR, Hermann: Die Hexe Drut 1909	55,000	1929
BRUNNGRABER, Rudolf: Radium 1936	55,000	1940
ERNST, Otto: Vom geruhigen Leben 1902	55,000	1927
ETTIGHOFER, P. C.: Das gefesselte Heer 1932	55,000	1938
GRIESE, Friedrich: Die Wagenburg 1935	55,000	1940
Das feste Herz. E Gabe dt Erzähler 1939	55,000	1940
HESSE, Hermann: Rosshalde 1914	55,000	1932
HUNNIUS, Monika: Menschen, die ich erlebte 1922	55,000	1940
KELLERMANN, Bernhard: Der 9. November 1920	55,000+	1929
KINAU, Rudolf: Steernkiekers 1917	55,000	1924
KLEPPER, Jochen: Der Vater 1937	55,000	1940
KOLBENHEYER, E. G.: Das gottgelobte Herz 1938	55,000	1940

TABLE A (con't.)

LAAR, Clemens: Kampf in der Wüste 1936	55,000+	1939
LÖNS, Hermann: Gesammelte Werke in 8 Bänden 1920	55,000	1940
MAY, Karl: Der alte Dessauer 1921	55,000	1940
MÜLLER-GUTTENBRUNN, Adam: D Glocken d Heimat 1910	55,000	1934
RILKE, R. M.: Geschichten vom Lieben Gott 1900	55,000	1936
ROSE, Felicitas: Die Erbschmiede 1926	55,000	1937
SAPPER, Agnes: Ohne den Vater 1915	55,000	1935
SCHÄFER, Wilhelm: D Fahrt in d Heiligen Abend 1935	55,000	1940
SCHIEBER, Anna: Ludwig Fugeler 1918	55,000	1938
SCHOBERT, Hedwig: Schwüle Stunden 1918	55,000+	1920
SKOWRONNEK, Richard: D Liebschaften d Käte Keller 1918	55,000	1922
SPIEGEL, E. v: U-Boot im Fegefeuer 1930	55,000	1940
STILGEBAUER, Eduard: Götz Krafft. D Gesch e Jugend in 4 Bänden, Bd III: Im engen Kreis 1904	55,000	1930
THOMA, Ludwig: Geschichten. E Auswahl 1917	55,000	1939
TRELLER, Franz: Der Letzte vom "Admiral" 1899	55,000	1939
WOLF, Friedrich: Kreatur 1925	55,000	1927
WRIEDE, Paul: Hamburger Volkshumor in Redensarten... 1924	55,000	1925
ZAHN, Ernst: Menschen 1900	55,000	1929
BAUDISSIN, Ida Gräfin: Durch Sturm und Not 1914	54,000	1919
BLOMBERG, Anna v: Reggfields Tochter 1900	54,000	1935
BLUNCK, Hans F.: Die Weibsmühle 1927	54,000	1940
BÖHME, Margarethe: Dida Ibsens Tagebuch. E Finale zum Tagebuch e Verlorenen 1907	54,000	1921

TABLE A (con't.)

BRAUN, Lily: Memorien einer Sozialistin, I: Lehrjahre 1909	54,000	1924
BREHM, Bruno v: Auf Wiedersehen, Susanne! 1940	54,000	1940
BUSCH, Fritz Otto: Zwei Jungens unter d Kriegsfahne (new series of Zwei Jungen bei der Reichmarine) 1933	54,000	1940
GINZKEY, Franz Karl: Der von der Vogelweide 1912	54,000	1933
GRABEIN, Paul: Du mein Jena (Vivat academia!) 1903	54,000+	1935
GRABEIN, Paul: Die Moosschwaige 1907	54,000	1935
GREINZ, Rudolf: Vorfrühling der Liebe 1925	54,000	1940
KINAU, Rudolf: Thees Bott dat Woterküken 1919	54,000	1930
KÜLPE, Frances: Kinder der Liebe 1912	c 54,000	1929
MARTIN, Marie: Deutsches Heimatglück 1917	54,000	1925
MAY, Karl: Aus dunklen Tann 1921	54,000	1940
MAY, Karl: Der Waldschwarze u a Erzn 1921	54,000	1939
BISCHOFF, Charitas: Bilder aus meinem Leben 1912	53,000	1938
EIPPER, Paul: Menschenkinder 1920	53,000	1935
EYTH, Max: Der Kampf um die Cheopspyramide... 1902	53,000+	1935
HAUPTMANN, Gerhart: Atlantis 1912	53,000	1925
KERN, Maximilian: Selbst der Mann c 1904	53,000	1931
PAUST, Otto: Land im Licht 1937	53,000	1940
SCHRECKENBACH, Paul: Wildefüer ?	53,000	1928
SCHUMACHER, Heinrich Vollrat: Kaiserin Eugenia 1913	53,000+	1929
SPECKMANN, Diedrich: Der Anerbe 1914	53,000	1921
STRATZ, Rudolf: Stark wie die Mark 1913	53,000	1928
WEBER, Alexander Otto: Durch die Lupe 1905	53,000	1924

TABLE A (con't.)

ZAHN, Ernst: Der Apotheker von Klein-Weltwil 1913	53,000	1926
ZAHN, Ernst: Was das Leben zerbricht 1912	53,000+	1922
ZWEIG, Stefan: Joseph Fouché 1930	53,000	1932
FOCK, Gorch: Fahrensleute. Neue Seegeschn 1914	52,000	1940
FOCK, Gorch: Hamborger Janmooten. Een lustig Book 1914	52,000	1925
GRAVENHORST, Traud: Heimweh des Herzens 1935	52,000	1940
GREINZ, Rudolf: Die Stadt am Inn 1917	52,000	1933
HUCH, Friedrich: Mao 1907	52,000	1928
KLEMM, Johanna: Waldasyl 1913	52,000+	1919
MANN, Heinrich: Die Jagd nach Liebe 1905	52,000+	1925
MANN, Heinrich: D Göttinnen oder d drei Romane der Herzogin von Assy 1902-1904		
1. Diana 1902	52,000+	1925
2. Minerva 1903	52,000+	1925
3. Venus 1904	52,000+	1925
SCHARRELMANN, Heinrich: Berni, III: Berni im Seebade 1918	52,000	1930
BOREE, Karl F.: Narren und Helden 1923	51,000	1925
BOSSI-FEDRIGOTTI, Anton Graf v: Standschütze Bruggler 1934	51,000	1936
FEDERER, Heinrich: Das Mätteliseppi 1916	51,000	1931
FRENSSEN, Gustav: Lütte Witt 1924	51,000	1930
GINZKEY, Franz Karl: Der Wiesenzaun 1913	51,000	1935
HEER, Jakob Christoph: Da träumen sie von Lieb u Glück 1910	51,000	1929
HERZOG, Rudolf: Gesammelte Werke, Reihe I, 6 Bde 1920	51,000	1929

TABLE A (con't.)

KEYSERLING, Eduard v: Am Südhang 1916	51,000	1924
OMPTEDA, Georg Frhr v: Excelsior 1910	51,000	1937
REISER, Hans: Cherpens Binscham d Landstreicher 1920	51,000	1937
ROSENHAYN, Paul: Die weisse Orchidee. 7 Abenteuer des Joe Jenkins 1917	51,000	1927
SEMSROTT, Albert: Das Buch von der "Möwe" 1928	51,000+	1940
SEMSROTT, Albert: Das Kaperschiff "Möwe" 1928	51,000	1940
SKOWRONNEK, Richard: Der Bruchhof 1903	51,000+	1939
TRELLER, Franz: Der Sohn des Gaucho 1901	51,000	1939
VOSS, Richard: Alpentragödie 1909	51,000+	1940
WASSERMANN, Jakob: Laudin und die Seinen 1925	51,000	1928
ADLERSFELD-BALLESTREM, E. v: Komtesse Käthe in d Ehe 1900	50,000	1939
BESTE, Konrad: D drei Esel d Doktorin Löhnefink 1937	50,000	1940
BLOEM, Walter: Brüderlichkeit 1922	50,000+	1922
BLOEM, Walter: Herrin 1921	50,000	1921
BLOEM, Walter: Die Schmiede der Zukunft 1913	50,000+	1913
BLOEM, Walter: Das verlorene Vaterland 1914	50,000+	1914
BOY-ED, Ida: Eine Frau wie du! 1913	50,000+	1922
BRÖGER, Karl: Bunker 17 1929	50,000	1940
BÜRKLE, Veit: Lasst den Frühjahr kommen 1940	50,000	1940
CAROSSA, Hans: D Schicksale Dr. Bürgers. Die Flucht 1930	50,000	1932
DINTER, Arthur: Die Sünde wider den Geist 1920	50,000	1920
DÖBLIN, Alfred: Berlin Alexanderplatz 1930	50,000	1933
DWINGER, E. E.: Spanische Silhouetten... 1937	50,000	1938

TABLE A (con't.)

ERDMANN, Gustav Adolf: S. M. S. "Emden" u sein Kommandant 1915	50,000	1916
ERNST, Otto: Hermannsland 1921	50,000	1922
FALKE, Gustav: Viel Feind, viel Ehr' 1915	50,000	1916
FEUCHTWANGER, Lion: Der jüdische Krieg 1932	50,000	1933
FISCHER-MARKGRAFF, E.: Sein Recht 1912	50,000	1919
FRANK, Gunnar: Der Weg zum Laster 1920	50,000	1930
FRENSSEN, Gustav: Der Weg unseres Volkes 1938	50,000	1940
GRABEIN, Paul: Der König von Thule 1907	c 50,000	1935
HARRER, Anny: Die Hölle der Verlorenen 1916	50,000	1917
HOLLÄNDER, Felix: Der Weg des Thomas Truck 1902	50,000+	1930
HUCH, Ricarda: Das Judengrab. Aus Bimbos Seelenwanderungen 1916	50,000	1932
IMMELMANN, Max: Meine Kampfflüge 1916	50,000	1916
KAERGEL, Hans Christoph: Die Berge warten 1935	50,000	1940
KELLERMANN, Bernhard: Der Tor 1909	50,000	1923
KESSLER, Johannes: Ich schwöre mir ewige Jugend 1935	50,000	1940
KÖHLER, Heinrich: Die Erbin 1912	50,000	1919
KOLL, Killian: Urlaub auf Ehrenwort 1937	50,000	1939
KRATZMANN, Ernst: D Lächeln des Magisters Anselmus... 1929	50,000	1929
LEHNE, Fr.: Trotzige Herzen ?	50,000	1918
LEHNE, Fr.: Das alte Lied ?	50,000	1918
MANN, Thomas: Unordnung und frühes Leid 1926	50,000	1930
MECHOW, Karl Benno v: Das Abenteuer 1930	50,000	1939

TABLE A (con't.)

MENZEL, Viktor: Schwurbrüder 1913	50,000	1925
MÜCKE, Hellmuth v: Emden 1915	50,000+	1915
NASO, Eckart v: Seydlitz 1932	50,000	1939
NEEFF, Adolf: Deutsche Kinder 1918	50,000	1918
OEHLER-HEIMERDINGER, Elisabeth: Gelitten u gestritten 1920	50,000	1920
ROSE, Felicitas: Der hillige Ginsterbruch 1928	50,000	1937
ROSEGGER, Peter: Werke, Gedenkausgabe, 6 Bde 1928	50,000	1931
ROSEN, Erwin: D dt Lausbub in Amerika, Tl II 1911	50,000+	1926
SCHÄFER, Wilhelm: Ein Mann namens Schmitz 1934	50,000	1939
SCHARRELMANN, Heinrich: Berni, II: Aus seiner ersten Schulzeit 1916	50,000+	1928
SCHMID, Hedda v: Die fünf Seemöwen 1916	50,000	1919
SCHNEIDER-FOERSTL, Josefine: D Liebe d Geigenkönigs Radanyi 1925	50,000	1930
SCHNITZLER, Arthur: Traum und Schicksal 1931	50,000	1931
STUTZER, Gustav: Meine Therese 1916	50,000+	1936
TUCHOLSKY, Kurt: Schloss Gripsholm 1931	50,000	1932
WEISMANTEL, Leo: Das unheilige Haus 1922	50,000+	1934
WERDER, Hans: Tiefer als der Tag gedacht 1907	50,000	1925
WERNER, Johannes: Boelcke d Mensch, d Flieger, d Führer d dt Jagdfliegerei 1932	50,000	1940
WINNIG, August: Die Hand Gottes 1938	50,000	1940
ZAHN, Ernst: Schattenhalb 1903	50,000	1929
ZILLICH, Heinrich: Zwischen Grenzen u Zeiten 1936	50,000+	1940
ZWEIG, Stefan: Marie Antoinette 1932	50,000+	1932

CHAPTER IV

TABLE B

More than two thousand and twenty titles by approximately five hundred and ninety authors are listed here. All of these books reached twenty-one thousand copies or twenty-one Auflagen, but not all were published between 1899 and 1940. Rather than render only a fraction of an author's works - where they began to be published before 1899 and continued to appear in this century - I chose to include all works which were successful to this degree written by the same author. The two prime examples of this are Ludwig GANGHOFER and Karl MAY.

This table enables one to follow the popularity of a title (to the extent that its popularity is mirrored in the number of copies or Auflagen printed) through the period 1915 to 1940. The authors are arranged alphabetically and their works descend from the most to the least popular. Should two titles indicate the same total, the more recently published is found first. Each title is followed by the date of its first publication and the designation of the type of literature (Roman, Erzählung, etc.) - should this have been ascertainable. The data from the DBV are given from the most recent (1936 to 1940) to the earliest (1915 to 1920) and in all but a very few cases the greatest figures found for a particular quinquenium are listed here. This arrangement was chosen in order to have the highest number of copies printed located closest to the title of the book.

The extent of an author's success with the reading public becomes immediately evident: (1) by the very fact that he is listed here, (2) by the number of his books which were successful enough to be included, and (3) by the number of copies which were printed of each of his works. It is also possible to determine in which quinquenium of this period a particular book experienced the greatest popularity.

Twenty-one thousand copies was chosen as the lowest limit, i. e. the minimum number of copies printed which a book had to reach in order to be included here. A great many titles attained twenty thousand by virtue of the first several printings, but do not appear again. This made twenty-one thousand a natural dividing line. Since the book clubs during the period concerned were considerably smaller in size and therefore in influence on the market and the public than those of today (the largest now in Germany being Bertelsmann Lesering with approximately 2.6 million members in 1960[1]), they did not affect the sales to any great extent. I therefore believe that a work of literature which was printed in more than twenty thousand copies before World War II was at least successful enough for some consideration.

The following examples may serve to enable the reader to gain the greatest possible advantage from the material presented here. The novels of Paul LANGENSCHEIDT are a clear indication of

---

[1]Langenbucher, p. 153.

a decline in popularity. Let me cite his Arme, kleine Eva which was published in 1907:

36/40	31/35	26/30	21/25	15/20
--	--	100T'30	85T'21	36T'16

The first ten years saw only thirty-six thousand copies printed, but the next six added fifty thousand more (averaging eighty-three hundred per year). Thereafter fewer were published each year (sixteen hundred and sixty-six) until the one hundred thousandth copy left the presses, and subsequently no information is found. Not one of the nine novels by LANGENSCHEIDT included in TABLE B was listed after 1930!

From the data found in the DBV for Hinter Pflug und Schraubstock by Max EYTH which appeared in 1899,

36/40	31/35	26/30	21/25	15/20
298T'37+	292T'35	278T'30	253T'25	180A'20

we see that from 1899 to 1920 this book averaged nine thousand copies printed per year. In the five years 1921 to 1925 a total of seventy-three thousand more were made. The number of copies printed per year continues to decrease until 1937 (when there is also an edition of unknown size by another publisher). It appears that this collection of Novellen became somewhat of a "standard" after having established itself on the market.[1]

---

[1] Currently the Universal-Bibliothek published by Philipp Reclam Jun. Verlag carries one of these Novellen (Berufstragik) under the title Die Brücke über die Ennobucht.

Should agreement ever be reached on a formula which one could apply for the determination of bestsellers (perhaps $B = X/t$, where X equals the number of copies and t the unit of time required to sell X-number of copies [and the time element should not be minimized], then B is the classification "bestseller", provided at least ten thousand, fifty thousand or one hundred thousand be sold in one, five or ten years), the material in TABLE B could readily be applied, and EYTH'S book would no doubt be included. For the five years 1921 to 1925 it averaged fourteen thousand six hundred copies per year. This is impressive, but assumes diminutive proportions when compared with Erich Maria REMARQUE'S <u>Im Westen nichts Neues</u> which reached nine hundred thousand copies during the first year (plus an edition of unknown quantity as is indicated by +). This illustrates the difficulty in establishing a set criterion of this type.

Instead of declining, <u>Der Wanderer zwischen zwei Welten</u> by Walter FLEX increases in popularity (notably after the Nazi regime had assumed power in Germany).

36/40	31/35	26/30	21/25	15/20
682T'40	340T'31	301T'28	255T'25	195T'20

The one hundred and ninety-five thousand copies which were printed during the first four years (averaging nearly forty-nine thousand per year) were increased by another one hundred and forty-five in the next seven years (averaging only twenty thousand seven hundred per year) and then experienced an addition of three hundred and forty-two thousand in the <u>nine</u> years from 1932 to 1940 (thus averaging thirty-eight thousand copies per year) - more than doubling all the printings of the previous fifteen years! It is obvious from these data that the greatest popularity of FLEX'S novel came fifteen years after its initial publication.

One more example is necessary to show how a book may remain available for some time without ever having achieved a major success. Otto ERNST'S Frieden und Freude (Humoristische Plaudereien) never reached more than twenty-three thousand copies:

36/40	31/35	26/30	21/25	15/20
--	s 26/30	23T'27	--	20T'20

Had there been adequate space in this study to show the entire entry from the DBV instead of only the highest figure in each period, one would see that 1-20 thousand were printed in 1920. The fact that no entry appeared again until 1927 indicates that the first twenty thousand copies had not yet been sold. Then in 1927 the total entry (21-23 thousand) shows that only three thousand more copies were published. Since all of these had not yet found buyers by the time the DBV for 1931/35 went to press there is the notation to refer to the DBV for 1926/30 where the still available copies were first listed. Apparently no more editions were printed within this period, for the 1936/40 DBV no longer lists this title.

The abbreviations used in TABLE B are found immediately in front of TABLE A (page 52). Where "ni", "nA" or "nAg" appear with only the year, there was no further information given in the DBV. However, one can be sure that there was an edition printed in that year.

Occasionally the title of a book may have been changed. If this has been detected the earlier title will then appear in parentheses following the more recent designation. For example:

UNGER, Hellmuth: Robert Koch (Helfer der Menschheit).

Where the key figures appear in Auflagen instead of thousands, the name of the publisher has been indicated either near the name of the work or in the column where the information is given. In reading from left to right the publisher mentioned published all such editions until another company is noted.

Finally, it should be kept in mind that the information which I have presented here stems almost exclusively from the DBV, the publishers' index. No claim is made that these data are absolutely comprehensive - for reasons mentioned earlier, but it is intended that this study be a sound beginning toward an effective listing of best-selling German prose fiction.

TABLE B

NAME	36/40	31/35	26/30	21/25	15/20
ADELT, Leonhard (1881-1945)					
Der Ozeanflug 1914 Nov	--	--	ni'29	40T'22	--
ADLERSFELD-BALLESTREM, Euphemia von (1854-1941) Published by Philipp Reclam Jun. Verlag.					
D weissen Rosen von Ravensberg 1897 R	127A'39	94A'35	79A'30	56A'25	19A'20
Trix 1903 R	63A'37	57A'35	52A'30	42A'25	30A'20
Komtesse Käthe 1894 Humn	57A'39	51A'35	42A'28	40A'24	35A'20
Komtesse Käthe in der Ehe 1900 Humn	50A'39	44A'35	34A'29	30A'24	23A'20
Die Falkner vom Falkenhof 1890 R	46A'39	41A'35	36A'30	27A'25	15A'20
Pension Malepartus 1901 R	40T'36	33A'35	27A'29	24A'24	18A'20
Major Fuchs auf Reisen 1905	33T'36	24A'35	20A'28	18A'24	12A'29
ALSEN, Ola (nd)					
Das Paradies der Frau nd Berliner-R	--	--	--	--	24T'18
ALVERDES, Paul (1897-)					
Kleine Reise. Aus e Tagebuch 1933	45T'40	20T'35			
Die Freiwilligen 1934 Hrsp	35T'40				
ARNAU, Frank (ie Heinrich Schmitt, 1894-)					
Kämpfer im Dunkel 1930 R	--	--	25T'30		
ARENS, Bernhard (1873-)					
Der Sohn des Mufti 1911 Erz	--	--	--	22T'23	16T'20

TABLE B (con't.)

NAME	36/40	31/35	26/30	21/25	15/20
L'ARRONGE, Hans (ie Aaron, 1838-1908)					
Zwei Wege 1919 R	--	--	--	--	25T'19
BAHR, Hermann (1863-1934)					
Die Hexe Drut 1909 R	--	--	55T'29	--	5A'14 S Fischer
Expressionismus 1914	--	--	--	25T'22	18T'20
BARTH, Rosa (-1958)					
Was Peterli als Bergführer erlebte 1927 Erz	35T'36	--	18T'30		
Hannerl vom Achensee 1929 Erz	30T'36	--			
BARTSCH, Rudolf Hans (1873-1952)					
Schwammerl 1912 R	--	236T'32	226T'29	190T'25	140T'19
D Gesch v d Hannerl u ihren Liebhabern 1913	--	91T'34	88T'28	85T'23	--
Zwölf aus der Steiermark 1908 R	--	91T'33	--	76T'23	61T'20
Vom sterbenden Rokoko 1909 Novn	ni'29	83T'34	79T'28	76T'24	56T'20
Frau Utta und der Jäger 1914 R	--	83T'32	63T'27	54T'22	--
Das deutsche Leid 1911 R	--	s 26/30	60T'29	--	50T'20
Seine Jüdin oder Jakob Böhmes Schusterkugel 1921 R	--	s 21/25	--	57T'22	
Die Haindlkinder 1908 R	--	ni'33	49T'27	--	--
Lukas Rabesam 1918 R	--	ni'33	46T'27	43T'22	30T'18

TABLE B (con't.)

NAME	36/40	31/35	26/30	21/25	15/20
BARTSCH, Rudolf Hans (con't.)					
Heidentum. D Gesch e Vereinsamten 1919	--	s 21/25	--	45T'22	25T'19
Bittersüsse Liebesgeschn 1910 Novn	--	--	--	43T'22	ni'19
Unerfüllte Geschichten 1916	--	--	41T'28	--	10T'16
Elisabeth Kött 1909 R	--	--	37T'27	--	--
BAUDISSIN, Ida Gräfin (nd)					
Durch Sturm und Not 1914 R	--	--	--	--	54T'19
BAUER, Franz (1901-)					
Auf d Jannshof stimmt was nicht 1932 Erz	29T'40				
BAUM, Vicki (1888-1960)					
Der Eingang zur Bühne 1920 R	--	146T'31	ni'29		
Hell in Frauensee 1927 R	--	141T'31	ni'29		
Student Chem Helen Willfüer 1929 R	--	105T'32			
Menschen im Hotel 1929 R	--	56T'31			
Zwischenfall in Lohwinkel 1930 R	--	30T'31			
Ferne 1926 R	--	30T'31	20T'27		
BEHRENS-LITZMANN, Anna (ie Anna Behrens, nd)					
Herbstgewitter 1915 R	--	--	--	--	62T'19

TABLE B (con't.)

NAME	36/40	31/35	26/30	21/25	15/20
BENRATH, Henry (ie Albert Henry Rausch, 1882-1949)					
Die Kaiserin Konstanza 1935 R	26T'40				
Die Kaiserin Galla Placida 1935 R	23T'40				
BEREND, Alice (ie A. Breinlinger, née Berend, 1878-1938)					
D Bräutigame d Babette Bomberling 1914 R	--	s 26/30	200A'30 S Fischer	11A'25	ni'15
Frau Hempels Tochter 1913 R	--	s 26/30	142A'28	130A'25	--
D Reise d Herrn Sebastian Wenzel 1912 R	--	--	129A'26	122A'25	
Spreemann & Co. 1916 R	--	58A'33	48A'28	42A'22	37A'20
Matthias Senfs Verlöbnis 1918 R	--	s 26/30	40T'29	--	20T'18
Die zu Kittelsrode 1917 R	--	--	38T'29	--	15T'17
BERENS-TOTENOHL, Josefa (1891-)					
Der Femhof 1934 R	160T'40	16T'35			
Frau Magdlene 1935 R	125T'40	12T'35			
BERGENGRUEN, Werner (1892-)					
D Grosstyrann u d Gericht 1935 R	40T'40				
BERNDORFF, Hans Rudolf (1895-)					
Spionage 1929 Erzn	--	79A'34 Franckh	55A'30 Dieck		

TABLE B (con't.)

NAME	36/40	31/35	26/30	21/25	15/20
BERSTL, Julius (1883-)					
Lachende Lieder. Dt Humor... 1909	--	--	--	21T'24	--
BERTHOLD, Theodor (1841-1909)					
Lustige Gymnasialgeschn c 1900	--	--	42A'27 Union	37A'23	31A'20
Aus Tertia und Sekunda 1909 Geschn	--	--	30A'29	21A'21	15A'19
BESTE, Konrad (1890-1958)					
D vergnügliche Leben d Doktorin Böhmfink 1934 R	122T'40				
D drei Esel d Doktorin Löhnefink 1937 R	50T'40				
BETSCH, Roland (1888-1945)					
Ballade am Strom 1939 R	41T'40				
BETTAUER, Hugo (1877-1925)					
Die Stadt ohne Juden 1922 R	--	--	--	55T'24	
BEUMELBURG, Werner (1899-)					
Sperrfeuer um Deutschland 1929 R	328T'40	166T'33	120T'29		
Die Gruppe Bosemüller 1930 R	170T'39	90T'35	30T'30		
Mit 17 Jahren vor Verdun 1931 R	142T'40	41T'35			
Donaumont 1923 R	135T'40	ni'35	s 21/25	2A'25	
Deutschland in Ketten 1931	77T'40	45T'33			

TABLE B (con't.)

NAME	36/40	31/35	26/30	21/25	15/20
BEUMELBURG, Werner (con't.)					
D König u d Kaiserin. Friedrich d Grosse und Maria Theresia 1937 R	66T'40				
Kampf um Spanien... 1939	60T'40				
Kaiser und Herzog... 1936	40T'40				
Preussische Novelle 1935	40T'40				
Reich und Rom... 1936	35T'40				
BEUTTEN, Hermann (ie Beuttenmüller, 1881-1960)					
Die Schönen von Baden-Baden. Heitere Badegeschn 1917	--	--	--	--	26T'18
BEYERLEIN, Franz Adam (1871-1949)					
Jena oder Sedan? 1903 R	--	--	270T'26	--	--
BIERBAUM, Otto Julius (1865-1910)					
Prinz Kuckuck. Leben, Taten, Meinungen u Höllenfahrt e Wüstlings 1907 R	--	--	ni'28	78T'22	32A'17
Zäpfel Kerns Abenteuer 1905	65T'40	s 26/30	45T'30	--	25T'18
Stilpe. R aus d Froschperspektive 1897	--	--	--	27A'23 Dt V-Anst	--
BINDING, Rudolf Georg (1867-1938)					
Der Opfergang 1912 Nov	--	360T'33	--	--	--
Unsterblichkeit 1921 Nov	--	100T'35	50T'28		

TABLE B (con't.)

NAME	36/40	31/35	26/30	21/25	15/20
BINDING, Rudolf Georg (con't.)					
Moselfahrt aus Liebeskummer 1932 Nov	--	90T'34			
Sankt Georgs Stellvertreter 1934 Leg	112T'40	89T'34			
Legenden der Zeit 1909	85T'40	--	--	53T'25	5T'20
Keuschheitslegende 1919	--	82T'34	60T'28	45T'25	
Die Geige 1911 vier Novn	--	47T'33	--	34T'35	14T'20
Das Heiligtum der Pferde 1935	34A'40 Gräfe & Unzer				
Reitvorschrift für e Geliebte 1926	ni'36	28T'34			
Erlebtes Leben 1928 Erz	--	26T'35			
BISCHOFF, Charitas (1848-1925)					
Amalie Dietrich. E Leben 1909 Erz	161T'40	132T'33	105T'28	85T'28	64T'20
Bilder aus meinem Leben 1912	53T'38	--	--	35T'22	29T'20
BLOEM, Walter (1868-1951)					
Kommödiantinnen 1914 R	280T'36	--	256T'29	--	--
Das eiserne Jahr 1911 R	--	--	(265T'28)	--	--
Kriegserlebnis-Tril in e Bd	205T'39				
Tl I: Vormarsch 1916	s above	125T'34	--	(120T'24)	50T'16
Tl II: Sturmsignal 1919	s above	40T'34	--	--	30T'19
Tl III: Das Ganze - halt! 1934	s above	ni'34			
Volk wider Volk 1912 R	--	--	ni'27	(171T'24)	--

TABLE B (con't.)

NAME	36/40	31/35	26/30	21/25	15/20
BLOEM, Walter (con't.)					
Die Schmiede der Zukunft 1913 R	--	--	ni'27	(170T'24)	--
Das verlorene Vaterland 1914 R	--	--	ni'27	(160T'24)	--
Der krasse Fuchs 1906 R	--	--	ni'27	112T'22	--
Das jüngste Gericht 1907 R	--	--	ni'27	(70T'24)	--
Gottesferne 1920 R	s 15/20	70T'32	--	(55T'24)	50T'20
Brüderlichkeit 1922 R	--	--	ni'27	50T'22	
Herrin 1921 R	--	--	--	50T'21	
BLOMBERG, Anna von (1858-1907)					
Reggfields Tochter 1900-1902 R	--	54T'35	--	14A'21 C Hirsch	--
Waldstille und Weltleid 1894	s 21/25	--	--	39A'21	--
BLUMENTHAL, Oskar (1852-1917)					
Lebensschwänke. Heitere Geschn 1914	--	--	--	--	30T'18
BLUNCK, Hans Friedrich (ie Johann, 1888-1961)					
Die grosse Fahrt 1935 R	139T'40	25T'35			
König Geiserich 1936 Erz	70T'39				
Die Weibsmühle 1927 R	54T'40				
Der Feuerberg 1934 Erz	40T'40				
Spuk und Lügen 1933 Geschn	30T'40	15T'35			

TABLE B (con't.)

NAME	36/40	31/35	26/30	21/25	15/20
BLUNCK, Hans Friedrich (con't.)					
Die Urvatersaga 1934	27T'38	20T'35			
BODENREUTH, Friedrich (ie Friedrich Jaksch, 1894-)					
Alle Wasser Böhmens fliessen nach Dtld 1937 R	190T'40				
BÖHME, Margarethe (1869-1939)					
Tagebuch einer Verlorenen... 1905	--	563T'31	552T'27	520T'22	330T'17+
Dida Ibsens Tagebuch. E Finale zum Tageb einer Verlorenen 1907	--	--	--	54T'21	s 1908
BÖTTCHER, Helmut Maximilian (1895-)					
Der Würfler 1926 R	23T'39	--			
BÖTTCHER, Maximilian (1872-)					
Krach im Hinterhaus 1936 R	25T'37				
BOHNAGEN, Alfred (1877-)					
Aufruhr in Giesekenberg 1938 R	49T'38				
BONSELS, Waldemar (1881-1952)					
D Biene Maja u ihre Abenteuer 1912 R	775T'38	760T'35	684T'28	584T'25	318A'20 Schuster & Loeffler
dass - with 12 multicolored pictures	790T'40[1]	755T'35	715T'29	545T'22	ni'20

[1]This figure represents the grand total for this book.

TABLE B (con't.)

NAME	36/40	31/35	26/30	21/25	15/20
BONSELS, Waldemar (con't.)					
Himmelsvolk 1915 Mär	445T'40	425T'31	--	400A'23 Dt V-Anst	295A'21 Schuster & L.
Indienfahrt 1916	--	--	350T'30	315T'25	166T'21
Menschenwege. Aus d Notizen e Vagabunden I 1918	--	--	--	153T'22	87T'21
Das Anjekind 1913 Erz	145T'40	--	s 15/20	--	70A'20
Wartalun. E Schlossgesch 1911	--	ni'31	--	119A'25 Dt V-Anst	57A'20 Schuster & L.
Eros u d Evangelien. Aus d Notizen e Vagabunden II 1920	--	--	--	115T'25	30T'21
Ave vita (Leben, ich grüsse Dich) 1905 Erz	--	--	--	90T'22	ni'18
Mario. E Leben im Walde 1939	87T'40				
Der tiefste Traum 1911 Erz	--	s 21/25	84T'26	82T'23+	7A'20
Mario und die Tiere 1928	60T'40	50T'35	40T'28		
Blut 1909 Erz	--	--	60T'26	58T'23	35A'20
Narren und Helden. Aus d Notizen e Vagabunden III 1923	--	--	--	51T'25	
BORCHART, Elsbeth (1878-)					
Des Weibes Waffen 1916 R	--	--	--	--	70T'19
BOREE, Karl Friedrich (1886-)					
Dor und der September 1931 R	--	65T'34			

TABLE B (con't.)

NAME	36/40	31/35	26/30	21/25	15/20
BOSSI-FEDRIGOTTI v Ochsenfeld, Anton Graf (1901-)					
Standschütze Bruggler 1934 R	51T'36				
D Vermächtnis der letzten Tage 1936 R	34T'37				
BOY-ED, Ida (1852-1928)					
Ein königlicher Kaufmann 1910 R	--	--	56T'26	50T'23	32A'20
Eine Frau wie du! 1913 R	--	--	ni'29	50T'22	--
BRANDENFELS, Hanna (ie Frau Eichemeyer, née Niclas, 1869-)					
Baroness Köchin 1899 R	--	--	28T'27	--	--
Das Kuckucksei 1911 R	--	--	26T'27	--	--
Der Stallbaron 1910 R	--	--	26T'27	--	--
Die Fee von Rabendorf 1901 R	--	--	21T'27	--	--
BRANDT, Rolf (1886-)					
Albert Leo Schlageter... 1926	93T'40	25T'31			
BRAUN, Lily (1865-1916)					
Im Schatten der Titanen... 1908	--	--	220T'29	140T'23	104T'20
Memoiren e Sozialistin, 2 Bde 1909-1911					
I: Lehrjahre	--	--	--	54T'24	48T'20
II: Kampfjahre	--	--	--	42T'24	--

TABLE B (con't.)

NAME	36/40	31/35	26/30	21/25	15/20
BRAUN, Otto (1897-1918)					
Aus nachgelassenen Schriften eines Frühvollendeten 1920	--	s 15/20	--	99T'22	45T'20
BRAUSEWETTER, Arthur (1864-1947)					
Mehr Liebe... 1919 Betrachtungen	--	--	--	100T'25	20T'20
Wer d Heimat liebt wie du 1916 R	--	95T'31	80T'30	--	
Die grosse Liebe ? R	--	36A'35 Reclam	31A'27	30A'24	22A'20
Stirb und Werde 1912 R	--	--	32T'29	--	30T'20
Zum Herrschen geboren 1904 R	--	32T'31	--	--	ni'19
Don Juans Erlösung 1915 R	--	30T'32	--	--	
BREHM, Bruno von (1892-)					
Apis und Este 1931 R	113T'40				
Weder Kaiser noch König... 1933 R	98T'40				
Das war das Ende 1932 R	78T'40				
Auf Wiedersehen, Susanne! 1940 R	54T'40				
BREHMER, Artur (1858-1923)					
Die kühne Fahrt d "Deutschland" c 1916 R	--	--	--	--	30T'17
BROCKDORFF, Gertrud Baronin von (1893-)					
D letzte Zarin. Alexandra Feodorowna 1917 R	71T'40	--	53T'30	--	ni'18

TABLE B (con't.)

NAME	36/40	31/35	26/30	21/25	15/20
BROD, Max (1884-)					
Tycho Brahes Weg zu Gott 1916 R	--	ni'31	77T'30+	52T'25	32T'17
BRÖGER, Karl (1886-1944)					
Bunker 17 1929 Erz	50T'40	24T'32			
Geschn vom Reservisten Anzinger 1939	30T'40				
BRONNEN, Arnolt (Ps: A. H. Schelle-Noetzel, 1895-1959)					
O. S. 1929 R	--	--	25T'29		
BRÜES, Otto (1897-)					
Das Gauklerzelt 1939 R	60T'40				
BRUNNGRABER, Rudolf (1901-1960)					
Radium. R e Elements 1936	55T'40				
Opiumkrieg 1939 R	48T'40				
BUCHHOLTZ, Hansgeorg (1899-)					
Der Musketier von Potsdam 1935	25T'40				
BÜRGEL, Bruno H. (1875-1948)					
Der Stern von Afrika 1921 R	60T'37	--	22T'26		
BÜRKLE, Veit (ie Karl H. Bischoff, 1900-)					
Lasst den Frühjahr kommen 1940	50T'40				
Bis zum Heimkehr im Sommer 1936 R	25T'39				

TABLE B (con't.)

NAME	36/40	31/35	26/30	21/25	15/20
BURG, Paul (ie Paul Schaumburg, 1884- zw 1952-58)					
Die Wetterstädter 1912 R	--	--	s 21/25	30T'25	3A'20
BURTE, Hermann (ie H. Strübe, 1879-1960)					
Vom Hofe, welcher unterging (from <u>Wiltfeber, der ewige Deutsche</u>) 1912	c 140T'39	6A'36 Diesterweg	--	20T'22	--
Wiltfeber, der ewige Deutsche 1912	74T'40	69T'35	40T'28+	--	25A'19
BUSCH, Fritz Otto (1890-)					
Flieger gegen England 1939	56T'40				
U-Boote gegen England 1939	56T'40				
Zwei Jungens bei d Reichsmarine (Zwei Jungens unter d Kriegsfahne) 1933	54T'40	33T'35			
U-Bootsfahrten 1934	39T'40				
Admiral Graf Spees Sieg u Untergang 1935	26T'40				
Wikinger 1934	25T'40				
Alarm! Deutsche Kreuzer! 1936	23T'40				
BUSCHBECKER, Karl Matthias (ie K. M. Busch, 1899-1942)					
... wie unser Gesetz es befahl 1936 R	58T'39				
BUSSE, Hermann Eris (1891-1947)					
Heiner und Barbara 1936 R	134A'40 P List				

TABLE B (con't.)

NAME	36/40	31/35	26/30	21/25	15/20
BUSSE, Hermann Eris (con't.)					
Bauernadel 1933 R-Tril	81A'38 P List	13A'33			
Der Tauträger 1938 R	28A'40				
BUSSE, Karl (nd)					
Trittchen. Aus d Aufzn e Verwundeten 1939	180T'40				
BUSSE, Karl (Ps: Fritz Döring, 1872-1918)					
Feuerschein 1915 Novn u Skn	--	--	--	--	30T'15
Die Wette 1906 Gesch	--	--	--	--	22A'17 Union
CAMILL, C. (ie Lotte Ochsner, earlier Lotte Neuter, 1865-)					
Leben 1912 Münchener-R	--	--	--	--	42T'17
CAROSSA, Hans (1878-1956)					
Der Arzt Gion 1931 Erz	82T'40	50T'33			
Geheimnisse des reifen Lebens 1936	65T'40				
D Schicksale Dr. Bürgers. D Flucht 1930 Erzn	--	50T'32			
Rumänisches Tagebuch (after 1938: Tagebuch im Kriege) 1924	45T'38	27T'34	10T'29		
Führung u Geleit. Lebensgedenkbuch 1933	40T'38	30T'34			
Eine Kindheit u Verwandlung e Jugend 1922, 1928, together 1933	35T'40	15T'35	12T'26	ni'22	

TABLE B (con't.)

NAME	36/40	31/35	26/30	21/25	15/20
CHRISTALLER, Helene (1872-1953)					
Gottfried Erdmann u seine Frau 1907 R	--	--	28A'27 Reinhardt	--	--
Albert Schweitzer. E Leben für Andere 1932	26T'36	23T'35			
Peterchen 1930 R	26T'37	s 26/30	5A'30		
CLAUSEN, Ernst Alexander (1861-1912)					
Das Haus am Markt 1911 R	--	42T'32	--	--	30T'20
Der Heiligen Kind 1916 R	--	--	--	40T'21	20T'16
CLÉMENT, Bertha (1852-1930)					
Libelle: I. Backfischzeit 1901	--	--	41A'28 Union	36A'23	30A'20
II. Lenz- u Brautzeit 1902	--	--	35A'28	31A'22	25A'20
Das Siebengestirn 1910	--	--	22A'26	18A'21	13A'19
Lebensziele 1907	--	--	22A'26	17A'21	14A'19
COLERUS, Egmont (1888-1939)					
Marco Polo (Zwei Welten. E Marco-Polo-R) 1926 R	25T'35	--			
COURTHS-MAHLER, Hedwig (1867-1950)					
Was Gott zusammenfügt... 1913 R	--	--	--	--	402T'19
Gib mich frei! 1912 R	--	--	ni'26	nA'25	402T'19
Des Anderen Ehre 1912 R	--	--	--	--	349T'19

TABLE B (con't.)

NAME	36/40	31/35	26/30	21/25	15/20
COURTHS-MAHLER, Hedwig (con't.)					
Die Testamentsklausel 1915 R	--	--	--	--	325T'19
Kathes Ehe 1914 R	--	--	nA'27	nA'24	342T'19
Lena Warnstetten 1916 R	--	--	--	--	295T'19
Die Bettelprinzess 1914 R	--	--	--	c 230T'24	180T'19
Die Assmanns 1917 R	--	--	ni'26	ni'25	210T'19
CZYGAN, Maria (nd)					
Deutsche Mädel 1917 Erz	--	--	--	--	40T'18
Sigrid 1916 Erz	--	--	--	--	40T'17
Vom Dämon der Unzucht gepackt. Gesch... 1913	--	--	--	--	40T'20
DAUMANN, Rudolf Heinrich (1896-1957)					
Das Ende des Goldes 1938 Utop-R	30T'38				
Gefahr aus dem Weltall 1938 Utop-R	21T'40				
DAUTHENDEY, Max (1867-1918)					
D acht Gesichter am Biwasee. Japanische Liebesgeschn 1911	125T'40	--	--	25T'22	--
Raubmenschen 1911 R	40T'40	20T'33	--	--	--
Die schönsten Geschichten 1919	--	30T'35	--	--	25T'19
DEHMEL, Richard (1863-1920)					
Zwei Menschen 1903 R in Romanzen	--	s 26/30	83A'27 S Fischer	79A'25	29A'17

TABLE B (con't.)

NAME	36/40	31/35	26/30	21/25	15/20
DEHMEL, Richard (con't.)					
Lebensblätter 1895 Novn in Prosa	--	s 21/25	--	21T'23	--
DELMONT, Joseph (1873-1935)					
Juden in Ketten (In Ketten) 1926 R	--	s 26/30	25T'29		
DIEHL, Ludwig (1866-1947)					
Suso 1921 R	108T'40	82T'32	--	54T'25	
DILL, Liesbet (ie Liesbet v Drigalski, née Dill, 1877-1962)					
Die Spionin 1917 R	--	--	60T'28	--	10T'17
Lo's Ehe 1903	--	--	--	25A'23 Morawe & Scheffelt	20T'18
DINTER, Arthur (1876-1948)					
Die Sünde wider das Blut 1917 R	--	260T'34	--	170T'21	5T'18
Die Sünde wider den Geist 1920 R	--	--	--	--	50T'20
Die Sünde wider die Liebe 1922 R	--	30T'28	--	25T'22	
DITTMER, Hans (L893-)					
Vom Ewigen im Heute 1933 Kurzgeschn	29T'40	13T'34			
DÖBLIN, Alfred (1878-1957)					
Berlin Alexanderplatz 1924 R	--	50A'33 S Fischer	40A'30		

TABLE B (con't.)

NAME	36/40	31/35	26/30	21/25	15/20
DÖRFLER, Peter (1878-1955)					
Als Mutter noch lebte 1912 R	86T'40	--	69T'30	46T'22	36T'20
Dämmerstunden 1916 Erz	--	37T'31	--	32T'22	21T'21
D Weltkrieg im schwäbischen Himmelreich 1915 Erz	c 28T'36	--	14A'27	--	13T'16
Der junge Don Bosco 1930 Erz	24T'40	8T'31			
Judith Finsterwalderin 1916 R	--	24T'33	--	7A'22	4A'18
Das Geheimnis des Fisches 1918 Erz	--	--	--	22T'25	15T'18
DOHNA-SCHLODIEN, Burggraf Nikolaus zu (1879-)					
Der "Möwe" zweite Fahrt 1917	--	--	--	--	150T'17
S. M. S. "Möwe" 1915	--	--	--	--	100T'16
DOMINIK, Hans (1872-1945)					
Ein Stern fiel vom Himmel 1934 R	179T'40	3A'35			
Land aus Feuer und Wasser 1939 R	167T'40				
Die Macht der Drei 1922 R	150T'40	100T'34	--		
Der Wettflug der Nationen 1934 R	128T'40	3A'35			
Atomgewicht 500 1935 R	102T'40				
Atlantis 1925 R	100T'40	s 21/25	--	30T'25	
Himmelskraft 1937 R	95T'40				
Die Spur des Dschingis-Khan 1923 R	93T'39	s 21/25	--		
Das stählerne Geheimnis 1934 R	90T'40				

TABLE B (con't.)

NAME	36/40	31/35	26/30	21/25	15/20
DOMINIK, Hans (con't.)					
Lebensstrahlen 1938 R	85T'40				
Der Brand der Cheopspyramide 1926 R	70T'40	s 26/30	20T'27		
Befehl aus dem Dunkel 1933 R	65T'40				
Kautschuk 1930 R	65T'40	--			
John Workmann, der Zeitungsboy... 1921 Erz	63T'38	nA'33	--		
Vistra, das weisse Gold Dtlds 1936 Gesch	60T'37				
Das Erbe der Uraniden 1928 R	60T'39	--			
DORN, Käthe (ie Rosa Springer, 1866-)					
Das weisse Kleid 1910 Gesch	--	--	--	148T'25	100A'20
Die schönsten Hände 1911 Erz	--	--	--	84A'25 E Müller	--
D Vaterunser in 9 Erzn dargestellt 1898	--	38T ?	35T'26	--	--
Leuchten müssen wir! Erz	--	--	--	35T'25	25T'20
Gesühnt Erz	--	30T'32	--	--	--
DORNAU, Charlotte von (ie Charlotte v Schauroth, earlier Ch. Laue, 1866-)					
Killmanns mit'm Strich... 1916 R	--	--	--	25A'22 Gerstenberg	15A'18
DREESEN, Willrath (1878-1950)					
Ebba Hüsing 1909 R	--	s 21/25	--	nA'21	68T'19

TABLE B (con't.)

NAME	36/40	31/35	26/30	21/25	15/20
DROSTE, Georg (1866-1935)					
Ottjen Alldag un sien Kaperstreiche... 1913	31T'37	--	26T'26	23T'24	18T'20
DUNCKER, Dora (1855-1916)					
George Sand. E Buch d Leidenschaft 1916 R	--	--	42T'30	--	
Die grosse Lüge 1901 R	--	--	ni'27	39T'21	--
DURIAN, Wolf (1892-)					
Kai aus der Kiste 1927 Gesch	67T'37	ni'34	20T'29		
DWINGER, Edwin Erich (1898-)					
Die letzten Reiter 1935 R	230T'40	75T'35			
Zwischen Weiss u Rot. D russ Trag 1930 R	225T'40	85T'35			
D Armee hinter Stacheldraht... 1929 R	200T'40	78T'35			
D Tod in Polen. D volksdt Passion 1940	150T'40				
Wir rufen Deutschland. Heimkehr u Vermächtnis 1932 R	110T'39	52T'35			
Auf halbem Wege 1939 R	110T'40				
Zug nach Sibirien 1933 Erz	100T'40	30T'35			
D namenlose Heer (from D Armee hinter...) 1935 R	70T'40				
Spanische Silhouetten... 1937	50T'38				
EBERMAYER, Erich (1900-)					
Befreite Hände 1938 R	23T'40				

TABLE B (con't.)

NAME	36/40	31/35	26/30	21/25	15/20
ECKHEL, Anna Hilaria v (ie A. H. Preuss, 1873-1948)					
Nanni Gschaftlhuber 1919 R	43T'36	32A'31 Bergstadt	27A'28	21T'25	6A'19
ECKMANN, Heinrich (1893-1940)					
Eira und der Gefangene 1935 R	68T'40				
Der Stein im Acker 1937 R	25T'40				
Das blühende Leben 1939 R	23T'40				
EICHACKER, Reinhold (1886-1931)					
Gaston und die Dirne 1919 R	--	--	30T'30	--	
Gaston, der Hochstapler 1919 R	--	--	30T'30	--	
Gaston und die Sängerin 1919 R	--	--	30T'30	--	
Briefe an das Leben... 1916 R	--	--	--	25T'23	7A'16
EICKE, Otto (nd)					
Der Ndjaro Krim-R	--	--	--	25T'24	--
EIPPER, Paul (1891-)					
Menschenkinder 1929	--	53A'35	40A'29 D Reimer		
Die gelbe Dogge Senta 1936 Gesch	40T'38				
Tiere sehen dich an 1928	--	--	40A'30		
Tierkinder 1929	--	--	30A'30		

TABLE B (con't.)

NAME	36/40	31/35	26/30	21/25	15/20
ENGEL, Georg (1866-1931)					
Die Last 1894 R	--	--	--	214T'23	--
Hann Klüth, der Philosoph 1905 R	--	--	ni'27	39A'24 Union	--
Die Herrin und ihr Knecht 1917 R	--	--	--	21A'23	5T'17
ENKING, Ottomar (1867-1945)					
Familie P. C. Behm 1902 R	--	--	21A'27 Schünemann	s 15/20	13A'18 C Reissner
ERDMANN, Gustav Adolf (nd)					
S. M. S. "Emden" und sein Kommandant 1915 Erz	--	--	--	--	50T'16
ERNST, Otto (ie O. E. Schmidt, 1862-1926)					
Asmus Sempers Jugendland 1905 R	--	190T'32	ni'28	160T'25	130T'20
Appelschnut 1906 hum Plaun	123T'40	101T'34	91T'29	65T'23	35T'17
Semper der Jüngling 1908 R	--	s 26/30	113T'30	110T'23	90T'20
Semper der Mann 1917 R	67T'38	s 21/25	--	65T'23	45T'20
Vom geruhigen Leben 1902 hum Plaun	--	s 26/30	55T'27	52T'23	49T'20
Hermannsland 1921 R	--	s 21/25	--	50T'22	
Vom grüngoldenen Baum 1909 hum Plaun	--	s 26/30	42T'27	--	44T'19
Ein frohes Farbenspiel 1900 hum Plaun	--	s 26/30	44T'27	--	36T'19
Aus meinem Sommergarten 1912 hum Plaun	--	s 26/30	35T'27	--	27T'19

TABLE B (con't.)

NAME	36/40	31/35	26/30	21/25	15/20
ERNST, Otto (con't.)					
Der süsse Willy oder Die Gesch e netten Erziehung before 1906	--	s 21/25	--	32T'23	--
August Gutbier oder Die sieben Weisen im Franziskanerbräu 1918	--	s 15/20	--	--	25T'18
Frieden und Freude 1920 hum Plaun	--	s 26/30	23T'27	--	20T'20
ERNST, Paul (1866-1933)					
Erdichtete Gespräche 1921	--	--	ni'31	2T'21	
Erdachte Gespräche. E Auswahl 1932	65T'39	35T'34			
Der Schatz im Morgenbrotsthal 1926 R	34A'39 P List	10A'33			
Heitere Welt 1936 Sieben Geschn	30T'39				
ERTL, Emil (1860-1935)					
D Leute vom blauen Guguckshaus 1905 R	27T'40	--	25T'26	22T'22	--
Erzähler, Der deutsche 1915 Erzn (Wilhelm von Scholz, ed)	--	--	--	--	36T'15
ESCHELBACH, Hans (1868-1948)					
D beiden Merks. E Schulgesch 1903 Nov	--	--	130T'30	--	--
Sonnensehnsucht 1916 R	24T'36	--	s 15/20	--	10A'18
ETTIGHOFER, Paul Coelestin (1896-)					
Verdun, das grosse Gericht 1936	330T'40				

TABLE B (con't.)

NAME	36/40	31/35	26/30	21/25	15/20
ETTIGHOFER, Paul Coelestin (con't.)					
Nacht über Sibirien... 1937	300T'40				
Eine Armee meutert... 1937	250T'39				
Gespenster am toten Mann 1931	240T'40				
Von der Teufelsinsel zum Leben 1932	100T'40				
Sturm 1918. Sieben Tage dt Schicksal 1938	100T'39				
Das gefesselte Heer 1932	55T'38				
ETTLINGER, Karl (Ps: Karlchen, 1882-1939)					
Aus fröhlichem Herzen Erzn	--	--	33T'28	--	--
Das Verhältnis 1920	--	--	26T'27	20T'22	10T'20
EWERS, Hans Heinz (1871-1943)					
Alraune. Gesch e lebenden Wesens 1911	--	--	ni'28	238T'22	228T'21
Horst Wessel. E dt Schicksal 1932	--	200T'34			
Das Grauen. Seltsame Geschn 1907	--	--	--	59T'22	--
Reiter in deutscher Nacht 1932	45T'36	40T'35			
Der Zauberlehrling oder Die Teufelsjäger 1909 R	--	--	--	45T'22	40T'20
Die Besessenen. Seltsame Geschn 1909	--	--	--	44T'25	29A'18
Grotesken 1910	--	--	--	40A'26 G Müller	--
Nachtmahr. Seltsame Geschn 1922	--	--	--	35T'22	

TABLE B (con't.)

NAME	36/40	31/35	26/30	21/25	15/20
EWERS, Hans Heinz (con't.)					
Hochnotpeinliche Geschichten 1902	--	--	--	--	22A'13
EYTH, Max (1836-1906)					
Hinter Pflug u Schraubstock... 1899 Erzn	298T'37+	292T'35	278T'30	253T'25	180A'20
Der Schneider von Ulm 1906 Gesch	nAg'37	113T'35	110T'30	99T'25	68T'20
D Kampf um d Cheopspyramide... 1902 R	nAg'37	53T'35	s 21/25	45T'25	25T'20
Lehrjahre	--	--	25T'30	20T'21	--
Der blinde Passagier (from Hinter Pflug und Schraubstock...) 1899 Erz	--	nA'31	2A'30 Buchners	ni'24	5T'16
FABER, Kurt (1883-1929)					
Rund um die Erde. Irrfahrten... 1924	--	23T'35	10T'27		
Unter Eskimos u Walfischfängern... 1916	--	23A'34 R Lutz	22A'30	19A'25+	13A'20
FALKE, Gustav (1853-1916)					
Viel Feind, viel Ehr' 1915	--	--	--	--	50T'16
D Stadt mit d goldenen Türmen 1912 R	--	--	--	24T'23	22T'20
FALLADA, Hans (ie Rudolf Ditzen, 1893-1947)					
Kleiner Mann, was nun? 1932 R	--	115T'35			
Wer einmal aus dem Blechnapf frisst 1934 R	--	30T'35			
Wolf unter Wölfen 1937 R	29T'40				

TABLE B (con't.)

NAME	36/40	31/35	26/30	21/25	15/20
FALLADA, Hans (con't.)					
Kleiner Mann, grosser Mann - alles vertauscht 1940 R	25T'40				
FEDERER, Heinrich (1866-1928)					
Berge und Menschen 1911 R	163T'36	152T'35	119T'29	90T'22	59T'19
Pilatus 1912 Erz	--	152T'35	93T'29	--	33T'20
D letzte Stündlein des Papstes 1914 Erz	138T'38	135T'35	--	110T'24	--
E Nacht in den Abruzzen. Mein Tarcisius Geschichtlein 1916	--	--	c 132T'27	60T'22	50T'18
Patria 1916 Erz	--	--	ni'30	60T'24	50T'18
In Franzens Poetenstube. Umbrische Reisekapitel 1918	--	--	59T'30	--	40T'18
Gebt mir meine Wildnis wieder. Umbrische Reisekapitel 1918	--	--	56T'29	50T'22	40T'18
Das Mätteliseppi 1916 Erz	--	51T'31	48T'27	42T'22	33T'19
Das Wunder in Holzschuhen 1919 Geschn	--	--	46T'30	--	40T'20
Regina Lob... 1925 R	45T'37	--	--		
Papst und Kaiser im Dorf 1924 R	--	41T'34	--		
Der Fürchtemacher 1919 Gesch	--	--	--	--	40T'20
Sisto e Sesto 1913 Erz	ni'39	--	--	--	40T'15
Jungfer Therese 1913 Erz	--	--	36T'30	27T'24	25T'19
Lachweiler Geschichten 1911	--	33T'31	29T'26	26T'24	25T'18

TABLE B (con't.)

NAME	36/40	31/35	26/30	21/25	15/20
FEDERER, Heinrich (con't.)					
Am Fenster. Jugenderinnerungen 1927	--	31T'31	21T'27		
Spitzbube über Spitzbube 1921 Erz	--	--	s 21/25	30T'21	
FEHRS, Johann Hinrich (1838-1916)					
Kattengold. Vertelln 1915	--	--	25T'26	--	15T'17
Ut Ilenbeck 1900 Vier Geschn	--	--	25T'28	--	--
FELDE, Max (ie Johann Kaltenboeck, 1853 - apparently still living in 1949)					
Der Arrapahu c 1900 Erz	34T'39	--	28A'27 Union	26A'25	19A'19
Addy, der Riflemann c 1901 Erz	--	--	27A'30	20A'22	16A'18
Villa Biberheim... 1903 Jagderle	--	--	26A'27	24A'25	19A'20
Das Gold von Sakramento 1917 Erz	--	21A'31	20A'27	17A'25	7A'19
FELDEN, Emil (1874-)					
Königskinder... 1914 R	--	--	30A'28 E Oldenburg	28A'22	18A'19
FENDRICH, Anton (1868-1949)					
Wir. Ein Hindenburgbuch 1917	--	--	--	--	145T'17
Mit d Auto an d Front. Kriegserle 1915	--	--	--	--	90T'17
An Bord. Kriegserle 1916	--	--	--	--	68T'17

TABLE B (con't.)

NAME	36/40	31/35	26/30	21/25	15/20
FERDINANDS, Carl (ie Karl Ferdinand v Vleuten, 1874-)					
Die Pfahlburg 1907 Erz	--	--	24T'28	23T'24	ni'20
Normanensturm 1908 Erz	--	--	21T'30	nA'21	--
FEUCHTWANGER, Lion (1884-1958)					
D hässliche Herzogin Margarete Maultasch 1923 R	--	--	150T'30		
Jud Süss 1917 R	--	ni'31	80T'29	ni'25	
Der jüdische Krieg 1932 R	--	50T'33			
Erfolg. Drei Jahre Gesch e Provinz 1930 R	--	25T'31			
FIGDOR, Karl (1881-1957)					
Die Herrin der Welt 1919 R	--	--	--	--	102T'20
FINCKENSTEIN, Ottfried Graf (1901-)					
Die Mutter 1938 R	100T'40				
FINCKH, Ludwig (1876-1964)					
Rapunzel 1909	194T'40	59T'31	57T'28	52T'25	33T'20
Der Rosendoktor 1906	154T'40	144T'32	142T'28	136T'25	94A'20
Die Reise nach Tripstrill 1911	63T'39	49T'33	47T'27	45T'22	35A'20
Der Bodenseher 1914	s 26/30	--	49T'26	45T'22	37A'20
Die Jakobsleiter 1920	s 26/30	--	31T'29+	29T'23	15A'21
Inselfrühling 1917 Erzn	--	--	--	23T'21	8T'17

TABLE B (con't.)

NAME	36/40	31/35	26/30	21/25	15/20
FINK, Georg (ie Kurt Münzer, 1879-1944)					
Mich hungert 1929 R	--	40T'32	25T'29		
FISCHER-GRAZ, Wilhelm (1846-1932)					
D Licht im Elendhaus (from <u>Grazer Novn</u>) 1903 Nov	--	--	125T'26	nA'24 ni'25	--
FISCHER-MARKGRAFF, Elisabeth (ie E. Fischer, née Markgraff, nd)					
Sein Recht 1912 R	--	--	--	--	50T'19
FLACK, Werner (nd)					
Wir bauen am Westwall. E Fronterl... 1939	45T'40				
FLAISCHLEN, Cäsar (1864-1920)					
Jost Seyfried 1905 R	--	--	122T'27	120T'24	--
FLAKE, Otto (1880-1963)					
Das Logbuch 1917 Erzn u Skn	--	--	--	27T'23	8A'17
Schritt für Schritt 1912 R	--	22A'32 S Fischer	--	12A'22	9A'20
FLEX, Walter (1887-1917)					
D Wanderer zw zwei Welten. E Krg-Erl 1917	682T'40	340T'31	301T'28	255T'25	195T'20
Vom grossen Abendmahl... 1915	139T'40	--	113T'28	104T'25	87T'20
Wallensteins Antlitz 1918 Gesch	80T'40	--	56T'27	43T'22	30T'20

TABLE B (con't.)

NAME	36/40	31/35	26/30	21/25	15/20
FLEX, Walter (con't.)					
D Kanzler Klaus v Bismarck 1914 Erz	57T'37	52T'28	47T'29	26T'21	21T'20
Wolf Eschenlohr 1919 Erz	--	56T'31	43T'26	11A'22	7A'20
Zwölf Bismarcks 1913 Zwölf Novn	--	34T'33	29T'30	21T'25	--
Novellen 1926	33T'40	20T'31	15T'28		
D Reiter u sein Junge vom Hautsee. Revanche 1939 Zwei Novellen	29T'40				
Der Schwarmgeist 1910 Erz	29T'39	25T'33	25T ?	--	ni'20
FOCK, Gorch (see also Hans Kinau, 1880-1916)					
Seefahrt ist not 1913 R	218T'36	207T'35	164T'26	155T'25	--
Hein Godenwind de Admirol v Moskitonien 1912 Gesch	73T'40	66T'30	--	62T'25	--
Sterne überm Meer. Tagebuchblätter u ... 1917	68T'40	58T'35	52T'26	--	
Nordsee 1916 Erzn	--	s 21/25	--	64T'26	5T'16
Schullengrieper u Tungenknieper... 1911 Geschn	64T'40	s 21/25	--	58T'25	--
Fahrensleute. Neue Seegeschn 1914	52T'40	s 26/30	48T'26	41T'22	--
Hamborger Janmooten. Een lustig Book 1914	--	s 21/25	--	52T'25	--
Ein Schiff! Ein Schwert! Ein Segel!... 1934	33T'40				
Schiff vor Anker 1920 Erzn	--	s 26/30	24T'26	21T'22	10T'20
Schiff ahoi! 1918 Ausgew Erzn	--	--	--	--	23T'18

TABLE B (con't.)

NAME	36/40	31/35	26/30	21/25	15/20
FORSTER, Hanna (ie Johanna Weis, née Forster, nd)					
Die Privatsekretärin 1916 R	--	--	--	90T'24	40T'16
FRANCK, Hans (1879-)					
Der Regenbogen 1927 7x7 Geschn	60T'36	s 26/30	11T'28		
Totaliter aliter 1933 Kurzgesch	35T'40	15T'35			
D Pentagramm der Liebe 1919 Fünf Novn	s 31/35	s 26/30	30T'27	8T'24	
Die Südseeinsel 1923 Nov	--	28T'35	14T'30		
FRANK, Gunnar (ie Karl Siber, 1890-)					
Der Weg zum Laster 1920 R	--	--	50T'30	--	
FRANK, Leonhard (1882-1961)					
Der Bürger 1924 R	--	--	94T'29	44T'24	
Der Mensch ist gut 1919	--	75T'35	--	--	50T'19
Bruder und Schwester 1929 R	--	--	40T'30		
Die Räuberbande 1914 R	--	--	30T'30	--	15T'20
Die Ursache 1916 Erz	--	--	25T'29	--	20T'20
FRANKE, Elisabeth (ie Elisabeth Loofs, née Francke, 1886-1931)					
Das grosse stille Leuchten 1912 Erz	--	--	--	30T'24	--
FRANZ, Arno (ie Franz Arno Kalklösch, 1880-1930)					
Sohr, der Knecht 1927 R	--	--	44T'30		

TABLE B (con't.)

NAME	36/40	31/35	26/30	21/25	15/20
FRANZOS, Karl Emil (1848-1904)					
Der deutsche Teufel 1916 R	--	--	--	40T'21	20T'16
Der Pojaz 1905 Gesch	--	s 26/30	25T'28	22T'23	17A'20
FREI, Friedrich (nd)					
Unser Fliegerheld Immelmann... c 1916	--	--	--	--	70T'16
S. M. S. "Möwe" c 1916	--	--	--	--	25T'16 nAg'16
FRENSSEN, Gustav (1863-1945)					
Jörn Uhl 1901 R	463T'39	416T'35	362T'29	288T'22	271T'20
Peter Moors Fahrt nach Südwest... 1906	253T'36	238T'34	215T'31	204T'25	191T'20
Hilligenlei 1905 R	239T'40	200T'35	190T'28	180T'23	165T'20
Die drei Getreuen 1898 R	--	193T'34	160T'26	151T'22	134T'20
Der Glaube der Nordmark 1936	170T'40				
Die Sandgräfin 1896 R	--	--	122T'29	108T'23	89T'20
Klaus Hinrich Baas 1909 R	--	--	114T'23	--	--
Die Brüder 1917 Erz	--	--	--	103T'22	94T'20
Dorfpredigten 1899-1903	--	--	97T'28	88T'21	--
Der Pastor von Poggsee 1921 R	--	97T'35	s 21/25	37T'22	
Der Untergang der Anna Hollmann 1911 Erz	91T'37	--	ni'29	73T'22	--
Dummhans 1929 R	65T'40+	--			
Lütte Witt 1924 Erz	--	--	51T'30	39T'25	

TABLE B (con't.)

NAME	36/40	31/35	26/30	21/25	15/20
FRENSSEN, Gustav (con't.)					
Der Weg unseres Volkes 1938	50T'40				
Grübeleien 1920	36T'39	33T'34	ni'28	25T'24	
Bismarck 1914 Epos	--	--	--	31T'23	
FROHNMEYER, Ida (1882-)					
Hansi 1921 Zwei Erzn	--	--	--	26T'22	
FUCHS-LISKA, Robert (1870-1935)					
Schamlose Seelen 1920 R	--	39T'32	s 21/25	ni'20	
GAGERN, Friedrich von (1882-1947)					
Ein Volk 1924 R	--	35T'31	--	15T'25	
Das nackte Leben 1923 R	23A'37 Parey	22A'35	--	4A'23	
GANGHOFER, Ludwig (1855-1920)					
Der laufende Berg 1897 R	--	500T'35	190T'29	181T'23	129T'20
Der Klosterjäger 1892 R	--	420T'32	301T'29	251T'22	206T'20
Der hohe Schein 1904 R	--	324T'35	164T'28	127T'22	114T'20
Der Dorfapostel 1900 R	--	332T'33	140T'28	127T'23	97T'20
Der Jäger v Fall 1883 R	300T'36	s 26/30	170T'27	148T'22	124T'20
Die Trutze v Trutzberg 1915 R	298T'37	117T'31	106T'27	96T'24	63T'20
Das Gotteslehen 1899 R	--	266T'34	ni'30	--	150T'21

TABLE B (con't.)

NAME	36/40	31/35	26/30	21/25	15/20
GANGHOFER, Ludwig (con't.)					
Der Unfried 1888 R	219T'36	s 26/30	157T'29	153T'23	117T'19
Schloss Hubertus 1895 R	--	s 26/30	216T'28	198T'22	163T'20
Der Mann im Salz 1906 R	--	213T'32	ni'30	109T'22	97T'21
Das Schweigen im Walde 1899 R	--	ni'31	205T'29	175T'25	95T'20
D Herrgottschnitzer aus Ammergau 1880 Gesch	ni'38	--	188T'29	163T'22	131T'20
Die Martinsklause 1894 R	--	s 21/25	--	177T'22	151T'21
Edelweisskönig 1886 R	--	ni'31	174T'29	160T'23	120T'16
Waldrausch 1908 R	--	172T'33	109T'28	96T'23	61T'20
Der Besondere u a Hochlandsgeschn 1893	152T'40	--	103T'29	93T'23	80T'20
Das neue Wesen 1902 R	--	s 26/30	141T'28	128T'23	--
Hochlandszauber 1931 Geschn	--	140T'35			
Der Ochsenkrieg 1914 R	--	134T'35	76T'28	64T'23	25T'19
Gewitter im Mai 1904 Nov	ni'39	--	110T'27+	100T'23	83T'19
Die Fackel-Jungfrau 1893 Bergsage	--	--	106T'27	91T'22	73T'18
Oberland 1887 Hochlandsgeschn	--	--	105T'29	94T'23	78T'20
Das grosse Jagen 1918 R	--	--	103T'29	86T'22	64T'20
Es war einmal 1889 moderne Märn	--	--	102T'27	82T'21	12A'20
Die Bacchantin 1897 R	--	s 26/30	92T'28	70T'22	59T'21
Die Sünden der Väter 1886 R	--	s 26/30	91T'29	69T'22	59T'21
Hubertusland 1912 Erzn	--	s 26/30	87T'29	75T'24	58T'20

TABLE B (con't.)

NAME	36/40	31/35	26/30	21/25	15/20
GANGHOFER, Ludwig (con't.)					
Damian Zagg 1906 Erzn	--	s 26/30	85T'29	65T'22	57T'20
Die Jäger 1905 Erzn	--	s 26/30	83T'29	63T'22	55T'20
Rachele Scarpa 1898 Nov	--	--	--	65T'24	11A'20
Lebenslauf eines Optimisten: 1. Buch der Kindheit 1909	--	s 26/30	61T'26 (40A)	32A'22	27A'20
Tarantella 1898 Nov	--	--	--	--	59T'20
Das Kind und die Million 1919 Gesch	--	--	57T'26	5T'22	
Lebenslauf eines Optimisten: 2. Buch der Jugend 1910	--	s 26/30	57T'29 (36A)	27A'22	22A'20
dass: 3. Buch der Freiheit 1911	--	s 26/30	53T'29 (32A)	23A'22	18A'20
Die liebe Kreatur 1913 Geschn	--	s 26/30	43T'29	34T'23	--
Bergluft 1883 Hochlandsgeschn	--	--	30T'29	27T'23	14A'20
Fliegender Sommer 1892	--	--	--	--	24T'20
Das wilde Jahr 1921 Fragmente aus dem Nachlass	--	--	--	23T'22	
Almer und Jägerleut 1885 Geschn	--	s 26/30	22T'29	17T'23	12T'20
GAST, Lise (ie Elisabeth Richter, 1908-)					
Junge Mutter Randi 1939 R	30T'40				

TABLE B (con't.)

NAME	36/40	31/35	26/30	21/25	15/20
GEISSLER, Horst Wolfram (1893-)					
Weiss man denn, wohin man fährt 1930 R	30T'37	25T'35			
GENZMER, Gertrud (nd)					
Jessika von Duden u a Novn 1912	--	--	--	--	22T'17
GEORGY, Ernst (ie Margarete Michaelson, 1873-1924)					
Jugendstürme 1900 R	--	--	--	59T'21	46T'16
GERSDORFF, Ada von (ie Ada Baronin v Maltzahn, 1854-)					
Durch Kampf zur Krone 1902 R	--	--	--	--	24T'20
GFELLER, Simon (1868-1943)					
Das Rötelein (from Gesch aus d Emmental) 1914 Erz	--	35T'34	--	--	ni'15
GILLHOFF, Johannes (1861-1930)					
Jürnjakob Swehn, der Amerikafahrer 1917 R	360T'40	255T'34	240T'29	176T'25	150T'20
dass - Eine Auswahl	90T'40	74T'34	50T'30		
GINZKEY, Franz Karl (1871-1963)					
Der von der Vogelweide 1912 R	--	54T'33	26T'27	23T'22	--
Der Wiesenzaun 1913 Nov	--	43T'35	39T'29	29T'25 nA'21	8T'20
GJELLERUP, Karl (1857-1919)					
Der Pilger Kamanita 1906 Leg-R	--	--	131T'28	120T'22	68T'20

TABLE B (con't.)

NAME	36/40	31/35	26/30	21/25	15/20
GJELLERUP, Karl (con't.)					
Die Weltwanderer 1911 R	--	s 21/25	--	23T'24	13T'20
GLAESER, Ernst (1902-1963)					
Jahrgang 1902 1928 R	--	100T'31	80T'28		
Frieden 1930 R (continuation of Jahrgang 1902)	--	--	25T'30		
GLASS, Luise (1857-1932)					
Gustel Wildfang c 1900 R	--	--	36A'28 Union	31A'23	26A'20
Das Montagskränzchen c 1899 R	--	--	36A'27	--	27A'20
Im Krähennest 1905 Erz	--	--	24A'27	22A'25	17A'20
Schwärmliesels Wunschglocke 1908 Erz	--	--	22A'30	--	15A'20
Annele 1902 R	--	--	--	--	21A'20
GLUTH, Oskar (1887-1955)					
Der verhexte Spitzweg 1928 R	71T'40	38T'34	25T'30		
Panks lachende Erben 1932 R	24T'40	8T'33			
GMELIN, Otto (1886-1940)					
Die junge Königin 1936 Erz	30T'40				
Germanenzug 1934 R (from Das neue Reich)	30T'40				
Das Angesicht des Kaisers 1927 R	30T'38	10T'35			
Das neue Reich 1930 R	26T'38	--			

TABLE B (con't.)

NAME		36/40	31/35	26/30	21/25	15/20
GOEDICKE, Elisabeth (1873-)						
Jens Larsen 1907 R		--	--	40T'26	--	--
GOLTZ, Joachim Frhr v der (1892-)						
Der Baum von Clery 1934 R		40T'40	15T'35			
Der Steinbruch 1938 R		25T'40				
GONTARD-SCHUCK, Margarete (nd)						
Seelenverkäufer. Erle einer Deutschen 1914		--	--	--	--	73T'20
GOOTE, Thor (ie Dr. Johannes M. Berg, 1899-)						
Wir fahren den Tod 1930		235T'40	--	20T'30		
Wir tragen das Leben 1932		75T'39				
Glühender Tag. Männer in d Bewährung 1940 Novn		35T'40				
GOTTBERG, Otto von (1867-1935)						
Die werdende Macht 1914 R		--	--	--	--	30T'18
GRABEIN, Paul (1869-1945)						
Die vom Rauen Grund 1913 R	(total)	c 171T'40				
	(Franke)	123T'40	--	48T'28	--	--
	(Grethlein)	--	--	48T'28	--	--
Ursula Drenck 1908 R	(total)	c 99T'35				
	(Globus)	s 31/35	34T'35	24T'28	--	--
	(Grethlein)	--	--	25T'28	--	--

TABLE B (con't.)

NAME	36/40	31/35	26/30	21/25	15/20
GRABEIN, Paul (con't.)					
Ursula Drenck (con't.) (Franke)	--	--	40T'28	--	--
Die Moosschwaige 1907 R	s 31/35	54T'35	44T'22	38T'22	--
Du mein Jena (Vivat academia!) 1903 R	s 31/35	54T'35	44T'29+	--	--
Der König von Thule 1907 R (total)	s 31/35	c 50T'35			
(Globus)	--	30T'35	20T'28	--	--
(Grethlein)	--	--	20T'28	--	--
Firnenrausch 1906 R	--	--	40T'28	--	--
Die Herren der Erde 1910 R	s 26/30	--	39T'29+	--	--
In Tropenglut u Urwaldnacht 1910	ni'39	--	27A'28 Union	21A'23	15A'20
Die Diamantensucher v Dorstfeldrank 1913	--	--	24A'27	17A'22	13A'19
Der Ruf des Lebens 1924 R	nA'39	--	21T'28	5T'24	
GRABENHORST, Georg (1899-)					
Die Reise nach Luzern 1939 Erz	40T'40				
Fahnenjunker Volkenborn 1929 R	30T'40	--	14T'29		
GRAESER, Erdmann (1870-1937)					
Koblanks 1922 R e Berliner Familie	--	--	45T'29		
Koblanks Kinder 1922 R e Berliner Familie	--	--	45T'29		
GRAF, Kurt (nd)					
Das fidele Kurt-Graf-Buch c 1921	132T'40	113T'35	90T'30	25T'23	

TABLE B (con't.)

NAME	36/40	31/35	26/30	21/25	15/20
GREINZ, Rudolf (1866-1942)					
Allerseelen 1910 R	146T'40	115T'34	105T'30	66T'25	--
Der Garten Gottes 1919 R	85T'40	61T'31	41T'28	38T'25	30T'19
Vorfrühling der Liebe 1925 R	54T'40	--	28T'28	25T'25	
Die Stadt am Inn 1917 R	--	52T'33	42T ?	36T'23	26T'19
Zauber des Südens 1929 R	45T'40	25T'35	20T'29		
Königin Heimat 1921 R	44T'40	s 26/30	33T'30	30T'23	
Das stille Nest 1908 R	--	s 26/30	43T'29	37T'23	--
Tiroler Bauernbibel 1907	37T'37	--	--	26T'23	21T'20
Äbtissin Verena 1915 R	--	s 26/30	33T'29	27T'23	22T'17
Über Berg u Tal. Ausgew lustige Tiroler-Geschn 1927	30T'40	--			
Das Haus Michael Senn 1909 R	--	s 26/30	30T'29	27T'23	--
Gertraud Sonnweber 1912 R	--	--	--	29T'25	--
Der Turm des Schweigens 1931 R	26T'40	16T'31	10T'31		
Die grosse Sehnsucht 1926 R	--	25T'32	23T'28		
Auf der Sonnseit'n 1911 Geschn	--	--	25T'28	22T'22	--
Fridolin Kristallers Ehekarren 1923 R	--	--	21T'28	18T'23	
Der Hirt von Zenoberg 1922 R	--	--	21T'29	18T'25	
Aus dem heiligen Landl 1909 Geschn	--	--	--	21T'22	--

TABLE B (con't.)

NAME	36/40	31/35	26/30	21/25	15/20
GRENGG, Marie (also Maria, 1899-)					
D Flucht zum grünen Herrgott 1930 R	40T'40	30T'35			
GRIESE, Friedrich (1890-)					
Die Wagenburg 1935 Erzn	55T'40				
Der Saatgang 1932 Erzn	45T'40	20T'33			
Alte Glocken 1925 Erz	38T'37	--	ni'29		
Die Weissköpfe 1939 R	25T'39				
GRIMM, Hans (1875-1959)					
Volk ohne Raum 1928 R	480T'40	315T'35	60T'30		
D Zug des Hauptmanns v Erckert 1932 R	230T'40	50T'34			
Der Ölsucher von Duala 1918	80T'40	35T'35	s 21/25	nA'22	
Luderitzland. Sieben Begebenheiten 1934	35T'40	20T'35			
Südafrikanische Novellen 1913	30T'40	20T'35	--	8T'21	--
GÜNTHER, Agnes (1863-1911)					
Die Heilige und ihr Narr 1913 R	125A'40 Steinkopf	115A'31	112A'29	96A'24	75A'21
Von d Hexe, die e Heilige war 1913 Erz	--	c 95T'31 (26A)	--	25A'25	85T'20+
HAARBECK, Lina (1871-1954)					
Geschn aus dem Rauhen Hause 1936	85T'40				

TABLE B (con't.)

NAME	36/40	31/35	26/30	21/25	15/20
HAAS, Rudolf (1877-1943)					
Matthias Triebl 1915 Gesch	--	60T'34	55T'26	49T'24	36T'20
Michel Blank u seine Liesel 1919 R	--	48T'32	38T'27+	35T'23	25T'20
Triebl der Wanderer 1916 Gesch	--	47T'32	--	45T'25	30T'20
HADINA, Emil (1885-1957)					
D graue Stadt - d lichten Frauen 1922 R	--	48T'33	28T'28	20T'24	
HAENSEL, Karl (1889-)					
Der Kampf ums Matterhorn 1929 R	--	--	35T'30		
HAGEL, Egino (nd)					
Der Gefangene auf Burg Hohenems Erz (Im Selbstverlag)	--	--	24T'26	--	--
HAGENBECK, Karl (1844-1913)					
Von Tieren u Menschen. Erinn u Erfahrungen 1908	34A'40 P List	ni'31	125A'30 P List	110T'22	ni'20
HALUSCHKA, Helene (1892-)					
Fröhliches Wissen um Adam u Eva 1934	25T'40				
HANDEL-MAZZETTI, Enrica Gräfin von (1871-1955)					
Jesse und Maria 1906 R	147T'36	s 26/30	90T'27	79T'21	70T'20
Meinrad Helmpergers denkwürdiges Jahr 1900 R	122T'38	s 26/30	98T'30	ni'25	44A'20

TABLE B (con't.)

NAME	36/40	31/35	26/30	21/25	15/20
HANDEL-MAZZETTI, Enrica Gräfin von (con't.)					
Die arme Margret 1910 R	--	s 26/30	117T'30	102T'22	ni'19 ni'17
Der deutsche Held 1920 R	83T'36	s 26/30	68T'30	52T'22	11T'20
Stephana Schwertner, Tl 3: Jungfrau und Märtyrin 1914 R	--	s 26/30	74T'27	63T'21	--
Stephana Schwertner, Tl 1: Unter d Richter von Steyr 1912 R	--	s 26/30	69T'27	58T'21	45A'20
Stephana Schwertner, Tl 2: D Geheimnis des Königs 1913 R	--	s 26/30	65T'27	54T'21	--
Brüderlein und Schwesterlein 1913 R	--	s 26/30	56T'27	--	ni'19 ni'17
Sand-Tril, Tl 1: Das Rosenwunder 1924 R	--	36T'34	ni'26	20T'24	
Ritas Briefe, Tl 2 1916	--	--	--	ni'24	29T'20
Frau Maria, Tl 1: Das Spiel v d 10 Jungfrauen 1929 R	--	s 26/30	22T'30		
HANSJAKOB, Heinrich (1837-1916)					
Im Schwarzwald 1901 Erzn	--	--	--	30T'24	--
Erzbeuern 1898 Erz	--	--	--	25T'22	21T'20
Waldleute 1897 Erz	--	--	--	23T'24	19T'20
HANSTEIN, Otfried von (1869-1959)					
Vom Segelschiffsjungen zum Lloyd Kapitän... 1928 Erinn	--	27T'33			

TABLE B (con't.)

NAME	36/40	31/35	26/30	21/25	15/20
HANSTEIN, Otfried von (con't.)					
Im Reiche d goldenen Drachen 1919	23T'31	--	--	ni'22	
HARBOU, Thea von (ie Frau Thea Lang, 1888-1954)					
Der Krieg u die Frauen 1913 Novn	--	--	--	--	100T'19
Die Flucht der Beate Hoyermann 1916 R	--	--	ni'28	43T'22	38A'20
Deutsche Frauen. Bilder stillen Heldentums (Dt Frauen im Kampfe des Lebens) 1914 Novn	--	--	--	25T'24	22T'20
HARDT, Ernst (ie Ernst Stöckhardt, 1876-1947)					
An den Toren des Lebens 1912 Nov	--	--	110T'28	--	--
HARRER, Anny (ie Annie Friedrich, nd)					
Die Hölle der Verlorenen 1916 R	--	--	--	--	50T'17
HAUPTMANN, Karl (1858-1921)					
Einhart der Lächler 1907 Erz	--	110A'33 P List	38T'28	35T'22	29T'20
HAUPTMANN, Gerhart (1862-1946)					
Der Ketzer von Soana 1918 Erz	172A'38 S Fischer	152A'32	146A'29	131A'25	105A'20
Der Narr in Christo Emanuel Quint 1910 R	--	s 21/25	83A'28	66A'22	54A'20
Die Insel der grossen Mutter... 1925 R	--	ni'31	75A'25	50A'25	
Atlantis 1912 R	--	s 26/30	53T'25	53A'25	40A'20

TABLE B (con't.)

NAME	36/40	31/35	26/30	21/25	15/20
HAUPTMANN, Gerhart (con't.)					
Bahnwärter Thiel. D Apostel. Novellistische Studien 1888, 1890	nA'39	--	ni'26	50A'22	ni'15
HAUSER, Heinrich (1901-1955)					
Im Kraftfeld von Rüsselsheim 1940	25T'41				
Brackwasser 1928 R	--	21T'35	14A'30		
HAUSMANN, Manfred (1898-)					
Lampioon. Abenteuer e Wanderers 1928 R	110T'39	70T'32			
Abel mit der Mundharmonika 1932 R	75A'40	61A'35 S Fischer			
Kleine Liebe zu Amerika. Reisebericht 1931	46A'36	42A'35	11A'31		
Die Frühlingsfeier 1924 Ges Novn	--	40T'32	--		
Salut gen Himmel 1929 R	32A'40	34A'35			
Ontje Arps 1934 Erz	23A'36	20A'34			
HEER, Jakob Christoph (1859-1925)					
Der Wetterwart 1905 R (total)	c 477T'40				
(Cotta)	387T'40	345T'32	335T'30	280T'25	150A'20
(Knaur)	--	435A'32			
An heiligen Wassern 1898 R (total)	c 458T'40				
(Cotta)	358T'40	328T'33	320T'30	270T'25	155A'20
(Knaur)	--	428A'33			
Der König der Bernina 1900 R	402T'40	356T'36	335T'30	285T'25	160A'20

TABLE B (con't.)

NAME	36/40	31/35	26/30	21/25	15/20
HEER, Jakob Christoph (con't.)					
Laubgewind 1908 R	320T'40	284T'36	270T'30	235T'25+	115A'20
Tobias Heider 1922 R	112T'40	108T'33	105T'28	100T'22	
Nick Tappoli 1920 R	--	95T'32	93T'26	90T'24	50A'20
Joggeli 1902 Gesch	88T'37	s 26/30	78T'28	75T'25	47A'21
Felix Notvest 1901 R	--	78T'35	76T'29	70T'25	37A'20
Der lange Balthasar 1915 R	--	s 26/30	67T'29	65T'25	45A'20
Heinrichs Romfahrt 1918 R	--	--	--	--	60A'18
Da träumen sie von Lieb u Glück 1910 Novn	--	s 26/30	51T'29	45T'24	30A'17
Was die Schwalbe sang 1916 Geschn	--	s 26/30	44T'28	41T'25	25A'17
HEIMBURG, Heino von (nd)					
U-Boot gegen U-Boot 1917	--	--	--	--	100T'17
HEIMBURG, Wilhelmine (ie Berta Behrens, 1850-1912)					
Aus d Leben meiner alten Freundin 1878 R	--	68A'33 Union	64A'30+	44A'23	31A'20
Lumpenmüllers Lieschen 1879 R	--	54A'32	45A'28+	32A'24	22A'20
Wie auch wir vergeben... 1907 R	--	48A'34	43A'29	31A'25	22A'20
Familie Lorenz 1911 R	--	43A'32	40A'30+	25A'23	20A'20
Trotzige Herzen 1897 R	--	43A'33	26A'26+	24A'23	19A'20
Kloster Wendhusen 1880 R	--	40A'32	36A'30+	24A'23	19A'20
Lore von Tollen 1889 R	--	39A'32	33A'30+	19A'22	15A'20

TABLE B (con't.)

NAME	36/40	31/35	26/30	21/25	15/20
HEIMBURG, Wilhelmine (con't.)					
Über steinige Wege 1908 R	--	38A'32	34A'29+	17A'22	14A'20
Herzenskrisen 1887 R	--	37A'32	34A'30+	17A'22	15A'20
Trudchens Heirat 1885 R	--	36A'32	21A'26+	19A'23	12A'19
Lotte Lore 1913 R	--	34A'33	--	32A'23	23A'19
Mamsell Unnütz 1893 R	--	22A'32	19A'25	17A'23	12A'20
Der Stärkere 1909 R	--	--	21A'27	19A'23	10A'19
Im Wasserwinkel 1900 R	--	21A'32	19A'26	18A'23	11A'19
Ein armes Mädchen 1884 R	--	21A'32	18A'25	17A'23	14A'20
HEIN, Alfred (1894-1945)					
Kurts Maler. E Lieblingsroman d dt Volkes 1922 (Courths-Mahler-Parodie)	--	--	--	999T'22	
HEINZE-HOFERICHTER, Mara von (ie Margarete, 1887-)					
Friedel Starmatz 1928 R	100T'36	100T'35	42T'30		
HERMANN, Georg (ie Georg H. Borchardt, 1871-1943)					
Jettchen Gebert 1906 R	--	159T'31	129T'29	118A'25	41A'15
Henriette Jacoby 1908 R	--	124T'32	102T'29	94A'35	31A'14
Aus guter alter Zeit 1913	--	--	30T'26	--	--
Heinrich Schön jun. 1915 R	--	--	--	26A'22 Dt V-Anst	5A'15

TABLE B (con't.)

NAME	36/40	31/35	26/30	21/25	15/20
HERWIG, Franz (1880-1931)					
Der grosse Bischof 1930 R	44T'38	39T'35			
Der Pfarrer zu Pferd 1923 Erz	--	--	21T'27	15T'23	
Herz, Das feste. E Gabe dt Erzähler (August Winnig, ed) 1939	55T'40				
HERZBERG, Margarete (nd)					
Die Intrigantin 1919 R	--	--	--	--	70T'19
Baroness Kläre 1915 R	--	--	--	7A'23 Munz	70T'15 (1-5A)
Lillis Vergeltung 1916 R	--	--	--	--	40T'17
HERZOG, Rudolf (1869-1943)					
Die Wiskottens 1905 R	615T'39	441A'32	361T'30	320T'23	185A'20
Die Stoltenkamps u ihre Frauen 1917 R	483T'41	417T'36	308T'30	280T'25	150A'20
Nur eine Schauspielerin 1897 R	--	--	425T'28	--	--
Die vom Niederrhein 1903 R	395T'40	276T'35	273T'30	240T'25	115A'20
Das grosse Heimweh 1914 R	389T'40	--	283T'30	250T'23	135A'20
Zum weissen Schwann 1897 R	--	--	341T'28	--	--
Die Burgkinder 1911 R	339T'38	316T'33	313T'30	285T'25	160A'20
Das Lebenslied 1904 R	321T'36	296T'32	291T'30	265T'25	130A'20
Hanseaten 1909 R	294T'36	269T'31	264T'28	246T'25	130A'20
Die Buben der Frau Opterberg 1921 R	265T'40	235T'31	230T'28	220T'25	

TABLE B (con't.)

NAME	36/40	31/35	26/30	21/25	15/20
HERZOG, Rudolf (con't.)					
Der Graf von Gleichen 1901 R	250T'40	177T'32	169T'27	121T'22	46A'19
Der Abenteuerer 1907 R	s 26/30	--	189T'28	170T'23	70A'20
Kameraden 1922 R	--	178T'32	175T'28	155T'25	
Wieland der Schmied 1924 R	--	155T'31	--	135T'25	
Jungbrunnen 1918 Novn	--	139T'35	--	105T'22	80A'19
Es gibt ein Glück 1910 Novn	--	115T'32	--	86T'23	--
Horridoh Lützow 1932 R	98T'40	nA'35			
Der alten Sehnsucht Lied 1906 Novn	--	83T'35	--	66T'23	16A'17
Die Welt in Gold 1913 Nov	--	71T'32	ni'26	60T'22+	35A'20
Das Fähnlein der Versprengten 1926 R	s 26/30	--	70T'26		
Kornelius Vanderwelts Gefährtin 1928 R	63T'38	--	60T'29		
Der Adjutant 1899 R	s 26/30	--	55T'28	42T'23	17A'17
Gesammelte Werke, Reihe 1, 6 Bde 1920 (Cotta)	s 26/30	--	51T'29	43T'25	20T'20
Wilde Jugend 1897 R	s 26/30	--	50T'29	--	--
Preussens Geschichte 1913	--	--	--	45T'24	40T'18
Das goldene Zeitalter 1897 R	--	45T'32	--	32T'25	14A'17
Über das Meer Verwehte 1934 R	33T'40				
Gesammelte Werke, Reihe 2, 6 Bde 1921 (Cotta)	s 26/30	--	33T'28	30T'25	
Germaniens Götter 1919	--	30T'33	--	--	

TABLE B (con't.)

NAME	36/40	31/35	26/30	21/25	15/20
HESSE, Hermann (1877-1962)					
Unterm Rad 1905 R	--	s 26/30	149A'30 S Fischer	122A'23	--
Knulp. 3 Geschn aus d Leben Knulps 1915	137A'40	129A'30	125A'29	112A'25+	
Peter Camenzind 1903 Erz	--	s 26/30	124A'30	115A'25	98A'20
Weg nach innen 1931 Vier Erzn	105A'40	90A'35			
Schön ist die Jugend 1916 Zwei Erzn	103A'37	100A'34+	92A'28	88A'25	
Demian 1919 Gesch	88A'37	s 26/30	78A ?	75A'25	
Narziss und Goldmund 1930 R	64A'40	55A'35	40A'30		
Rosshalde 1914 R	--	55A'32	--	52A'25	30A'18
Der Steppenwolf 1928 R	42A'40	40A ?	35A'28		
Gertrud 1910 R	--	--	ni'27	42A'24 A Langen	36A'10
Die Marmorsäge 1907	--	--	--	40T'17	--
Siddhartha 1922 Indische Dtg	36A'37 S Fischer	34A'35	33A'29	18A'25	
Märchen 1919 Erzn	--	--	31A'30	24A'22	5A'19
In der alten Sonne 1914	--	s 21/25	31A'27	27A'24	--
HESSIG, H. (ie Herta Kärger, formerly Hessig-Stahl, nd)					
Vom Baum der Erkenntnis 1913	--	--	--	nA'24	24T'16

TABLE B (con't.)

NAME	36/40	31/35	26/30	21/25	15/20
HEUBNER, Rudolf (1867-)					
Der heilige Geist. R in zwei Teilen					
1. Jakob Siemering & Co. 1917 (total)	--	c 76T'34 38T'34	nAg 38T'27	35T'22	5T'17
2. Jakob Siemerings Erben 1918 (total)	--	c 71T'34 33T'34	nAg 38T'27	30T'23	15T'18
HEYCK, Hans (1891-)					
Friedrich Wilhelm I. Amtmann u Diener Gottes auf Erden 1936	40T'36				
HEYKING, Elisabeth von (1861-1925)					
Briefe, die ihn nicht erreichten 1903 R	--	--	ni'28	102A'25 Paetel	96A'20
Der Tag Anderer 1905 R	--	--	s 21/25	26A'25	--
HINDENBURG, Paul von (v Beneckendorff, 1847-1934)					
Aus meinem Leben 1920	--	170T'33	146T'29	139T'25	12A'20
HINRICHS, August (1879-1956)					
Das Volk am Meer 1929 R	48T'40	26T'33			
Das Licht der Heimat 1920 R	34T'40	24T'35	19T'28	15T'22	
Die Hartjes 1924 R	24T'39	19T'35	14T'28	10T'25	
HIRSCHBERG-JURA, Rudolf (ie Rudolf Hirschberg, 1867-)					
Heddas Heirat 1916 R	--	--	--	nA'24	25T'20

TABLE B (con't.)

NAME	36/40	31/35	26/30	21/25	15/20
HIRSCHFELD, Georg (1873-1942)					
Der Patrizier 1919 R	--	--	ni'27	--	25T'19
HOCH, Christa (ie Frau Pia Sophie Rogge, née Börner, 1878-1955)					
Soldatentöchter 1912 Offiziergeschn	--	--	--	--	70T'19
HOECHSTETTER, Sophie (1878-1943)					
Königin Luise 1926 R	31T'39	22T'31			
Passion 1911	--	--	nAg'25	nAg 26T'21	--
HÖCKER, Paul Oskar (1865-1944)					
Kleine Mama 1910 R	70T'37	--	--	--	--
Fräulein Doktor 1898 R	--	--	--	--	67A'19 P List
D reizendste Frau - ausser Johanna 1935 R	60T'40				
Zwischen Hochzeit und Heirat (Die junge Exzellenz) 1914 R	58T'37	--	--	--	--
Ein Liller Roman 1916	--	--	--	--	40T'17
HOFER, Klara (ie Klara Höffner, 1875-1955)					
Alles Leben ist Raub 1913	--	s 26/30	34T'30	28T'25	11A'20
Maria im Baum 1912 Erz (total)	c 28T'40 7T'40	21T'31	--	--	ni'16

TABLE B (con't.)

NAME	36/40	31/35	26/30	21/25	15/20
HOFFENSTHAL, Hans von (ie Hans v Hepperger, 1877-1914)					
Lori Graff 1909 R	--	--	65T'30	61T'25	--
Moj 1914 R	--	--	--	43T'22	--
HOFFMANN, Hans (1848-1909)					
Spätglück. Sturmwolken 1901 Zwei Erzn	--	--	103T'28	--	--
HOFMANNSTHAL, Hugo von (1874-1929)					
Dt Erzähler 1912 Ausgew v H. von H.	40T'40	28T'35	--	13T'21	--
HOLESCH, Ditha (ie Editha, 1901-)					
Der schwarze Hengst Bento 1937 R	30T'39				
HOLLÄNDER, Felix (1867-1931)					
Das letzte Glück 1896 R	--	--	ni'26	69A'24 S Fischer	--
Der Weg des Thomas Truck 1902 R	--	--	50T'30	ni'20	10A'20
Der Eid d Stephan Huller 1912 R	--	--	ni'26	45T'23	--
Frau Ellin Röte 1893 R	--	--	ni'26	37A'24	--
Die Briefe des Fräulein Brandt 1917 R	--	--	ni'26	33A'25 R Mosse	30T'19
Der Tänzer 1918 R	--	--	ni'26	30T'24	5A'18
HOLM, Korfiz (1872-1942)					
Herz ist Trumpf 1917 R	33T'40	21T'35	18T'28	--	15T'18

TABLE B (con't.)

NAME	36/40	31/35	26/30	21/25	15/20
HOUBEN, Heinrich Hubert (1875-1945)					
Der Ruf des Nordens 1928	245T'40	224T'33			
HUCH, Felix (1880-1952)					
Der junge Beethoven 1927 R	60T'40	34T'34	25T'28		
HUCH, Friedrich (1873-1913)					
Pitt u Fox, die Lebenswege der Brüder Sintrup 1909 R	--	--	150T'27	130T'22	88T'18
Geschwister 1903 R	--	s 26/30	75A'27 S Fischer	70A'21	--
Mao 1907 R	--	--	52A'28	48A'24	--
Wandlungen 1905 R	--	46A'31	--	44A'24	ni'16
HUCH, Ricarda (1864-1947)					
Lebenslauf d heiligen Wonnebald Pück 1905 Erz	--	95T'31	--	--	--
D Judengrab. Aus Bimbos Seelenwanderungen 1916 Zwei Erzn	--	50T'32	--	--	
Erinn v Ludolf Ursleu d Jüngeren 1893 R	49T'36	s 26/30	ni'30	41T'25	31A'20
Der letzte Sommer 1910 Erz	--	40T'33	14T'27	9T'22	6T'20
Michael Unger (Vita somnium breve until 1913) 1902 R	37T'40	34T'35	31T'30	28T'25	8A'20
Fra Celeste 1899 Erz	--	30T'32	ni'29	ni'24	--
D Leben d Grafen Federigo Confalonieri 1910	26T'38	23T'33	--	18T'25	--

TABLE B (con't.)

NAME	36/40	31/35	26/30	21/25	15/20
HUCH, Ricarda (con't.)					
Aus der Triumphgasse 1902 Skn	--	--	--	23T'24	20T'20
HÜBENER, Helene (1843-1918)					
Es muss doch Frühling werden 1888 Erz	--	--	75T'28	65T'23	52A'20
Die drei Freundinnen 1893 Erz	--	--	47T'28	--	7A'20
Maria und Lisa 1903 Erz	--	--	45T'26	--	5A'19
Licht und Schatten 1902 Erz	--	--	38T'28	24T'21	3A'19
Gesühnte Schuld 1898 Erz	--	--	38T'28	--	25T'20
Nur treu 1895 Vier Erzn	--	--	37T'28	40T'23 (6A)	5A'19
Grossmütterchen 1901 Erz	35T'37	--	30T'28	30T'23 (4A)	3A'17
Im Rosenhaus 1910 Erz	--	--	33T'28	30T'23 (4A)	3A'19
Aus dem Leben einer Waise 1912 Erz	--	--	30T'28	30T'23 (4A)	3A'19
Unter einem Dach 1897 Erz	--	--	28T'28	30T'23 (4A)	--
Tante Hedwig 1904 Erz	--	--	25T'28 (4A)	25T'23 (3A)	--
Die Nachbarn 1914 Erz	--	--	22T'28	24T'23 (3A)	2A'19

TABLE B (con't.)

NAME	36/40	31/35	26/30	21/25	15/20
HUGGENBERGER, Alfred (1867-1960)					
Die Bauern von Steig 1913 R	35T'38	--	31T'28	28T'23	25T'20
HULDSCHINER, Richard (1872-1931)					
Fegefeuer 1922 R	--	s 26/30	25T'27	20T'22	
HUNNIUS, Monika (1858-1934)					
Meine Weihnachten 1922 Erz	94T'39	--	60T'30		
Mein Onkel Hermann... 1922 Erinn	58T'40 Salzer	--	10A'30 Salzer	3A'25	
dasselbe mit Bildnis des Onkels	13A'37 Salzer	--	--	--	
Mein Weg zur Kunst 1925	--	57T'35	11A'30	6T'25 (2A)	
Menschen, die ich erlebte 1922	55T'40	42T'31	38T'30		
Mein Elternhaus 1935	30T'40	10T'35			
Bilder aus d Zeit d Bolschewikenherrschaft in Riga 1921	26T'38	23T'33	18T'27	12T'22	
Baltische Frauen von einem Stamm 1930	21T'40	16T'30			
HUONDER, Anton (1858-1926)					
D Schwur d Huronenhäuptlings 1894 Erz	--	--	c 43T'27 (18A)	38T'22 (16A)	14A'19 Herder
E rote u e weisse Rose... 1896 Erzn	--	--	--	40T'23 (16A)	12A'19

TABLE B (con't.)

NAME	36/40	31/35	26/30	21/25	15/20
HUONDER, Anton (con't.)					
Die Rache des Mercedariers 1910 Erz	--	--	--	26T'23 (8-11A)	26T'17 (9-10A)
Der Findling von Hong Kong 1909 Erz	--	--	c 26T'28 (11A)	21T'22 (9A)	16T'18 (7A)
D heilige Brunnen v Chitzen-Itza 1908 Erz	--	--	c 26T'28 (11A)	21T'22 (9A)	16T'18 (7A)
HYAN, Hans (1868-1944)					
Die Verführten 1911 R	--	--	--	--	28T'20
ILG, Paul (1875-1957)					
Probus 1922 R	--	--	--	30T'22	
IMMELMANN, Max (1890-1916)					
Immelmann, d Adler v Lille (ed Franz Immelmann) 1934	nAg 57T'40				
Meine Kampfflüge. Selbsterlebt u selbsterzählt 1916	--	--	--	--	50T'16
ITZINGER, Karl (1888-1948)					
D Blutgericht am Haushammerfeld oder... 1933 R	45T'40				
Ums Letzte. D Ende e dt Kampfes um Freiheit, Glaube u Heimat 1937 R	30T'40				

TABLE B (con't.)

NAME	36/40	31/35	26/30	21/25	15/20
ITZINGER, Karl (con't.)					
Es muss sein. D Kampf e dt Volkes um Freiheit, Glaube u Heimat 1936 R	30T'40				
JACQUES, Norbert (1880-1954)					
Piraths Insel 1917 R	--	--	ni'26	--	32A'20 S Fischer
JÄGER, Paul (1869-)					
Das schöne Morgenlicht 1929	31T'38	--	10T'30		
Christsonne 1931 Weihnachtsgeschn	30T'38	23T'35			
JANSEN, Werner (1890-1943)					
Robert d Teufel (D irdische Unsterblichkeit) 1924 R	208T'40	--	205T'29	75T'24	
Das Buch Treue 1916 Nibelungen-R	149T'40	--	130T'29	100T'23	13T'17
Geier um Marienburg 1925 R	121T'40	--	110T'29	100T'25	
Das Buch Liebe 1918 Gudrun-R	120T'40	107T'32	99T'27	--	35T'20
Das Buch Leidenschaft 1920 Amelungen-R	87T'40	--	74T'29	--	25T'20
Heinrich der Löwe 1923 R	64T'40	--	50T'28	40T'24	
Verratene Heimat 1932 R	37T'40	12T'32			
Die Kinder Israels 1927 Rassen-R	23T'40	--			
JELUSICH, Mirko (1886-)					
Cromwell 1934 R	158A'40 Speidel	40A'35			

TABLE B (con't.)

NAME	36/40	31/35	26/30	21/25	15/20
JELUSICH, Mirko (con't.)					
Caesar 1929 R	96A'40 Speidel	49A'35			
Der Löwe 1936 R	78A'40				
Hannibal 1934 R	77A'40	32A'34			
Der Soldat 1939 R	40A'40				
JERUSALEM, Else (ie Else Widakowich, 1877-)					
Der heilige Skarabäus 1909 R	--	--	40A'26 S Fischer	--	26A'16
JOHST, Hanns (1890-)					
Mutter ohne Tod. D Begegnung 1933 Zwei Erzn	140T'40	30T'34			
Maske und Gesicht 1935	35T'40				
Consuela. Aus d Tagebuch... 1925	30T'40	--	5T'25		
Die Torheit einer Liebe 1931 R	25T'40	s 26/30			
JÜNGER, Ernst (1895-)					
In Stahlgewittern. E Kriegstageb 1920	c 60T'40 (20A)	16A'35 Mittler	13A'31	18T'24 (6A)	
Auf den Marmorklippen 1939 R	23T'40				
JÜNGER, Nathanael (ie Johannes Rump, 1871-)					
J. C. Rathmann und Sohn 1913 R	26T'37	--	--	23T'22	18T'19

TABLE B (con't.)

NAME	36/40	31/35	26/30	21/25	15/20
JÜNGER, Nathanael (con't.)					
Hof Bokels Ende 1907 R	--	--	s 21/25	23T'21	13T'18
JÜRGENS, Ludwig (1893-)					
Stadt im Seewind 1931 R	--	25T'36			
JUNG, Hermann (1901-)					
Krieg unter Wasser. D Opfertod d Fünftausend 1939	24T'40				
JUNGNICKEL, Max (1890-vermisst)					
Ins Blaue hinein 1917 R	--	25T'32	--	--	11A'18
Kunterbuntes Heimweh (D lachende Soldatenbuch) 1915	--	--	--	23A'21 Wiechmann	22A'18
JUST, Wilhelm (1864-)					
Graf Udos Seele 1924 R	--	--	24A'29 Frawin	23A'25 Sonnemann	
KÄLIN, Karl (also KAELIN, 1870-1950)					
In den Zelten des Mahdi 1904 Erz	--	--	--	27T'23	21T'20
KAERGEL, Hans Christoph (1889-1946)					
Die Berge warten 1935 Erz	50T'40				
Einer unter Millionen 1936 R	42T'40				

TABLE B (con't.)

NAME	36/40	31/35	26/30	21/25	15/20
KAERGEL, Hans Christoph (con't.)					
Der Volkskanzler... 1935	27A'38 J Beltz	15A'35			
KÄSTNER, Erich (1899-)					
Fabian 1932 Gesch	--	30T'32			
KAHLE, Karl (1884-1958)					
Hermann Löns und die Frauen 1926	--	--	22T'26		
KAHLENBERG, Hans von (ie Helene Kessler, née v Monbart, 1870-)					
Nixchen. E Beitrag zur Psychologie d höheren Töchter 1899 Nov	--	--	--	100T ?	--
Verliebte Geschichten	--	--	--	--	30T'18 2A'13
KAISER, Isabelle (1866-1925)					
Die Friedensucherin 1908 R	27A'36 Bachem	--	--	22A'21 Cotta	16T'19 Bachem
KAMPE, Otto (nd)					
Ein Korb voll Kirschen 1914 Kl Geschn	--	172T'34	112T'30	7A'25	3A'20
Robinson 1913 Erz	165T'37	135T'33	75T'29	6A'25	
Schelmenstreiche, lustige Geschn... 1925	40T'36	30T'31	20T'29		

TABLE B (con't.)

NAME	36/40	31/35	26/30	21/25	15/20
KARLCHEN (ie Karl Ettlinger, 1882-1939)					
Aus fröhlichen Herzen (including the next two titles) Erzn	--	--	33T'28	--	--
D Tagebuch eines Glücklich-Verheirateten. Unterschlagen u mitgeteilt 1906 Erz	--	--	s above	26T'23	--
Fräulein Tugendschön, d edle Gouvernantin u a Humn 1909	--	--	s above	25T'23	--
Unsere Donna. D Tagebuch e modernen Dienstmädchens 1907 Erz	--	--	--	24T'23	--
KARLIN, Alma Maximiliane (1891-1950)					
Im Banne der Südsee. Als Frau allein... 1930	--	30T'33			
Erlebte Welt, d Schicksal e Frau... c 1930	--	30T'33			
Einsame Weltreise. D Tragödie e Frau 1929	--	30T'32			
KARRASCH, Alfred (1893-)					
Parteigenosse Schmiedecke 1934 R	71T'40	60T'34			
KATH, Lydia (ie Frau Lydia Knop, née Kath, 1906-)					
Jomsburg 1934 E Wikingergesch	31T'40				
KATTERFELD, Anna (ie Anna Ilgenstein, 1880-)					
Die Stadt der Barmherzigkeit... 1930	--	s 26/30	25T'30		
KELLER, Paul (1873-1932)					
Waldwinter 1902 R	518T'38	433T'35	293A'29	250A'23	50A'16

TABLE B (con't.)

NAME	36/40	31/35	26/30	21/25	15/20
KELLER, Paul (con't.)					
Ferien vom Ich 1915 R	--	371T'35	271A'29	241A'24	44A'17
Der Sohn der Hagar 1907 R	--	328A'31 Bergstadtv.	232A'29	214A'24	139A'20
Die Heimat 1904 R	--	207T'35	169A'27	161A'24	81A'20
Hubertus 1918 R	--	192A'31	--	172A'24	110A'20
Das letzte Märchen 1905 Mär-R	--	142A'31	--	121A'23	71A'20
Die Insel der Einsamen 1913 R	--	141A'31	--	121A'23	--
Gold u Myrrhe 1898 Erzn u Skn Tl 1	c 121T'37 nF 51T'37	60T'33	55T'27	49T'21 1-10A'23	37T'18
Die alte Krone 1909 R	--	119A'34	ni'29	102A'23	29A'17
In fremden Spiegeln 1920 R	--	118A'31	--	97A'23	30A'20
Stille Strassen 1912 Erzn	--	98A'32	--	68A'22	52A'20
Die fünf Waldstädte 1910 Erzn	--	96A'32	96A'29	70A'24	59A'20
D königliche Seminartheater u a Geschn 1916	--	85A'32	85A'29	59A'23	26A'17
Altenroda 1921 Gesch	--	80A'32	--	30A'21	
Grünlein 1915 E dt Kriegsgesch	--	--	71A'27	--	8A'15
Von Hause. E Päckchen Humor aus d Werken Paul Kellers mit Bildern 1917	--	--	59A'29	51A'21	10A'17
Marie Heinrich 1926 R	--	--	45A'28		
Die vier Einsiedler 1923 R	--	45A'33	--	35A'24	
In deiner Kammer 1903 Geschn	s 26/30	--	c 44T'29 24T'29	nF 5T'25	20T'20

TABLE B (con't.)

NAME	36/40	31/35	26/30	21/25	15/20
KELLER, Paul (con't.)					
Titus u Timotheus u d Esel Bileam 1927 R	--	--	30A'27		
Die drei Ringe 1924	--	--	s 21/25	30A'24	
Ulrichshof 1929 R	--	28A'34			
Das Niklasschiff 1907 Neue Erzn (total)	--	c 28T'32			
(Schöningh)	--	23T'32	--	19T'21	14T'18
(Bergstadtverlag)	--	--	--	5T'25	--
KELLERMANN, Bernhard (1879-1951)					
Der Tunnel 1913 R	358A'40 S Fischer	343A'35	253A'28	238A'24	200A'20
Yester und Li 1904 R	183A'37	--	--	168A'25	--
Ingeborg 1906 R	131A'36	s 26/30	128A'28	110A'22+	45T'17
Das Meer 1910 R	--	--	96A'29	92A'25	63A'18
Der 9. November 1920 R	--	--	55A'29	51A'22+	34A'21
Der Tor 1909 R	--	s 21/25	--	50A'23	20A'17
Ein Spaziergang in Japan 1910	--	--	s 21/25	23T'22	3A'20 P Cassierer
KENNICOTT, Mervyn Brian (ie Gertrud Hamer, née v Sanden, 1881-1940)					
Das Herz ist wach... 1934	100A'36 nA'40	3A'34 Wunderlich			
KERN, Maximilian (1877-)					
Selbst der Mann c 1904	--	53A'31 Union	48A'26	38A'22	29A'20

TABLE B (con't.)

NAME	36/40	31/35	26/30	21/25	15/20
KERN, Maximilian (con't.)					
Im Labyrinth des Ganges c 1904 Erzn	35A'37 Union	33A'32	30A'27	26A'22	19A'20
In der Wildnis d Gran Chaco 1909	--	28A'31	--	22A'23	17A'20
Unter Mongolen u Wilden 1917	--	--	25A'28	21A'25	12A'19
Das Erbe des Pharao 1911	--	--	24A'30	20A'25	14A'20
Der Zwingherr von Celebes 1914	--	--	23A'30	17A'22	12A'20
KESSLER, Johannes (nd)					
Ich schwöre mir ewige Jugend 1935 Erinn	50A'40 P List				
KESSLER, Walter (ie Gunther Haupt, 1904-)					
Und eines Tages öffnet sich die Tür. Briefe zweier Liebenden 1939	36T'40				
KEYSERLING, Eduard von (1858-1918)					
Beate und Mareile 1903 E Schlossgesch	--	ni'33	--	68A'25 S Fischer	
Am Südhang 1916 Erz	--	ni'33	--	51A'24	
Im stillen Winkel 1918 Erz	--	ni'33	--	32A'24	
KINAU, Jakob (1884-)					
Die See ruft 1924 R	29T'39	s 21/25	--	9T'24	

TABLE B (con't.)

NAME	36/40	31/35	26/30	21/25	15/20
KINAU, Rudolf (1887-)					
Blinkfüer. Helle u düstere Biller 1918 Skn	--	78T'34	75T'29	65T'21	25T'20
Steernkiekers 1917 Erz	--	--	--	55T'24	30T'20
Thees Bott dat Woterküken 1919 Erz	--	54T'30	49T'27	46T'25	17T'20
Laterne. En bebern Licht ut Nacht un Dok 1920 R	--	42T'30	37T'27	35T'24	10T'20
Strandgoot 1921 Skn	--	--	--	24T'21	
KIPP, Friedrich (1878-1953)					
Die Waldheimat d Donatus Quind 1927 R	--	25T'31			
KIRCHSTEIGER, Hans (1852-1932)					
Das Beichtsiegel 1905 R	--	--	--	35A'24 Anzengruber	s 10/12
KIRSCHWENG, Johannes (1900-1951)					
Der Widerstand beginnt 1934 Nov (total)	c 36T'37				
(Hausen Verlag)	nA 18T'37	18A'34			
KLABUND (ie Alfred Henschke, 1890-1928)					
Bracke 1918 Eulenspiegel-R	--	120T'32	--	ni'24	5A'18
Borgia 1928 R	--	95T'31	40A'29		
Pjotr 1923 R	--	60T'32	ni'29		

TABLE B (con't.)

NAME	36/40	31/35	26/30	21/25	15/20
KLEMM, Johanna (Hanna Clemens, nd)					
Waldasyl 1913 R	--	--	--	nA'21	52T'19
KLEPPER, Jochen (1903-1942)					
Der Vater 1937 R	55T'40				
KNEIP, Jakob (1881-1958)					
Hampit der Jäger 1927 R	69A'39 P List	61A'33			
dass - Eine Auswahl 1933 R	10T'39				
KNITTEL, John (ie Hermann Knittel, 1891-)					
Via Mala 1934 R	143T'40	24T'35			
Therese Etienne 1927 R (W. Krüger)	20T'36	--			
(O. Füssli)	4A'37	3A'35	2A'30		
KOCH, Henny (1854-1929)					
Mütterchen Sylvia c 1905 Erz	--	--	38A'27 Union	33A'23	24A'19
Die ins Leben lachen 1908 Erz	--	36A'33	34A'26	--	27A'20
Im Lande der Blumen 1912 Erz	--	--	24A'26	19A'22	15A'20
Die verborgene Handschrift Erz	--	--	22A'26	19A'21	11A'19
KOEBNER, Franz Wolfgang (1887-)					
Die Nonne u d Halekin 1917	--	--	--	41T'21	

TABLE B (con't.)

NAME	36/40	31/35	26/30	21/25	15/20
KOEBNER, Franz Wolfgang (con't.)					
Maria Evere. D Gesch e Komödiantin 1917	--	--	--	31T'21	21T'19
KÖHLER, Heinrich (1852-1920)					
Die Erbin 1912 R	--	--	--	--	50T'19
Margarete 1914 Gesch	--	--	--	nA'24	37T'20
KOHLENEGG, Viktor von (ie V. von Kohl-Kohlenegg, 1872-1940)					
Der Katzentisch 1913 R	--	--	--	44T'22	--
KOHNE, Gustav (1871-)					
Waffenschmied des Volkes 1933 R	32T'37				
KOLBENHEYER, Erwin Guido (1878-1962)					
D Begegnung auf d Riesengebirge 1933 Nov	110T'40	60T'35			
Meister Joachim Pausenwang 1910 R	100T'40	25T'34	--	15T'26	
Karlsbader Novelle 1786 1934	90T'40	20T'34			
Paracelsus, R in drei Tln 1. Die Kindheit d Paracelsus 1917	60T'40	35T'35	25T'30	15T'23	
Das gottgelobte Herz 1938 R	55T'40				
Paracelsus, R in drei Tln 2. Das Gestirn d Paracelsus 1921	45T'40	30T'35	20T'28		
Amor Dei 1908 R	45T'40	35T'33	25T'29	18T'23	45A'17 G Müller

TABLE B (con't.)

NAME	36/40	31/35	26/30	21/25	15/20
KOLBENHEYER, Erwin Guido (con't.)					
Paracelsus, R in drei Tln 2. Das dritte Reich d Paracelsus 1926	43T'40	18T'34	10T'27		
KOLL, Killian (ie Walter-Julius Bloem, 1898-1945)					
Urlaub auf Ehrenwort 1937 Geschn	50T'39				
Die unsichtbare Fahne 1938 R	35T'40				
KOSSAK, Margarethe (1855-)					
Die Erbtante 1912 Krim-R	--	--	--	46T'25	30A'19
KRAFT, Zdenko von (1886-)					
Sonnwend des Glückes 1917 R	s 15/20	--	23T'28	--	
KRAMARZ, Maria (nd)					
Dies Mädel ist Hanne - später bist du es 1937	35T'40				
KRANE, Anna Freiin von (1853-1937)					
Magna peccatrix. Die grosse Sünderin 1908 Leg-R	--	--	31A'30 Bachem	26A'22	20T'20
Die Leidensbraut 1921 Gesch	--	--	--	30A'24	
Das Schweigen Christi 1915 R	--	--	--	21T'21	11T'19

TABLE B (con't.)

NAME	36/40	31/35	26/30	21/25	15/20
KRATZMANN, Ernst (1889-1950)					
Das Lächeln des Magisters Anselmus oder... 1927 R	s 26/30	--	50T'29		
KRAZE, Friede Henriette (Ps: Heinz Gumprecht, 1870-1936)					
Die magischen Wälder... 1933 R	110T'39	14T'33			
Land im Schatten 1929 R	40T'39	30T'34	8A'30		
Das wahre Gesicht... 1925 Erz	--	33T'34	25T'26	25T'25	
Die Freiheit des Kolja Iwanov 1927 R	--	25T'35			
KREHMCKE, Karl (nd)					
Auf eigenen Füssen 1912 R	--	--	--	--	35T'19
KRETZER, Max (1854-1941)					
Der Mann ohne Gewissen 1905 R	--	--	195T'29	--	--
Treibende Kräfte 1903 R	--	--	--	45T'21	--
Der Millionenbauer 1891 R	--	--	30T'26	--	25T'19
KRICKEBERG, Elisabeth (1860-)					
Siddys Ehekontrakt 1917 R	--	--	--	c 90T'23 (3A)	60T'19 (2A)
KRIEGER, Arnold (1904-1965)					
Mann ohne Volk 1934 R	102T'39+				

TABLE B (con't.)

NAME	36/40	31/35	26/30	21/25	15/20
KRIEGER, Hermann (1866-)					
Familie Hahnekamp 1913 R	--	--	23T'30	--	--
KRÖGER, Theodor (1897-1958)					
Das vergessene Dorf... 1934	325T'39				
Heimat am Don 1937 R	140T'38				
KRÖGER, Timm (1844-1918)					
Im Nebel (from Leute eigener Art) 1906	--	--	80T'26	--	--
Bohnen und Speck (Neun Novn) 1906 Geschn	--	33T'34	ni'27	30T'18	--
Neun Novellen - Auswahl 1906	--	--	ni'27	30T'18	
KRONBERG, Max (nd)					
Jugend am Start 1929 R	--	--	40T'29		
Hallo! Leo heiratet 1929 R	--	--	30T'29		
KRÜGER, Hermann Anders (1871-1945)					
Gottfried Kämpfer 1904 R	--	--	82T'30	--	33T'16
KÜCHLER, Kurt (1883-1925)					
Steuermann Holk 1919 R	--	--	--	--	25T'20
KÜLPE, Frances (née James, 1862-1946)					
Mutterschaft 1907 R	153T'40	131T'33	116T'29	--	17A'20

TABLE B (con't.)

NAME	36/40	31/35	26/30	21/25	15/20
KÜLPE, Frances (con't.)					
Kinder der Liebe 1912 Gesch (total)	--	--	c 54T'29		
(G. Müller)	--	--	25T'29	--	--
(P. Franke)	--	--	29T'29	--	--
Doppelseele 1910 R	--	--	27T'29	22T'23	--
Ring 1914 R	--	--	22T'29	--	--
KÜMMEL, Konrad (1848-1936)					
Auf der Sonnenseite, 1. Bdchen 1903	--	--	c 30T'29 (12A) Herder	--	28T'20 (10-11A)
Das arme Bäschen 1916 Volkserzn	--	--	--	--	23T'20
Der Rock des armen Mannes 1914 Volkserzn	--	--	--	--	23T'20
Das schwarze Lieserl 1914 Volkserzn	--	--	--	--	23T'20
Die vier Musikanten 1914 Volkserzn	--	--	--	--	23T'20
Im Talbachkirchlein 1914 Volkserzn	--	--	--	--	23T'20
KÜNKEL, Hans (1896-1956)					
Ein Arzt sucht seinen Weg 1939 R	25T'40				
KULL, Franz (nd)					
Fünf Jahre Fremdenlegionär... 1921	--	--	--	450T'23	
KUNTZE, Paul Heinrich (1883-)					
Das Volksbuch unserer Kolonien 1938	150T'40				

TABLE B (con't.)

NAME	36/40	31/35	26/30	21/25	15/20
KUNTZE, Paul Heinrich (con't.)					
Volk und Seefahrt 1939	75T'40				
KURZ, Isolde (1853-1944)					
Vanadis. Schicksalsweg e Frau 1931 R	62A'37+ Wunderlich	34A'35			
Nächte von Fondi 1922 Geschn	30T'38	ni'35	27T'29	16T'25	
Aus meinem Jugendland 1918	--	--	24T'27	22T'22	19T'20
Florentiner Novellen 1890	21T'37	ni'35	19T'29	15T'21	10A'20
KUTZLEB, Hjalmar (1885-1959)					
Sperrkampf und Jagdzauber 1934 Erzn	41T'40	7T'35			
KYBER, Manfred (1880-1933)					
Unter Tieren, Bd I 1912 Geschn	200T'38	172T'34	130T'28	45T'22	7T'16
Neue Tiergeschichten (Unter Tieren, Bd II) 1926 Geschn	--	70T'35	25T'28		
Märchen 1920	ni'40	35T'32	30T'28	20T'22+	
LAAR, Klemens (ie Eduard Koebsell, 1906-1960)					
Der Kampf um die Dardanellen 1936	91T'40				
Kampf in der Wüste 1936	55T'39+				
Der grosse Marsch 1939	25T'40				

TABLE B (con't.)

NAME		36/40	31/35	26/30	21/25	15/20
LAND, Hans (ie Hugo Landsberger, 1861-after 1935)						
Stürme 1921 R	(total)	--	--	--	c 58T'22	
	(Union)	--	--	--	48A'22	
	(Seifert)	--	--	--	10T'21	
Stadtsanwalt Jordan 1915 R		--	--	58T'30	50T'22	
Wanda. Geschn v schlimmen Mädeln c 1917		--	--	--	--	30T'17
Das Mädchen mit dem Goldhelm 1918 R		--	--	--	--	25T'18
LANDSBERGER, Arthur (1876-1933)						
Lu, die Kokette 1914		--	--	71T'28	--	ni'18
Raffke & Cie. Die neue Gesellschaft 1924, 1917 Re		--	--	--	47T'24	
Wie Satan starb 1919 R		--	--	--	--	30T'19
LANGENSCHEIDT, Paul (1860-1925)						
Arme, kleine Eva 1907 R		--	--	100T'30	85T'21	36T'16
Ich habe dich lieb! 1909 R		--	--	84T'30	59T'24	23T'16
Du bist mein! 1910 R		--	--	74T'28	65T'22	20T'16
Blondes Gift 1911 R		--	--	72T'30	57T'22	--
Um Nichts! 1903 R		--	--	--	34T'20	--
Graf Cohn 1908 R		--	--	--	33T'22	14T'16
Eine dumme Geschichte 1908 R		--	--	28T'25	24T'25	--
Beate 1919 R		--	--	--	--	25T'21

TABLE B (con't.)

NAME	36/40	31/35	26/30	21/25	15/20
LANGENSCHEIDT, Paul (con't.)					
Diplomatie der Ehe 1919 R	--	--	24T'27	--	15T'20
LANGEWIESCHE, Wilehlm (1866-1934)					
Jugend u Heimat. Erinn e 50jährigen 1916	--	--	--	(75T'25)	55T'18
Wolfs. Geschn um ein Bürgerhaus, zwei Tle: 1. Buch: Im Schatten Napoleons 1919	--	--	s 15/20	(60T'25)	40T'19
2. Buch: Vor Bismarcks Aufgang 1919	--	--	s 15/20	(60T'25)	40T'19
LANGSDORFF, Werner (nd)					
U-Boote am Feind... 1937	150T'40				
Flieger am Feind... 1934	70T'40	25T'35			
LAUFF, Joseph von (1855-1933)					
Pittje Pittjewitt 1903 R	--	--	32T'29	29T'22	24T'20
Anne-Suzanne 1915 R	--	--	34T'29	30T'22	26T'20
Die Tragikomödie im Hause d Gebrüder Spier 1924 Niederrheinische Geschn	--	30T'32	--		
Sinter Klaas 1921 R	--	--	29T'28	22T'22	
Die Brixiade... 1915 Kom-Epos	29T'37	28T'35	23T'29	15T'22	8T'18
Schnee 1919 R	--	--	--	27T'23	25T'20
Kevelaer 1910 R	--	27T'35	--	24T'24	14T'20
Juffer Beetje. Qualen 1925 Zwei Novn	--	--	--	25T'25	
Frau Aleit 1905 R	--	--	--	25T'24	18T'19

TABLE B (con't.)

NAME	36/40	31/35	26/30	21/25	15/20
LAUFF, Joseph von (con't.)					
Die Tanzmamsell 1907 R	--	--	--	--	24T'20
Sergeant Feuerstein 1917 R	--	--	--	--	21T'18
LE FORT, Gertrud Freiin von (1876-)					
Die ewige Frau... 1934	47T'40	25T'35			
Die Letzte am Schafott 1931 Nov	25T'40	15T'35			
LEHMANN, Arthur Heinz (1909-1956)					
Hengst Maestoso Austria 1939 Gesch	43T'40				
LEHNE, Fr. (ie Helene Butenschön, 1874-1957)					
Ein Frühlingstraum 1906 Erz	345T'40	nAg'33 nA'31	nA'30	--	nAg'16 35T'16
Die geborene Krause 1915 R	--	--	ni'27	c 165T'22 (8A)	130T'20 (7A)
Das alte Lied R	--	--	--	--	50T'18
Trotzige Herzen R	--	--	--	--	50T'18
LEIP, Hans (1893-)					
Herz im Wind 1934 Geschn	25T'40				
Jan Himp und die kleine Brise 1934 R	24T'38				
LETTOW-VORBECK, Paul (1870-)					
Heia Safari! 1920	151T'40	--	60T'28	50T'22	

TABLE B (con't.)

NAME	35/40	31/35	26/30	21/25	15/20
LETTOW-VORBECK, Paul (con't.)					
Meine Erinnerungen aus Ostafrika 1920	68T'38	--	--	58T'26	
LEUTZ, Ilse (Ps: I. L. Harrison, 1896-)					
Schloss Ohnesorge 1924 R	s 31/35	45T'35	35T'29	25T'24	
LEVIN, Julius (1862-1935)					
D Lächeln d Herrn v Golubice-Golubicki 1915 R	--	--	--	35A'25 S Fischer	
LICHTENBERGER, Franz (1881-1944)					
Reinecke Fuchs (nach Simrock neuerzählt) 1911	110T'36	90T'31	70T'30	3A'25	--
LIENHARD, Friedrich (1865-1929)					
Oberlin 1910 R	--	169T'35	--	123A'22	84A'20
Thüringer Tagebuch 1903	--	105T'35	--	83A'23	43A'20
Der Spielmann 1913 R	--	s 21/25	--	90A'22 Greiner & Pfeiffer	70A'20
Westmark 1919 R	--	s 15/20	--	--	31A'20
Wasgaufahrten. E Zeitbuch 1895	--	s 26/30	--	25A'22	20A'20
LILIENFEIN, Heinrich (1879-1952)					
Im stillen Garten 1915 Erzn	ni'39	--	--	35T'23	10T'15

TABLE B (con't.)

NAME	36/40	31/35	26/30	21/25	15/20
LINDENLAUB, Georg (nd)					
D Wölflinge u d Fischfänger c 1928 Erz	43A'39 J Beltz	29A'35	9A'30		
Der tolle Hugbald c 1928 Erz	26A'38	20A'35	8A'30		
LINKE, Johannes (1900-vermisst 1945)					
Ein Jahr rollt übers Gebirg 1934 R	38T'40				
LINKER, Hans Willi (ie Johannes Wilhelm Linker, 1896-1958)					
Spiel in Flandern 1936 Nov	25T'40				
LOBSIEN, Wilhelm (1872-1947)					
Klaus Störtebeker 1927 Erz	77T'39	--			
Der Halligpastor 1914 R	--	--	30T'28	22T'22	17T'20
LÖHNDORFF, Ernst Friedrich (Ps: Peter Dandoo, 1899-)					
Unheimliches China. Reisebericht 1939	30T'40				
Afrika weint 1930	--	30T'33	+'30		
LÖNS, Hermann (1866-1914)					
Der Wehrwolf. E Bauernchronik 1910	565T'39+	440T'35	351T'28	271T'25	90T'19
Das zweite Gesicht 1912 R	435T'39	386T'35	--	290T'21	--
Mümmelmann. E Tierbuch	--	360T'35	--	173T'25	ni'18
dass - Auswahl	--	--	ni ?	--	--
Mein braunes Buch. Haidbilder 1907 Skn	--	--	--	130T'23	66T'18

TABLE B (con't.)

NAME	36/40	31/35	26/30	21/25	15/20
LÖNS, Hermann (con't.)					
Mein grünes Buch. Jagdschiln 1901 Skn	s 31/35	nAg'34	ni'28	110T'25	65T'19
Isegrimms Irrgang 1916 Geschn	95T'38	--	--	--	
Der zweckmässige Meyer 1911 Hum	95T'37	--	s 11/14	72T'24	--
Das Tal der Lieder u a Schiln	--	--	--	80T'25	26T'16
Aus Forst und Flur. Vierzig Tiernovn	--	73A'35 Voigtländer	64A'26	59A'25	40A'20
Das Lönsbuch Erzn, Schiln	s 31/35	s 26/30	ni'28	60T'25	35T'20
Kraut u Lot. E Buch für Jäger u Heger 1911	--	--	--	58T'22	ni'18
Ges Werke, 8 Bde 1920 (Hesse & Becker)	55T'40	--	43T'30	21T'24	
Frau Döllmer. Hum-sat Plaun von Fritz von der Leine	s 26/30	--	ni'28	48T'25	30T'17
Im flammenden Morgenrot... 1933	--	35T'34			
Der letzte Hansbur 1909 R	1A'39 nA'40	--	s 15/20	--	30T'17
Löns-Gedenkbuch von Friedrich Castelle 1917	ni'39	--	--	26T'25	
LORENZ, Helmut (1889-)					
Die versunkene Flotte 1926 R	s 31/35	30T'35	19T'29		
LUCKNER, Felix Graf von (1881-1966)					
Seeteufel. Abenteuer... 1921	392T'38	330T'35	270T'30		
Seeteufel erobert Amerika 1928	114T'37	85T'33	75T'29		

TABLE B (con't.)

NAME	36/40	31/35	26/30	21/25	15/20
LUDWIG, Emil (1881-1948)					
Wilhelm der Zweite 1926	--	--	200T'29	53T'26	
Napoleon 1925	--	--	189T'31	41A'25	
Juli 14. 1929	--	--	120T'29		
Genie und Charakter... 1924	--	80T'32	s 21/25	24A'25	
Bismarck. Gesch e Kämpfers 1911 (total)	--	--	c 56T'27+		
(Zsolnay)	--	ni'32	44T'27+	--	--
(Cotta)	--	--	--	12A'21	--
(S. Fischer)	--	--	--	--	9A'17
Goethe 1920 Drei Bde (total)	--	--	--	c 40T'28	
(Zsolnay)	--	ni'31	s 21/25	--	
(Cotta)	--	--	--	12A'22	
(Rowohlt)	--	--	--	28T'26	
D Fahrten d "Emden" u d "Ayesha" 1916	--	--	--	--	32T'16
D Fahrten d "Goeben" u d "Breslau" 1916	--	--	--	--	25T'16
LUSERKE, Martin (1880-)					
Das schnellere Schiff 1934 Erz	35T'39				
LUX, Joseph August (1871-1947)					
Grillparzers Liebesroman... 1912 R	s 26/30	--	62T'30	--	--
Lola Montez 1912 R	--	--	59T'30	--	--
Franz Schuberts Lebenslied 1915 R	--	--	23T'28	--	5T'15

TABLE B (con't.)

NAME	36/40	31/35	26/30	21/25	15/20
MALTZAHN, Elisabeth von (ie Frau Elisabeth Wengel, née Maltzahn, 1868-)					
Das heilige Nein 1912 R	74A'36 F Bahn	73A'33	71A'29	66A'24	48A'20
Das ist gewisslich wahr 1910 R	--	46A'33	45A'29	42A'25	36A'20
Wenn ich die Sonne grüsse... 1916 R	--	--	--	35T'23	30T'20
Osanna in excelsis! 1905 Erz	--	30A'35	26A'26	25A'25	17A'20
Getraute Treue 1902 Erz	--	22A'35	21A'30	20A'22	13A'20
Wenn Mütter sündigen... 1920 R	--	21A'35	--	19A'21	12A'20
Contra naturam? 1913 R	--	--	21A'26	20A'22	15A'20
MANN, Heinrich (1871-1950)					
D Kaiserreich: 1. D Untertan 1911 (total)	--	c 260T'31			
(Zsolnay)	--	105T'31	--	--	--
(7-Stäbe-Verlag)	--	--	155T'29	--	--
(K. Wolff)	--	--	--	--	7T'18
Im Schlaraffenland 1901 R	--	--	115T'29	65T'25	40T'17
Die Armen 1912 R	--	65T'31	--	--	50T'17
Die Jagd nach Liebe 1905 R	--	ni'32	--	52T'25	15T'16
D Göttinnen oder D drei Re d Herzogin v Assy					
1. Diana 1902	--	ni'32	--	52T'25	17T'17
2. Minerva 1903	--	ni'32	--	52T'25	17T'17
3. Venus 1904	--	ni'32	--	52T'25	17T'17
Professor Unrat od D Ende e Tyrannen 1906 R	--	--	ni'30	47T'25	12T'17

TABLE B (con't.)

NAME	36/40	31/35	26/30	21/25	15/20
MANN, Heinrich (con't.)					
Mutter Marie 1927 R	--	ni'30	45T'30		
Die kleine Stadt 1908 R	--	--	--	37T'25	20T'17
Zwischen den Rassen 1907 R	--	--	--	37T'25	14T'16
MANN, Thomas (1875-1955)					
Buddenbrooks 1901 R	(1,305T'36)	1,165A'32 S Fischer	1,085A'30	159A'25	99A'18
Königliche Hoheit 1909 R	--	148A'32	98A'30	82A'25	32A'15
Der Zauberberg 1925 R	(135A'36)	s 26/30	125A'30	34A'25	
D kl Herr Friedemann u a Novn 1898	--	s 26/30	107A'30	96A'25	ni'20
Tonio Kröger 1914 Nov	--	99A'35+	85A'30	49A'25	--
Der Tod in Venedig 1913 Nov	--	s 26/30	80T'30	68A'25	23A'16
Das Wunderkind 1903 Nov	--	s 26/30	75A'27	70A'25	--
Unordnung und frühes Leid 1926 Nov	--	s 26/30	50A'30		
Friedrich u d grosse Koalition 1916	--	43A'31	--	41T'24	25T'16
Mario und der Zauberer 1930 Nov	--	s 26/30	30A'30		
Betrachtungen eines Unpolitischen 1918	--	26A'35	--	24A'25	6A'18
Die Geschichte Jakobs 1933 R	--	25A'33			
Bekenntnisse des Hochstaplers Felix Krull 1924 R	--	25T'26+	20T'25		

TABLE B (con't.)

NAME	36/40	31/35	26/30	21/25	15/20
MARÉS, Frau Jolanthe (ie Selma Reichel, nd)					
Lilli. E Sittenbild aus Berlin-W 1914 R	--	--	--	--	30T'19
Lillis Ehe 1914 R	--	--	--	--	30T'19
Mütterreigen c 1915 Gesch	--	--	--	--	25T'20
MARIE-MADELEINE (ie M-M Baronin v Puttkamer, née Günther, 1881-)					
Die Kleider der Herzogin 1906 R	--	30T'31	--	--	--
Ihr schlechter Ruf 1914 R	--	--	ni'28	27T'22	25T'20
Marsch nach Hause, Der (Dt Humoristen) Heitere Geschn v Rosegger, Raabe, Reuter, Roderich 1903	--	s 26/30	105T'27	--	20T'17
MARTI, Ernst Otto (1903-)					
Menschen am Berge 1939 R	25T'40				
MARTIN, Kurt (1891-)					
Der Fall Tolstikoff 1917 Krim-R	--	--	--	30T'23	
MARTIN, Marie (1856-1926)					
Deutsches Heimatglück. E Jugendleben auf d Lande 1917	--	--	s 21/25	54T'25	
MATTHIAS, Karl (1838-1903)					
Mit vollen Segeln 1901 Erz	--	--	29A'27 Union	22A'21	17A'19

TABLE B (con't.)

NAME	36/40	31/35	26/30	21/25	15/20
MAY, Karl (1842-1912)					
Winnetou I 1893 Erz	360T'39	273T'34	182T'26	--	88T'16
Old Surehand II 1895 Reiseerz	350T'40	166T'33	106T'26	100T'25	--
D Schatz am Silbersee 1894 Erz	330T'40	202T'35	118T'27	--	--
Winnetou II 1893 Erz	320T'39	249T'32	173T'26	--	--
Winnetou III 1893 Erz	301T'39	238T'32	168T'26	--	--
Old Surehand I 1894 Reiseerz	265T'40	174T'34	112T'26	85T'25	--
Durchs wilde Kurdistan 1892 Reiseerz	262T'40	198T'33	148T'26	--	--
Der Schut 1893 Reiseerz	260T'40	200T'33	138T'26	--	--
Durch die Wüste 1892 Reiseerz	c 255T'39 (32A)	242T'35	171T'26 (25A)	--	90T'15
Von Bagdad nach Stambul 1892 Reiseerz	244T'40	187T'33	142T'26	--	67T'16
In d Schluchten d Balkan 1892 Reiseerz	232T'40	177T'33	137T'26	--	53T'16
Durch d Land d Skipetaren 1892 Reiseerz	225T'40	173T'33	133T'26	--	62T'16
Unter Geiern 1914 Erz	195T'38	156T'33	90T'27	--	--
Der Ölprinz 1897 Erz	182T'38	144T'34	92T'27	--	22T'16
Die Sklavenkarawane 1893 Erz	180T'40	120T'32	82T'27	--	22T'16
Auf fremden Pfaden 1897 Reiseerz	175T'40	130T'33	100T'27	--	--
Am stillen Ozean 1894 Reiseerz	175T'40	125T'34	102T'26	--	54T'16
Halbblut u a Erzn 1916	170T'40	108T'35	65T'27	--	
Das Vermächtnis d Inka 1895 Erz	168T'38	134T'34	80T'27	--	--

TABLE B (con't.)

NAME	36/40	31/35	26/30	21/25	15/20
MAY, Karl (con't.)					
Am Rio de la Plata 1894 Reiseerz	160T'37	138T'34	111T'26	102T'25	--
In den Kordillern 1894 Reiseerz	158T'37	137T'34	110T'26	102T'25	--
"Ich" aus dem Nachlass 1917	c 154T'40 (14A)	12A'33	10A'26	--	
Orangen und Dateln 1893 Erz	150T'39	120T'33	106T'26	100T'25	--
Kapitan Kaiman u a Erzn 1897	143T'37	128T'31	106T'27	--	--
Der blaurote Methusalem 1892 Erz	140T'37	120T'32	82T'27	--	--
Winnetous Erben 1910 Reiseerz	135T'39	110T'35	82T'28	--	--
Im Reiche d silbernen Löwen II 1898 Erz	122T'39	96T'33	90T'28	64T'25	--
Im Reiche d silbernen Löwen 1898 Reiseerz	120T'37	94T'28	94T'28	--	--
Im Lande d Mahdi I 1896 Reiseerz	116T'37	100T'34	86T'26	79T'25	--
Im Reiche d silbernen Löwen III 1898 Erz	111T'39	87T'33	82T'28	73T'25	--
Im Lande d Mahdi II 1896 Reiseerz	111T'37	96T'34	82T'26	75T'25	--
Weihnacht 1897 Reiseerz	110T'36	98T'33	93T'28	85T'25	--
Im Lande der Mahdi III 1896 Reiseerz	110T'37	95T'34	81T'26	74T'25	--
Im Reiche d silbernen Löwen IV 1898 Erz	107T'39	83T'33	78T'28	70T'25	--
Satan und Ischariot I 1897 Reiseerz	--	105T'33	83T'28	74T'25	--
Satan und Ischariot II 1897 Reiseerz	--	102T'33	80T'28	71T'25	--
Satan und Ischariot III 1897 Reiseerz	--	100T'33	80T'28	71T'25	--
Am Jenseits 1899 Reiseerz	--	92T'31	85T'27	--	--
Ardistan und Dschinnistan 1909 Reiseerz	--	--	82T'28	--	13T'16

TABLE B (con't.)

NAME	36/40	31/35	26/30	21/25	15/20
MAY, Karl (con't.)					
Trapper Geierschnabel 1923 R	74T'39	55T'32	37T'28	25T'23	
Und Friede auf Erden 1904 Reiseerz	72T'39	65T'28	65T'28	--	--
Der schwarze Mustang Erz	--	69A'32 Union	63A'27	--	41A'19
Der sterbende Kaiser 1923 R	65T'39	47T'33	37T'28	25T'23	
Benito Juarez 1923 R	60T'39	45T'34	37T'28	25T'23	
Vom Rhein zur Mopimi 1923	60T'40	--	37T'28	25T'23	
Schloss Rodriganda 1923 R	58T'40	--	37T'28	25T'23	
Der alte Dessauer 1921 Humn	55T'40	46T'31	40T'27	20T'25	
Aus dunklem Tann 1925 Erzn	54T'40	46T'31	40T'27	20T'25	
Der Waldschwarze u a Erzn 1921	54T'39	46T'31	40T'27		
Die Liebe der Ulanen III 1930	45T'39	ni'32	ni'30		
Ardistan u Dschinnistan II 1909 Reiseerz	--	--	--	43T'25	--
Das Buschgespenst 1935 Erz	40T'39				
Zobeljäger und Kosak 1934 R	40T'40				
Im Tal des Todes 1934 R	40T'39				
Der Derwisch 1933 R	40T'40				
Die Juweleninsel 1927 R	38T'39	28T'33	20T'27		
In Mekka 1923 Reiseerz	37T'36	--	25T'27	15T'23	
Der Weg nach Waterloo (Die Liebe der Ulanen I) 1930 R	--	ni'32	30T'30		

TABLE B (con't.)

NAME	36/40	31/35	26/30	21/25	15/20
MAY, Karl (con't.)					
D Sohn d Bärenjägers c 1894, 1928 Erz	--	30T'32	20T'28 (1A'28)		
Allah il Allah! 1931 Reiseerz	--	28T'31			
Zepter und Hammer 1927 R	28T'37	--	20T'27		
Der Fremde aus Indien 1939	25T'39				
Professor Vitzliputzli u a Erzn 1927	23T'36	--	15T'27		
Das Zauberwasser u a Erzn 1927	23T'36	--	15T'27		
MAYER, Erich August (1894-1949)					
Gottfried sucht seinen Weg 1929 R	33T'40	22T'31			
Flammen 1928 R	22T'40	14T'32			
MECHOW, Karl Benno von (1897-1960)					
Vorsommer 1934 R	95T'40	40T'34			
Das Abenteuer 1930 R	50T'39	15T'33			
Sorgenfrei 1934 Erz	40T'39	20T'34			
Der unwillkommene Franz 1933 Erz	30T'40	15T'33			
MEIER-GRAEFE, Julius (1867-1935)					
Vincent van Gogh 1921 R	--	29T'32	ni'28	7T'25	
MENZEL, Viktor (1865-)					
Schwurbrüder 1913 Kosaken-R	--	--	--	50T'25 (4A)	2A'20

TABLE B (con't.)

NAME	36/40	31/35	26/30	21/25	15/20
MESCHENDÖRFER, Adolf (1877-)					
Die Stadt im Osten 1933 R	30T'40	15T'34+			
METZGER, Hanny (ie Johanna, 1888-)					
Die aus zwei Welten kamen 1919 R	--	--	--	--	25T'19
MEYER-FÖRSTER, Wilhelm (1862-1934)					
Karl Heinrich 1900 Erz (Dt V-Anstalt)	--	--	--	--	31T'19
(Heckners V.)	--	--	--	4A'20	--
Heidenstamm 1901 R	--	--	--	--	23A'20 Dt V-Anst
MEYRINK, Gustav (1868-1932)					
Der Golem 1915 R	--	191T'31	s 15/20+	ni'21	150T'17
Das grüne Gesicht 1916 R	--	--	s 15/20	--	95T'21
Walpurgisnacht 1917 R	--	--	s 15/20	--	90T'20
MEZGER, Max (1876-1940)					
Monika fährt nach Madagaskar 1931 Erz	36T'40	ni'33			
MIEGEL, Agnes (1879-)					
D Fahrt d sieben Ordensbrüder 1933 Erz	70T'39	30T'35			
Unter hellem Himmel 1936 Geschn	60T'40				
MILLER, Arthur Maximilian (1901-)					
Das Jahr der Reife 1931 R	27T'36				

TABLE B (con't.)

NAME	36/40	31/35	26/30	21/25	15/20
MOLO, Walter R. von (1880-1958)					
Fridericus-Trilogie R (together)	485T'36	100T'31	--	10T'24	--
1. Fridericus 1918	--	--	--	50T'22	20T'18
2. Luise 1919	--	--	--	28T'22	20T'19
3. Das Volk 1921	--	--	--	25T'21	
Der Schiller-Roman 1918	100A'35 nS-A J Beltz	100A'32 Holle & Co	59T'26+	--	20T'18
Ein Deutscher ohne Deutschland 1931 R	--	30T'35			
MOMMA, Wilhelm (1880-1930)					
Waffenbrüder 1915 Erz	--	--	--	--	23T'15
MORAHT, Robert (1884-)					
D Versenkung d "Danton" 1917 Erle	--	--	--	--	30T'17
MORGENSTERN, Christian (1871-1914)					
Stufen. E Entwicklung in Aphorismen und Tagebuchnotizen 1916	--	--	--	38T'22	ni'18
MOSZKOWSKI, Alexander (1851-1934)					
Die unsterbliche Kiste 1907 Witze	--	--	--	116T'22	95T'18
MÜCKE, Hellmuth von (1881-)					
Ayesha 1915 Erz	--	--	332T'27	--	

TABLE B (con't.)

NAME	36/40	31/35	26/30	21/25	15/20
MÜCKE, Hellmuth von (con't.)					
Emden 1915 Erz	--	--	--	ni'17	50T'15
MÜHSAM, Erich (1878-1934)					
Gerechtigkeit für Max Hoelz! 1926	--	--	45T'26		
MÜLLER-GUTTENBRUNN, Adam (1852-1923)					
Der grosse Schwabenzug 1913 R	61T'40	--	30T'27	27T'23	11T'14
Die Glocken der Heimat 1910 R (total)	--	c 55T'34 35T'34	S-A 20T'29	31T'25	23T'20
Der kleine Schwab 1910 Abenteuer	31T'39	--	ni'26	--	15T'16
Barmherziger Kaiser 1916 R	--	29T'34	26T'26	--	10T'16
Lenau, das Dichterherz der Zeit 1. Sein Vaterhaus 1919 R	--	--	28T'26	25T'22	10T'19
Meister Jakob und seine Kinder 1918 R	25T'37	--	--	20T'22	15T'18
Es war einmal ein Bischof 1912 R	--	--	25T'30	23T'23	12T'16
Joseph der Deutsche 1917 R	--	s 26/30	24T'29	21T'23	10T'17
Die Madjarin 1896 Erz	--	--	23T'28	--	--
MÜLLER-HENNIG, Erika (nd)					
Wolgakinder 1934 Gesch	97T'40	2A'35			
Wolgakinder im Baltenland c 1936	25T'39				
Abenteuer um Saratow c 1936 Erz	22T'39				

TABLE B (con't.)

NAME	36/40	31/35	26/30	21/25	15/20
MÜLLER-PARTENKIRCHEN, Fritz (ie Fritz Müller, 1875-1942)					
Kramer & Friemann 1920 R	109T'40	ni'34	--	12T'22	
Die Firma 1935 R	56T'40	28T'35			
Heul', wenn's Zeit ist! c 1936 Gesch	33T'40				
Kaum genügend 1927 Schulgeschn	26T'40	--	16T'30		
MÜNZER, Kurt (1879-1944)					
D Ladenprinz od Das Märchen vom Kommis 1914 R	--	--	--	32T'22	13A'19
MUSCHLER, Reinhold Conrad (1882-1957)					
Die Unbekannte 1934 Nov	220T'36	150T'35			
Bianca Maria 1924 R	--	60T'31	45T'28	22T'25	
Ivola 1936 Nov	40T'36				
Insel der Jugend 1930 R	35T'37	20T'31			
Diana Beata 1938 R	30T'39				
Basil Brunin 1928 R	24T'38	20T'31	20T'30		
NASO, Eckart von (1888-)					
Seydlitz 1932 R	50T'39	3A'32			
NECKE, Max (nd)					
Dt Weihnachtsgeschn (Weihnachtsgeschn) 1909	--	58T'32	45T'26	40T'22	ni'14

TABLE B (con't.)

NAME	36/40	31/35	26/30	21/25	15/20
NECKE, Max (con't.)					
Unter gutem Stern (Luxus-Ag von Deutsche Weihnachtsgeschn) 1909	--	--	--	40T'22	--
NEEFF, Adolf (1871-1942)					
Kleines Sternbüchlein c 1916	130T'40	--	--	--	110T'18
Kurzweil c 1916	110T'40	--	--	--	100T'18
Vom alten Fritz c 1916 Anekn	95T'39	--	--	--	85T'18
Anekdoten von Bismarck 1917	60T'40	--	--	--	40T'17
Deutsche Kinder, e Heimatbüchlein... 1918	--	--	--	--	50T'18
Germanen. Von ihrem Leben u Gemüt 1918	--	--	--	--	40T'18
NERGER, Karl August (nd)					
S. M. S. "Wolf" und "Wölfchen" 1919	--	--	--	--	100T'19
NEUBAU, Robert (nd)					
Kriegsgefangen - über England entflohen c 1916	--	--	--	--	70T'16
NEUMANN, Alfred (1895-1952)					
Der Teufel 1926 R	--	132T'32	120T'30		
Rebellen 1929 R	--	--	45T'29		
Der Held 1930 R	--	30T'31			
Guerra 1929 R	--	--	30T'29		
König Haber 1926 Erz	--	--	25T'29++		

TABLE B (con't.)

NAME	36/40	31/35	26/30	21/25	15/20
NEUMANN, Robert (1897-)					
Mit fremden Federn 1927 Parodien	--	--	25T'30		
NIESE, Charlotte (1854-1935)					
Um die Weihnachtszeit u a Erzn 1905	--	--	110T'30	ni'23	--
Das Lagerkind 1914 Erz	73T'40	nA ?	ni'26	--	ni'20
NOLDEN, Arnold (ie Wilhelm Pferdekamp, 1901-)					
Auf Schiffen, Schienen,... 1930 R	200T'38	ni'35			
NORDSTRÖM, Clara Elisabeth (1886-1962)					
Lillemor 1936 R	31T'40				
Kajsa Lejondahl 1935 R	29T'40	9T'35			
Ruf der Heimat 1938 R	26T'40				
Frau Kajsa 1935 R	25T'40	7T'35			
OBERKOFLER, Joseph Georg (1889-)					
Der Bannwald 1939 R	70T'40				
OBERLÄNDER, Adolf (nd)					
Heiteres und Ernstes 1917	--	--	s 21/25	79T'23	
OEHLER-HEIMERDINGER, Elisabeth (ie Elisabeth Oehler, 1884-1955)					
Gelitten und gestritten 1920 Geschn	--	--	50T'24	30T'24	

TABLE B (con't.)

NAME	36/40	31/35	26/30	21/25	15/20
OEHRLEIN, Ernst (nd)					
Die Rose von St. Pauli (Jan Feltens Liebesabenteuer) c 1918 Hamburger-Sittenbild	--	65T'32	--	--	50T'20
OLDENBURG-JANUSCHAU, Elard von (nd)					
Erinnerungen 1936	40T'40				
OMPTEDA, Georg Freiherr von (1863-1931)					
Excelsior 1910 R	51T'37	49T'35	44T'30	36T'25	--
Deutscher Adel um 1900, R in 3 Bdn: 1. Sylvester von Geyer 1897	--	--	--	27T'22	--
2. Eysen 1899	--	--	--	25T'22	--
OSTWALD, Hans (1873-1940)					
Das Zillebuch 1929	--	--	110T'29		
Der Urberliner in Witz, Humor u Anek 1927	86T'40	--	10T'27		
PAASCHE, Hans (1881-1920)					
Fremdenlegionär Kirsch... 1916	--	--	--	--	250T'18
D Forschungsreise des Afrikaners L. M. ins innerste Deutschland... 1921	--	--	c 58T'29 (7A)	50T'25 (6A)	
PANY, Leonore (1877-)					
Gegen den Strom 1916 R	--	--	--	--	80T'19
Theaterkinder 1917 R	--	--	--	--	37T'17

TABLE B (con't.)

NAME	36/40	31/35	26/30	21/25	15/20
PAPKE, Käthe (1872-1951)					
Das Forsthaus im Christianental 1920 Erz					
(total)	c 71T'40				
(Christliche Verlagshaus)	43T'40	--	--	--	--
(G. Koezle)	28A'37	26A'35	22A'30	15A'25	4A'20
Die Letzten von Rötteln 1912 Erz	40T'37	32A'33	27A'30	--	15A'20
Nur eine Erzieherin 1915 Erz	s 26/30	--	25A'28	12A'22	10A'20
Wettergasse 18 1918 Gesch	22T'37	15A'31	14A'28	--	6A'20
PAUL, Adolf (1863-1943)					
Die Tänzerin Barberina 1915 R	95T'38	--	--	30T'24	28A'21
PAUST, Otto (nd)					
Volk im Feuer 1935 R	90T'40+				
Land im Licht 1937 R	53T'40				
PHILIPPI, Felix (1851-1921)					
Jugendliebe 1917 R	--	s 21/25	--	125T'25	80T'20
Cornelie Arendt 1915 R	--	s 21/25	--	75T'25	50T'20
Das Schwalbennest 1919 R	--	s 21/25	--	60T'25	45T'20
Monica Vogelsang 1913 Vier Novn	--	s 21/25	43T'26	--	30T'20
Die Ehrenreichs 1918 R	--	s 21/25	--	s 1918	40T'20
Hotel Gigantic 1915 R	--	--	37T'26	--	34T'20
Die Sieger 1914 R	--	--	--	36T'22	--

TABLE B (con't.)

NAME	36/40	31/35	26/30	21/25	15/20
PHILIPPI, Felix (con't.)					
Liebesfrühling 1920 R	--	--	30T'28	--	
PIETSCH, Otto (1874-)					
Das Gewissen der Welt 1915 R	--	s 26/30	23T'30	20T'23	15A'19
PLEYER, Wilehlm (1901-)					
Die Brüder Tommahans 1937 R	65T'40				
Der Puchner. E Grenzlandschicksal 1934 R	45T'40	10T'35			
Im Gasthaus zur dt Einigkeit! 1937 Geschn	25T'40				
PLÜSCHOW, Gunther (1886-1931)					
Die Abenteuer d Fliegers v Tsingtau... 1916	--	--	610T'27	--	100T'16
Segelfahrt ins Wunderland... 1926	90T'39	58T'35			
PONTEN, Joseph (1883-1940)					
Der babylonische Turm... 1918 R	--	62T'32	17T'25	--	15T'20
Der Meister 1919 Nov (total)	c 61T'40				
(Insel)	45T'40+	ni'33	--	--	
(Schaffstein)	--	--	--	1-10T'22	
(Dt V-Anst)	--	--	--	--	1-6T'19-'20
Die Stunde Heidelbergs 1935 Erz	25T'40				
Auf zur Wolga. Schicksal dt Auswanderer (from Wolga, Wolga) 1931 R	25T'39	5T'31			

TABLE B (con't.)

NAME	36/40	31/35	26/30	21/25	15/20
POPERT, Hermann Martin (1871-1932)					
Helmut Harringa 1910 Gesch	--	--	c 315T'30 (49A)	310T'25 (48A)	190T'18 (38A)
PRELLWITZ, Gertrud (1869-1942)					
Vom Wunder des Lebens 1909 Dtg	--	--	147T'26	137T'22	67T'20
Vorfrühling (Drude Tl I) 1920 R	--	--	--	45T'24	
PRESBER, Rudolf (1868-1935)					
Mein Bruder Benjamin 1919 Gesch	100T'37	100T'33	80T'28	71T'25	40T'20
Von Leutchen, die ich liebgewann 1905 Skn	--	--	64T'27	62T'25	49A'20
Der silberne Kranich 1921 R	--	--	--	40T'21	
Die Zimmer d Frau Sonnenfels 1924 Novn	--	--	34A'25 Eysler	2A'24	
Der Rubin der Herzogin 1915 R	ni'37 ni'37	ni'33	ni'28 ni'29	32A'22 Dt V-Anst	24A'19
Die bunte Kuh 1911 R	--	--	--	30T'23	22A'20
Von Kindern u jungen Hunden 1906 Novn	--	--	--	30A'25	28A'20
Haus Ithaka 1926 R	--	--	24T'28		
RAINALTER, Erwin Herbert (1892-1960)					
In Gottes Hand 1937 R	44T'37				
RANDENBORGH, Elisabeth von (1893-)					
Neu ward mein Tagwerk... 1933 R	35T'37	10A'35			

TABLE B (con't.)

NAME	36/40	31/35	26/30	21/25	15/20
RANDENBORGH, Elisabeth (con't.)					
Die harte Herrlichkeit 1934 R	32T'40	5A'35			
Amries Vermächtnis 1935 Erz	24T'40	4A'35			
RANTZAU, Adeline Gräfin zu (1867-1927)					
Hans Kamp 1905 R	--	s 15/20	--	29T'21	7T'16
RANTZAU, Lilly Gräfin zu (1895-)					
Kamerad Frau 1937 R	40T'39				
REDWITZ(-SCHMÖLZ), Marie Freiin von (1856-1933)					
Der Liebe Dornenpfad 1918 R	--	--	--	--	90T'19
Meeresrauschen u Herzensstürme 1918 R	--	--	--	--	60T'19
REIMANN, Hans (1889-)					
Sächsische Miniaturen (including <u>D Paukerbuch</u>) 1918	--	ni'31	30T'28	15T'22	4T'18
D Dame mit d schönen Beinen u a Grotn 1916	--	--	--	21T'22	2A'16
REIMMICHL (ie Sebastian Rieger, 1867-1953)					
Weihnacht in Tirol. Volksbuch mit Bildern 1911	33T'38	28T'31	--	20T'24	9T'18
Die Glocken von Hochwald 1917 R	--	26T'32	--	15T'24	10T'17
Aus den Tiroler Bergen 1898 Geschn	--	s 15/20	--	25T'25	10T'17
Das Heimweh 1920 Erz	--	24T'35	20T'28	15T'24	10T'20

TABLE B (con't.)

NAME	36/40	31/35	26/30	21/25	15/20
REIMMICHL (con't.)					
Die schwarze Frau 1909 R	23T'36	s 15/20	--	17T'25	9T'18
Bergschwalben 1904 Geschn	--	s 15/20	--	23T'24	12T'19
REISER, Hans (1888-1946)					
Cherpens Binscham der Landstreicher 1920 Novn	51A'37 P List	8T'26	s 15/20	--	2T'20
REITZENSTEIN, Hans-Joachim Frhr von (1881-1935)					
Das Mysterium der Liebe. Silhouetten aus zwei Welten 1917 Novn	--	--	--	--	28T'18
REMARQUE, Erich Maria (ie Erich Paul Remark, 1898-)					
Im Westen nichts Neues 1929 R	--	ni'30	900T'29+		
Der Weg zurück 1931 R	--	75T'31			
RENN, Ludwig (ie Arnold Friedrich Vieth v Golssenau, 1889-)					
Krieg. Erlebnisbericht 1928	--	155T'31	100T'29		
REUTER, Gabriele (1859-1941)					
Ellen von der Weiden 1900 R	--	--	65A'29 S Fischer	62A'23	--
Frauenseelen 1901 Novn	--	--	--	48A'24	--
Der Amerikaner 1907 R	--	--	--	40A'24	ni'16
Aus guter Familie... 1895 Gesch	--	28A'31	ni'20	--	--

TABLE B (con't.)

NAME	36/40	31/35	26/30	21/25	15/20
RICHTER, Hans (1898-)					
Der Kanal 1923 R	30T'38	s 21/25	--		
RICHTHOFEN, Manfred Frhr von (1892-1918)					
Der rote Kampfflieger (E Heldenleben) 1917	420T'38 Ullstein	ni'33	--	--	350T'17
(Winkler)	3A'36	--	--	--	--
(Dt Verlag)	ni'39	--	--	--	--
RILKE, Rainer Maria (1875-1926)					
Die Weise von Liebe und Tod des Cornets Christoph Rilke 1899 Erz	ni'40	500T'34	350T'27	200T'21	--
Briefe an einen jungen Dichter 1929	--	140T'32			
Briefe an eine junge Frau 1930	--	90T'33			
Auguste Rodin 1903	--	60T'34	48T'28	45T'24	30T'20
Geschn vom Lieben Gott 1900 Erzn	55T'36	50T'31	42T'28	33T'22	23T'20
D Aufzn d Malte Laurids Brigge 1910 R	38T'38	35T'34	25T'27	20T'22	17T'20
RITTER, Paul (1887-)					
U-Bootsgeist 1935 Abenteuer	26T'40	10T'35			
RODA RODA, Alexander (ie Sandor Friedrich Rosenfeld, 1872-1945)					
Die verfolgte Unschuld 1914	--	--	--	--	62T'18
Der Schnaps, der Rauchtabak u d verfluchte Liebe 1908 R	--	--	47T'28	37A'24	30A'20

TABLE B (con't.)

NAME	36/40	31/35	26/30	21/25	15/20
RODA RODA, Alexander (con't.)					
Von Bienen, Drohnen und Baronen 1908	--	--	--	32A'25 Rikola	s 1908
So jung und schön... 1918	--	--	--	--	30T'18
Eines Esels Kinnbacken (Schwefel über Gomorrha) 1906	--	--	--	28T'22	--
500 Schwänke. Karikatur v W. Trier 1912	--	--	--	24A'22 Eysler	s 11/14
Summler, Bummler, Rossetummler 1909 Geschn	--	--	--	21A'24	--
ROM, Thé von (ie Theodore von Rommel, 1871-)					
Freie Menschen 1907 R	--	--	--	--	22T'16
ROMBACH, Otto (1904-)					
Adrian, der Tulpendieb 1936 R	63T'40				
ROSE, Felicitas (ie Rose Mörsberger, 1862-1938)					
Heideschulmeister Uwe Karsten 1909 R	500T'37	420T'34	299T'28	192T'21	--
Der Mutterhof 1918 R	200T'39	125T'34	--	--	
Der Tisch der Rasmussen 1920 R	100T'39	64T'32	--	--	16T'20
Das Lyzeum in Birkholz 1917 R	96T'37	85T'32	--	--	12T'18
Der graue Alltag u sein Licht 1922 R	79T'37	58T'32	--	20T'22	
Die Eiks von Eichen 1908 R	71T'37	65T'32	60T'29	--	--
Erlenkamp Erben 1924 R	--	64T'32	--	30T'24	

TABLE B (con't.)

NAME	36/40	31/35	26/30	21/25	15/20
ROSE, Felicitas (con't.)					
Meerkönigs Haus 1917 R	61T'37	56T'32	--	--	
Pastor Verden 1912 Heide-R	57T'40	44T'35	26T'28	23T'25	15A'20
Die Erbschmiede 1926 R	55T'37	--	20T'26		
Der hillige Ginsterbruch 1928 R	50T'37	--	20T'28		
Die Wengelohs 1929 R	39T'37	--			
Drohnen 1912 Gesch	38T'37	35T'32	30T'23	--	--
D Haus mit d grünen Fensterläden 1930 R	32T'37	--			
Bilder aus den vier Wänden 1910	32T'37	29T'30	--	--	--
Die jungen Eulenrieds 1936 R	25T'37				
Die vom Sunderhof 1932 R	25T'37				
ROSEGGER, Hans Ludwig (1880-1929)					
Die Verbrecherkolonie (new printing 1910: Lebensschicksal eines Einsamen) 1907 Tageb	--	--	--	--	42T'20
ROSEGGER, Peter (1843-1918)					
Als ich noch d Waldbauernbub war I 1902 Erz	--	384T'33	364T'30	307T'25	--
Als ich noch d Waldbauernbub war II 1902 Erz	--	300T'31	290T'29	250T'25	--
Als ich noch d Waldbauernbub war III 1902 Erz	--	260T'31	250T'29	205T'22	--

TABLE B (con't.)

NAME	36/40	31/35	26/30	21/25	15/20
ROSEGGER, Peter (con't.)					
D Schriften des Waldschulmeisters 1875	--	248A'33 Staackmann	248A'30	180A'25	--
Erdsegen... 1900 R	126T'40	123T'33	s Werke	60T'25	ni'15
Peter Mayr, d Wirt an der Mahr 1893 Gesch	--	116T'33	64T'28	61T'25	--
Jakob der Letzte 1888 Gesch	--	116T'33	86T'28	63T'25	--
Alpensommer 1909	--	92T'33	42T'25	39T'23	--
Das ewige Licht 1896 Erz	--	90T'33	--	87T'23	ni'15
Die Abelsberger Chronik 1907	--	86T'33	36T'27	33T'23	--
Der Adlerwirt von Kirchbrunn 1907	--	--	--	ni'22	80T'20
Heidepeters Gabriel 1886 Gesch	--	s 26/30	79A'28	74A'22	--
I. N. R. I. Frohe Botschaft eines armen Sünders 1905	--	78T'31	--	75T'24	30T'15
Waldheimat, 1. D Waldbauernbübel 1877 Erz	--	78A'33	--	75A'25	ni'19
Der Gottsucher 1883 R	--	s 26/30	76A'26	73A'24	--
Sonnenschein 1901	--	73T'33	48T'26	45T'23	ni'20
Waldheimat, 2. Der Guckinsleben 1877 Erz	--	72T'33	72A'30	69A'25	ni'19
Nixnutzig Volk 1906	--	71T'33	46T'25	43T'23	--
Weltgift 1903	--	60T'33	ni'29	35T'34	ni'15
Die Försterbuben 1908 R	--	57T'33	57T'28++	54T'24	ni'16
Martin der Mann 1889 Erz	--	57T'33	57A'29	34A'23	--
Das Buch der Novellen, Bd I 1872	--	s 21/25	--	51A'23	--

TABLE B (con't.)

NAME	36/40	31/35	26/30	21/25	15/20
ROSEGGER, Peter (con't.)					
Werke, Gedenkausgabe, 6 Bde (H. L. Rosegger, ed) 1928	--	50T'31	45T'30		
Mein Himmelreich 1900	--	s 21/25	--	47T'24	ni'16
Dorfsünder 1887	--	s 26/30	43A'29	40A'23	--
Mein Weltleben, Bd I 1897	--	s 21/25	--	42T'24	--
D Älpler in ihren Wald- u Dorfgeschn 1886	--	s 26/30	41A'27	38A'23	--
D Buch d Novellen, Bd II zw 1872-1886	--	s 21/25	--	39A'24	ni'15
Ausgewählte Erzählungen 1910	--	--	--	38T'22	--
D Buch d Novellen, Bd III 1886	--	s 21/25	--	38A'24	ni'16
Volksleben in Steiermark... 1875	--	s 21/25	--	36A'23	--
Die beiden Hänse 1911	--	s 21/25	--	35T'24	ni'16
Das Sünderglöckel 1904	--	s 21/25	--	35T'24	ni'15
Der Schelm aus den Alpen 1890	--	s 26/30	34A'29	31A'23	--
Das Buch von den Kleinen 1910	--	--	s 21/25	33T'24	ni'16
Sonderlinge 1875	--	s 21/25	--	32A'22	ni'15
Kindheitswege d Waldbauernbuben 1926 Erz	31T'39	--	25T'29		
Waldheimat, 3. D Schneiderlehrling 1877 Erz	--	s 26/30	31T'26	28T'23	ni'19
Heimgärtnerstagebuch 1913	--	s 21/25	--	30T'24	15T'17 nF'17
Mein Weltleben, Bd II 1897	--	s 21/25	--	29T'24 nF'24	--

TABLE B (con't.)

NAME	36/40	31/35	26/30	21/25	15/20
ROSEGGER, Peter (con't.)					
Waldheimat, 4. D Student auf Ferien 1919 Erz	--	s 26/30	28T'25	25T'23	
Höhenfeuer 1887	--	s 21/25	--	27A'22	ni'15
Werke, 6 Bde, Neue Folge 1929	--	25T'33			
Mit Tieren und Menschen 1919 Erz	25T'39	--	25T'30	--	
Steirische Geschichten 1903	--	--	--	25T'21	--
ROSEN, Erwin (ie Erwin Carlé, 1876-1923)					
Orgesch 1921	--	--	--	100T'21	
Der dt Lausbub in Amerika, Bd I 1911	--	--	60A'26 R Lutz	59A'25	44A'20
Der dt Lausbub in Amerika, Bd II 1911	--	--	50A'26	49A'25	36A'20
Der dt Lausbub in Amerika, Bd III 1911	--	--	44A'26	43A'25	31A'20
dass - Volksausgabe in e Bd 1924	40A'40	32A'34	30A'30	17A'25	
In der Fremdenlegion 1909	--	39A'34	37A'29	32A'24	26A'20
ROSEN, Franz (ie Margarethe von Sydow, 1869-)					
Eines grossen Mannes Liebe 1910 R	--	--	25T'29	8A'22	6A'20
ROSENHAYN, Paul (1877-1929)					
Elf Abenteuer d Joe Jenkins 1916 Det-Gesch	--	--	56T'27	50T'21	15T'16
Die weisse Orchidee 1917 Sieben Abenteuer des Joe Jenkins	--	--	51T'27	40T'21	20T'17

TABLE B (con't.)

NAME	36/40	31/35	26/30	21/25	15/20
ROSENHAYN, Paul (con't.)					
Die drei auf der Platte 1919 Sechs Abenteuer des Joe Jenkins	--	--	40T'27	--	20T'19
Der Mitternachtsbesuch 1922 Krim-R	--	--	25T'30		
ROSNER, Karl Peter (1873-1951)					
Der König. Weg und Wende 1921 R	--	--	118T'30	115T'23	20T'21
Mit d Armee v Falkenhayn gegen d Rumänen 1917	--	--	--	--	30T'17
Die drei Fräulein v Wildenberg 1914 R	--	--	24T'28	22T'25	--
Es spricht die Nacht 1911 Spukgeschn	--	22T'21	--	--	--
Georg Bangs Liebe 1906 R	--	--	22T'27	14T'25	--
ROTH, Joseph (1894-1939)					
Hiob 1930 R	--	25T'33			
ROTHACKER, Gottfried (ie Bruno Nowak, 1901-1940)					
Das Dorf an der Grenze 1936 R	200T'40				
Die Kinder von Kirwang 1939 Erz	32T'40				
ROTHMUND, Toni (1877-1956)					
Caroline Schlegel 1926 R	46A'40 Reclam	32A'35	24A'30		
RUBATSCHER, Maria Veronika (1900-)					
Maria Ward. E kl Buch v e grossen Frau 1927	32T'37				

TABLE B (con't.)

NAME	36/40	31/35	26/30	21/25	15/20
RÜST, Edela (ie Emma Reichel, 1857-1931)					
Die Liebeskämpfer 1905 R	--	--	--	--	40T'20
SALOMON, Ernst von (1902-)					
Die Geächteten 1930 R	104T'39	20T'33			
Die Kadetten 1933 Autobiographie	38T'39				
SALTEN, Felix (ie Siegmund Salzmann, 1869-1945)					
Bambi. E Lebensgesch aus d Walde 1923	--	--	35T'30		
SANDER, Ulrich (1892-)					
Das Feldgraue Herz 1933	40T'40	ni'34			
SAPPER, Agnes (1852-1929)					
Die Familie Pfäffling 1906 Gesch	400T'40	300T'35	250T'28	200T'25	100T'19
Werden u Wachsen. Erlebnisse d grossen Pfäfflingskinder 1910 Gesch	210T'37	190T'35	140T'26	118T'23	70T'20
Frieder. D Gesch vom kl Dummerle 1920	--	--	110T'30	50T'22	10T'20
Das kleine Dummerle u a Erzn 1904	110T'38	92T'35	82T'29	--	40T'20
Frau Pauline Brater 1908	--	--	82T'29	37A'25	22A'19
Ohne den Vater 1915 Erz	--	55T'35	--	45T'23	
Das Enkelhaus 1917	46T'40	--	39T'30	26T'22	2A'20
Lieschens Streiche u a Erzn 1907	--	--	30T'29	23T'22	3A'20

TABLE B (con't.)

NAME	36/40	31/35	26/30	21/25	15/20
SCHÄFER, Wilhelm (1868-1952)					
D dreizehn Bücher d dt Seele 1922 Prosa-Epos	170T'40	90T'35	37T'29	32T'25	
Die Anekdoten 1935	80T'40++	25T'35			
Die Fahrt in den Heiligen Abend 1935	55T'40				
Ein Mann namens Schmitz 1934 Nov	50T'39	20T'34			
Die Missgeschickten 1932	35T'40	20T'35			
Lebenstag eines Menschenfreundes 1915 R	--	--	34T'27	24T'23	4A'16
Die Badener Kur 1939 Nov	30T'40				
Hundert Historchen 1940	25T'40				
Wendekreis neuer Anekdoten 1937	25T'40				
Anckemanns Tristan 1936 Nov	25T'40				
SCHAFFNER, Jakob (1875-1944)					
Konrad Pilater 1910 R (total)	--	--	c 74T'29		
(7-Stäbe-Verlag)	s 26/30	s 26/30	63T'29	--	--
(Union)	--	--	11A'28	8A'25	--
Grobschmiede u a Novn 1917	--	--	--	46A'21 S Fischer	
Der Dechant von Gottesbüren 1917 R	25T'33	s 21/25	--	22A'25	10T'17
Die Weisheit der Liebe 1919 R	23T'36	s 26/30	19A'29	18T'25	15T'19
Die Glücksfischer 1925 R	22T'36	s 26/30	13A'27	8A'25	

TABLE B (con't.)

NAME	36/40	31/35	26/30	21/25	15/20
SCHARRELMANN, Heinrich (1871-1940)					
Berni, 1: E kl Junge. Was er sah u hörte, als er noch nicht zur Schule ging 1916	55T'37	--	67T'29	3A'22	
Berni, 3: Berni im Seebade 1918	--	--	52T'30	20T'21	10T'18
Berni, 2: Aus seiner ersten Schulzeit 1916	45T'35	--	50T'28	3A'22	
Aus Heimat u Kindheit u glücklicher Zeit. Geschn aus d Stadt Bremen 1925 (Beltz)	2A'37	ni'31	--		
(Westermann)	--	--	48T'29	5T'25	
Heute und vor Zeiten 1905 Geschn	--	--	21T'29	--	--
SCHARRELMANN, Wilhelm (1875-1950)					
Grossmutters Haus u a Geschn 1913	--	--	28T'28	--	--
In der Pickbalge 1934 R	--	23T'34			
SCHAUMANN, Ruth (ie Ruth Fuchs, née Schaumann, 1899-)					
Amei. Eine Kindheit 1932	48T'38	29T'35			
SCHENZINGER, Karl Aloys (1886-1962)					
Anilin 1936 R	505T'40				
Der Hitlerjunge Quex 1932 R	244T'40	120T'34			
Metall 1939 R	120T'39				
SCHICKELE, René (1883-1940)					
Das Erbe am Rhein, R-Tril 1. Maria Capponi 1925	--	22A'31 S Fischer	15T'26		

TABLE B (con't.)

NAME	36/40	31/35	26/30	21/25	15/20
SCHIEBER, Anna (1867-1945)					
...und hätte die Liebe nicht 1912 Gesch	180T'36	175T'34	165T'30	130T'23	110T'20
Alle guten Geister... 1905 R	153T'38	150T'34	140T'28	--	110A'20
Amaryllis u a Geschn 1914	--	95T'33	90T'29	--	70T'20
Annegret. E Kindergesch 1922	75T'37	--	60T'30	20T'22	
Ludwig Fugeler 1918 R	55T'38	--	35A'29	--	14A'18
Heimat 1915 Erzn	--	48T'31	--	45T'23	41T'19
Bille Hasenfuss. Wie er sich u d Gänserich bezwang 1926	--	--	40T'30		
Das Kind 1916 Erz	--	--	--	--	40T'20
Des Lebens- u Liebesgarten u a Geschn 1919	--	--	35T'26	--	30T'20
Sonnenhunger. Gesch v d Schattenseite 1903	--	--	32T'27	--	26T'20
Wanderschuhe u a Erzn 1911	--	--	--	30T'23	--
Warme Herzen c 1918 Geschn	--	--	25T'28	--	13T'19
SCHIEKER-EBE, Sofie (ie Sophie Schieker, 1892-)					
Was tun, Sibylle? 1930	24T'40	4A'35			
SCHIROKAUER, Alfred (1880-1934)					
Ferdinand Lassalle. E Leben für Freiheit u Liebe 1912 R	--	--	68T'30	--	31T'19
Mirabeau 1921 R	--	22T'31	--	10T'21	

TABLE B (con't.)

NAME	36/40	31/35	26/30	21/25	15/20
SCHLEICH, Karl Ludwig (1859-1922)					
Besonnte Vergangenheit. Lebenserinn 1859-1919 1921	469T'40	365T'35	255T'30	63T'25	
Es läuten d Glocken, Phantasien über den Sinn des Lebens 1912	--	ni'31	84A'30 Concordia	39A'25	5A'20
SCHLICHT, Freiherr von (ie Wolf Graf von Baudissin, 1867-1926)					
Erstklassige Menschen 1904 R	--	--	--	--	49T'20
Graf Udo Bodo 1905 R	--	--	--	42T'25	--
D süssen kl Mädchen. Wie sie lieben 1911	--	--	--	s 15/20	39A'20 M Seyfert
Ein Kampf 1899 Erz	--	--	--	39T'25	--
Unverstandene Frauen 1912	--	--	--	--	35A'20
Aus der Schule geplaudert 1897 Humn	--	--	--	32T'25	--
Humoresken u Erinnerungen 1896	--	--	--	32T'25	--
Wenn Frauen lieben 1916 hum Plaun	--	--	--	--	30A'20
Die Frau u meine Frau 1910 Geschn	--	--	--	--	24A'20
Seine Hoheit 1907 Humn u Satn	--	--	--	24T'25	--
Exzellence Seyffert 1901 R	--	--	--	--	24A'19
SCHLIPPENBACH, Gabriele von (Ps: Herbert Rivulet, 1847-)					
Subotins Erbe 1904 Krim-R	--	--	--	46T'25	30A'19

TABLE B (con't.)

NAME	36/40	31/35	26/30	21/25	15/20
SCHMID, Hedda von (ie Frau Hedda von Riesemann, 1864-)					
Die fünf Seemöwen 1916 Erz	--	--	--	--	50T'19
D Spitzen d Herzogin 1918 Erz (Munz & Co)	--	--	--	2A'23	--
(Dt Drucks- u Verlagshaus)	--	--	--	--	30T'18 (1A)
Ein Steppenkind 1915 Erz	--	--	--	--	30T'16
SCHMIDT, Franz von (1895-)					
Ich heisse Viktor Mors... 1937 R	70T'38				
SCHMITTHENNER, Adolf (1854-1907)					
Das deutsche Herz 1908 R	59T'39	50T'33	42T'30	37T'25	27T'20
Vergessene Kinder 1910 letzte Erzn	--	--	22T'30	10T'25	--
(Dt V-Anst)	--	--	--	--	5A'19
SCHMÖCKEL, Hermann (1866-)					
Martin Luther. Lebensbild 1916	265T'38	--	--	--	25T'16
Hindenburg. Ein Lebensbild 1915	249T'37	245T'34	--	--	20T'15
Die Leute von Kluckendorf 1911 Erzn	--	--	s 21/25	35T'22	30T'18
SCHMÜCKLE, Georg (1880-1948)					
Engel Hiltensperger 1930 R	47T'38	9T;31			
SCHNEIDER-FOERSTL, Josefine (ie Josephine Schneider, 1885-)					
D Liebe des Geigenkönigs Radanyi 1925 R	--	--	50T'30		

TABLE B (con't.)

NAME	36/40	31/35	26/30	21/25	15/20
SCHNITZLER, Arthur (1862-1931)					
Der Weg ins Freie 1908 R	--	s 21/25	136T'29	45A'24	33A'18
Reigen. Zehn Dialoge 1900	--	ni'31	100T'23	68T'21+	--
Frau Berta Garlan 1901 Nov	--	--	ni'29	80A'25 S Fischer	--
D griechische Tänzerin u a Novn 1904	--	--	--	61A'21	--
Fräulein Else 1924 Nov	--	--	60T'28	11T'24	
Traum und Schicksal 1931 Sieben Novn	--	50A'31			
Casanovas Heimfahrt 1918 Nov	--	s 26/30	49A'29	1-4A'21 ill Ag	15A'18
Therese. Chronik e Frauenlebens 1928 R	--	s 26/30	35A'29		
Traumnovelle 1926	--	s 26/30	30A'27		
Doktor Gräsler, Badearzt 1917 Erz	--	--	ni'30	29A'22	
Leutnant Gustl 1901 Nov	--	s 26/30	26A'26	--	--
SCHOBERT, Hedwig (ie Baronin Hedwig von Bode, née Harnisch, 1857-1919)					
Schwüle Stunden 1918 R	--	ni'31	s 15/20	--	55T'20
Treibholz 1916 R	--	ni'31	s 15/20	--	25T'20
SCHÖTTLER, Horst (1874-1942)					
Der Plauderer, 4 Bde, 1. Finessen vom Leben, Lieben, Lachen 1910	--	--	--	41T'25	25T'20
Der Plauderer, 4 Bde, 2. Weib - Wahn - Wahrheit 1912	s 21/25	--	--	25T'22	--

TABLE B (con't.)

NAME	36/40	31/35	26/30	21/25	15/20
SCHOLZ, Wilhelm von (1874-)					
Die Pflicht 1932 Nov	74A'40 P List	15A'35			
Perpetua... 1926 R	--	45A'33	5T'26		
see also Erzähler, Der deutsche					
SCHRECKENBACH, Paul (1866-1922)					
Der König von Rothenburg 1911 Gesch	--	134T'35	124T'30	79T'25	--
Der böse Baron von Krosigk 1907 R	87T'40	78T'33	58T'28	52T'24	37T'20
Um die Wartburg 1913 R	--	76T'33	51T'28	48T'25	--
Die letzten Rudelsburger 1913 R	--	68T'33	46T'29	43T'25	--
Der getreue Kleist 1910 R	--	67T'33	62T'30	35T'25	--
Der deutsche Herzog 1915 R	--	57T'34	33T'29	30T'23	--
Die von Wintzingerode 1905 R	--	57T'33	32T'28	29T'25	--
Michael Meyenburg R	--	56T'33	31T'29	29T'22	24T'20
Wildefüer R	--	--	53T'28	50T'25	40T'20
Eiserne Jugend 1921 R	--	48T'33	41T'29	35T'22	
Markgraf Gero 1916 R	--	35T'34	32T'27	29T'25	21T'19
Die Pfarrfrau von Schönbrunn 1911 Erz	--	25T'31	20T'26	15T'21	9T'17
SCHRECKENBACH, Wolfgang (1904-)					
Die Stedinger. D Heldenlied e Bauernvolkes 1936 R	70T'40+				

TABLE B (con't.)

NAME	36/40	31/35	26/30	21/25	15/20
SCHROEDER, Matthias Ludwig (1904-1950)					
Alle Achtung! Männer! 1936 Geschn	25T'40				
SCHRÖER, Gustav (1876-1949)					
Heimat wider Heimat 1929 R	210T'40	68T'34	15T'29		
Um Mannesehre 1932 R	185T'40				
Der Heiland vom Binsenhofe 1918 R	95T'37	44T'35	--	11T'25	10T'20
Der Schelm von Bruckau 1938 R	82T'40				
Die Flucht aus dem Alltag 1924	70T'40	40T'32	30T'30	11T'25	
Das Land Not 1928 R	--	60T'33			
Sturm im Sichdichfür 1928 R	45T'38	--	30T'30		
Das Schicksal der Käthe Rotermund 1937 R	35T'40				
Frau Käthe Werner 1928	35T'40	20T'31	3A'29		
Der Hohlofenbauer 1927 R	31T'36	--	21T'30		
Der erste dt Weihnachtsabend 1939 Erz	30T'40				
Die Siedler vom Heidebrinkhofe 1932	--	30T'35			
Der Schulze von Wolfenhagen. Gesch e Dorfes 1921	29T'40	24T'35	16T'28		
Der rechte Erbe 1929 R	26T'38	21T'35			
Schicksalshände 1931 R	25T'39	21T'35			
Die Lawine von St. Thomas 1939 R	23T'39				
Die Leute aus Dreisatale 1920 R	23T'40	20T'35	14T'27	11T'24	

TABLE B (con't.)

NAME	36/40	31/35	26/30	21/25	15/20
SCHRÖER, Gustav (con't.)					
Das Wirtshaus zu Kapelle 1919 R	21A'36 Hesse/Becker	14A'32	7A'29	4A'23	3A'20
SCHROTT-FIECHTL, Hans (1867-1938)					
Die Herzensflickerin 1912 R	--	--	--	100T'24	25T'19
SCHROTT, Henriette (ie Frau H. Pelzel, Edle v Staffalo, née Schrott, 1877-)					
Jakob Brunner 1910 R	--	--	34T'26	--	29T'20
SCHUK, Pankraz (1877-1951)					
Der Weg nach Mayerling 1919 R	--	--	28T'30	26T'22	
SCHULZE-BERGHOF, Paul (1873-1947)					
Die schöne Sabine 1916 R	23T'37	--	--	14T'22	4T'16
SCHULZE-SMIDT, Bernhardine (1846-1920)					
Drei Freundinnen 1903 Erz	--	--	31A'28 Union	--	27A'19
Lissy 1900 Erz	--	--	27A'26	--	22A'20
Schattenblümchen 1901 Erz	--	--	--	21A'22	17A'20
SCHUMACHER, Heinrich Vollrat (1861-1919)					
Liebe u Leben d Lady Hamilton 1910 R	--	--	179T'29	ni'24	--
Lord Nelsons letzte Liebe 1911 R	--	--	165T'29	ni'24	--
Kaiserin Eugenia. D Weg zum Thron 1913 R	--	--	53T'29	ni'24	--

TABLE B (con't.)

NAME	36/40	31/35	26/30	21/25	15/20
SCHWERIN, Karl (ie Karl Trotsche, 1862-1920)					
Söhne der Scholle 1913 R	--	--	--	36A'23 Reissner	15T'18
Wilde Rosen und Eichenbrüche 1901 Erzn	--	--	--	--	29T'20
SCHWERIN, Otto (1890-1936)					
Der Kurier des Presidenten 1920 Krim-R	--	--	42T'29	--	
Das rote Licht 1920 Krim-R	--	30T'31	--	--	
SCHWIETZKE, Bruno (1896-)					
...starben in Flandern 1938	35T'40				
SEELIGER, Ewald Gerhard (1877-)					
Peter Voss d Millionendieb oder... 1913 R	--	300T'35	270T'27+	--	ni'20
Bark Fortuna od Mandus Frixens erste Reise 1909 R	--	--	66T'30	--	37T'19
SEIDEL, Ina (1885-)					
Das Wunschkind 1930 R	310T'40	160T'35			
Lennacker, d Buch e Heimkehr 1938 R	120T'40				
Unser Freund Peregrin 1940 Erz	30T'40				
Der Weg ohne Wahl 1933 R	30T'40	26T'35			
Die Fürstin reitet 1929 Erz	22T'36	18T'35			

TABLE B (con't.)

NAME	36/40	31/35	26/30	21/25	15/20
SELL, Sophie Charlotte (1864-1943)					
Weggenossen 1911 R	262T'40	25A'31	21A'30	17A'25	12A'20
SEMSROTT, Albert (nd)					
Der Durchbruch der "Möwe" 1928	56T'40	nAg'35			
Das Kaperschiff "Möwe" 1928	51T'40	nAg'35			
Das Buch von der "Möwe" (contains the two books listed above)	51T'40				
Hein Spuchtfink, d Bremer Schiffsjunge 1934 Erz	30T'40				
Hein Spuchtfink auf grosser Fahrt 1934 Erz	26T'40				
SEXAU, Richard (1882-)					
Im Felde u Daheim 1915 Erzn (together with Richard Riess)	--	--	--	--	32T'17
SIEVERS, Karl (nd)					
Dudo, der Fischer Erz	45A'40 Beltz	31A'35	9A'30	--	--
SIMPSON, Margot von (1888-)					
Fürst Woronzeff 1930 R	--	204T'34	ni'30+		
Reiterin in Tag und Traum 1938 R	22T'39				

TABLE B (con't.)

NAME	36/40	31/35	26/30	21/25	15/20
SKOLASTER, Hermann (1877-)					
Schwester Beata. Schicksale e Zirkus-prinzessin 1938	110T'40				
SKOWRONNEK, Fritz (1858-1939)					
Die süsse Not 1918 R	--	--	ni'28	28T'21	15T'18
Fegefeuer R	--	--	--	28T'21	14T'17
SKOWRONNEK, Richard (1862-1932)					
Die Sporck'schen Jäger 1912 R	--	--	100T'29+	ni'22	--
D Liebschaften der Käte Keller 1918 R	--	--	--	55T'22	
Der Bruchhof 1903 R	51T'39	33T'35	ni'27	--	15A'17
Muttererde (Morgenrot u Die schwere Not) 1934 Zwei Re	30T'38				
Morgenrot 1916 R	s above	--	ni'28	--	18T'16
Die schwere Not 1916 R	s above	--	ni'28	--	ni'16
SLEZAK, Leo (1873-1946)					
Meine sämtlichen Werke u Der Wortbruch in einem Band 1934	68T'40	18T'35			
Meine sämtlichen Werke 1922	--	--	53T'28	31T'22	
Der Wortbruch 1928	--	--	31T'28		
SÖRENSEN, Wulf (ie Frithjof Fischer-Sörensen, 1899-)					
Die Stimme der Ahnen 1933 Dtg	75T'36+	34T'35			

TABLE B (con't.)

NAME	36/40	31/35	26/30	21/25	15/20
SOHNREY, Heinrich (1859-1948)					
D Leute aus d Lindenhütte. Niedersachsens Waldhofgeschn					
1. Friedesinchens Lebenslauf 1886	110T'40	ni'35	99T'31	85T'24	70T'18
2. Hütte und Schloss 1886	75T'36	--	66T'27	63T'24	60T'20
Der Bruderhof 1897 R	54T'39	48T'35	45T'30	40T'26	35T'19
Fusstapfen am Meer 1927 R	--	49T'35	37T'29		
Im grünen Klee - im weissen Schnee 1903 Dorfgeschn	--	s 26/30	--	41T'26	--
Die hinter den Bergen 1894 Gestalten u Geschn	--	--	39T'27 (14A)	--	13A'20
Wenn die Sonne aufgeht 1910 Geschn	37T'36	--	35T'27	--	--
Philipp Dubenkropps Heimkehr 1888 Gesch	--	--	36T'29	30T'25	18T'20
Draussen im Grünen 1912 Geschn	--	--	35T'27	--	--
SOMMER, Rolf (nd)					
Fliegerhauptmann Oswald Boelcke. E dt Heldenleben 1916	--	--	--	--	80T'18
SONNECK, Rita (nd)					
Graf von Brühl 1920 R	--	--	22T'30	--	
SONNLEITNER, A. Th. (ie Alois Tlučhoř, 1869-1939)					
D Höhlenkinder im Heimlichen Grund 1918 R	121A'40 Franckh	101A'35	84A'30	46A'25	

TABLE B (con't.)

NAME	36/40	31/35	26/30	21/25	15/20
SONNLEITNER, A. Th. (con't.)					
D Höhlenkinder im Pfahlbau 1919 R	96A'40	82A'35	69A'30	28A'25	3A'20
D Höhlenkinder im Steinhaus 1920 R	84A'40	70A'35	55A'30	33A'25	
D Höhlenkinder in ihrer Steinzeit (from <u>Die Höhlenkinder im Heimlichen Grund</u>) 1926	39A'40	33A'32	28A'30		
Die Hegerkinder von Aspern 1923	--	--	--	36T'23	
D Höhlenkinder in der Sintflut (from <u>Die Höhlenkinder im Pfahlbau</u>) 1926	34A'38	27A'34	24A'30		
D Höhlenkinder auf der Sonnleiten (from <u>Die Höhlenkinder im Steinhaus</u>) 1926	25A'37	22A'34	19A'30		
Kojas Haus der Sehnsucht 1922	22A'38	21A'34	20A'30	13A'25	
SPECK, Wilhelm (1861-1925)					
Der Joggeli 1907 Erz	--	s 21/25	--	69T'24	59T'18
Zwei Seelen 1904 Erz	--	s 26/30	45T'26	43T'23	37T'20
Ein Quartettfinale (Aushalten!) 1908 Nov	--	--	--	30T'19	10T'15
SPECKMANN, Diedrich (1872-1938)					
Heidjers Heimkehr 1904 Erz	274T'40	250T'31	241T'28	235T'23	174T'19
Heidehof Lohe 1906 R	--	208T'32	196T'29	170T'23	135T'20
Das goldene Tor 1907 Erz	--	115T'34	s 15/20	87T'21	77T'19
Die Heidklause 1919 Erz	--	--	106T'28	78T'23	58T'20
Herzensheilige 1909 R	99T'36	--	--	81T'22	66T'20

TABLE B (con't.)

NAME	36/40	31/35	26/30	21/25	15/20
SPECKMANN, Diedrich (con't.)					
Neu-Lohe 1920 R	86T'39	--	s 21/5	60T'23	30T'20
Geschwister Rosenbrock 1912 R	85T'39	--	74T'27	71T'21	51T'20
Erich Heydenreichs Dorf 1913 Erz	--	--	--	58T'22	37T'19
Der Anerbe 1914 Erz	--	--	--	53T'21	43T'20
Jan Murken 1922 R	43T'37	--	s 21/25	12T'22	
SPERL, August (1862-1929)					
Die Söhne des Herrn Budiwoj 1896 hist R	--	--	38T'27	41T'22	26T'20
D Fahrt nach d alten Urkunde 1893 Geschn	--	--	--	31T'25	20T'17
Burschen heraus! 1913 R	--	c 28T'31 (13A)	--	26T'25 (12A)	15T'17 (7A)
Hans Georg Portner 1902 R	--	--	27T'30	25A'24	22A'20
SPEYER, Wilhelm (1887-1952)					
Der Kampf der Tertia 1928 Erz	--	s 26/30	25T'28		
SPIEGEL, Edgar Frhr v (v u z Peckelsheim, nd)					
Kriegstagebuch U 202 1916	360T'38	--	--	--	50T'16
Oberheizer Zenne, d letzte Mann d "Wiesbaden" 1917	160T'38	--	--	--	100T'17
U-Boot im Fegefeuer 1930	55T'40	s 26/30			

TABLE B (con't.)

NAME	36/40	31/35	26/30	21/25	15/20
SPIESS, Johannes (1888-)					
Wir jagten Panzerkreuzer 1938 Krg-Ab	37T'40 (Steiniger)				
(U-Boot Abenteuer 1932) (Hobbing)	--	1-2A'32			
SPILLMANN, Joseph (1842-1905)					
E Opfer d Beichtgeheimnisses 1896 Erz	c 88T'40+ (42A)	39A'35 Herder	37A'28	82T'23 (34A)	62T'20 (26A)
Die Marienkinder 1892 Erz	--	--	c 50T'27+ (22A)	46T'22 (20A)	18A'20
Liebet eure Feinde! 1891 Erz	ni'39	--	c 48T'26 (21A)	--	44T'20 (19A)
Lucius Flavus 1898 R	--	--	44T'26+	--	40T'20
Kämpfe und Kronen 1894 Erz	--	--	--	43T'22 (18A)	14A'20
Der Neffe der Königin 1893 Erz	--	--	c 43T'26 (18A)	--	38T'20 (16A)
Tapfer und treu 1897 R	--	c 38T'31 (16A)	c 34T'26 (15A)	--	c 32T'20 (13A)
Die Sklaven des Sultans 1895 Erz	--	--	c 36T'26 (16A)	--	34T'20 (14A)
Die koreanischen Brüder 1899 Gesch	ni'39	--	35T'26	--	29T'20
Selig die Barmherzigen! 1900 Erz	ni'39	--	--	33T'23 (14A)	11A'20
Der Zug nach Nicaragua 1897 Erz	ni'39	--	--	33T'23 (15A)	12A'20

TABLE B (con't.)

NAME	36/40	31/35	26/30	21/25	15/20
SPILLMANN, Joseph (con't.)					
Die Brüder Yang u die Boxer 1905 Erz	--	--	--	32T'23 (13A)	9A'19
Die beiden Schiffsjungen 1902 Erz	--	--	c 32T'26 (13A)	--	26T'20 (11A)
Das Fronleichnamsfest d Chiquiten 1901 Erz	ni'39	--	c 32T'26 (13A)	--	26T'20 (11A)
Um das Leben einer Königin 1900 R	--	--	--	32T'23	27T'20
Die Goldsucher c 1900 Erz	--	--	--	32T'22 (13A)	9A'19
Die Wunderblume von Woxindon 1893 R	--	--	ni'25	32T'24	27T'20
Wolken u Sonnenschein 1888 Novn u Erzn	--	--	c 32T'26 (13A)	--	23T'20 (11A)
Der schwarze Schuhmacher 1903 Erz	--	--	--	26T'24	22T'20
SPITTELER, Carl (1845-1924)					
Die Mädchenfeinde 1907 Gesch	35T'38+	25T'34	--	15T'24	12T'20
Imago 1906 R	21T'37	--	--	20T'22	15T'19
SPÖRL, Heinrich (1887-1955)					
Man kann ruhig darüber sprechen... 1937 Plaun	210T'39				
Die Feuerzangenbowle 1933 Erz	173T'40				
Wenn wir alle Engel wären 1936 Erz	60T'39				

TABLE B (con't.)

NAME	36/40	31/35	26/30	21/25	15/20
SPRINGENSCHMID, Karl (1897-)					
Helden in Tirol 1934 Geschn	26A'40 Franckh	7A'35			
STARK, Adolf (nd)					
Im Banne der Leidenschaft 1913 Krim-R	--	--	--	40A'20 Henschel	--
STEGEMANN, Hermann (1870-1945)					
Der Kampf um den Rhein 1924	--	61T'35	58T'27	50T'25	
Die Krafft von Illzach 1913 R	--	--	36T'30	--	27A'20
Der gefesselte Strom 1914 R	--	23T'31	--	21T'25	--
STEGUWEIT, Heinz (1897-)					
Der Jüngling im Feuerofen 1932 R	140T'40	50T'34			
Heilige Unrast 1936 R	100T'40				
Frohes Leben 1934 Geschn	70T'40				
Die Saskia mit d leichten Glanz 1940 Nov	30T'40				
Ihr vielgeliebten Schätze 1939 R	26T'40				
STEHR, Hermann (1864-1940)					
Der Heiligenhof 1918 R	213A'40 P List	167T'35	20T'26	s 15/20	5A'18 S Fischer
Peter Brindeisener 1924 R	98A'40 P List	76T'27	15T'27 Horen V	20A'24 F Lintz V	

TABLE B (con't.)

NAME	36/40	31/35	26/30	21/25	15/20
STEHR, Hermann (con't.)					
Drei Nächte 1909 R	85T'36	89T'35	14T'28	11A'24+	
Nathanael Maechler 1929 R	--	47T'29			
An d Tür des Jenseits 1932 Zwei Novn	40T'38	25T'34			
Leonore Griebel 1900 R (P List)	--	39A'30	--	--	--
(Horen-Verlag)	--	--	39T'30	--	--
(F Lintz)	--	--	--	34A'21	--
Der Geigenmacher 1926 Gesch	28A'38 P List	13A'30+	6T'27		
STEIN, Lola (ie Lola Stern, 1885-1959)					
Der gute Kamerad 1918 R	--	--	--	c 60T'23 (2A)	30T'18 (1A)
STEINART, Arnim (ie Friedrich Otto Arnim Loofs, 1886-1930)					
Der Hauptmann 1916 Erz	--	--	--	27T'25	25A'18
STERNEDER, Hans (1889-)					
Der Wunderapostel 1924 R	--	35T'32	30T'30	15T'25	
Der Bauernstudent 1921 R	--	33T'33	25T'27	21T'24	13T'22
Der Sonnenbruder 1922 R	--	23T'32	20T'28	15T'25	
STEUBEN, Fritz (see also Erhard Wittek, 1898-)					
Der fliegende Pfeil 1930 Erz	46T'40	16A'35	4A'30		
Der rote Sturm 1931 Erz	37T'40	12A'35			

TABLE B (con't.)

NAME	36/40	31/35	26/30	21/25	15/20
STEUBEN, Fritz (con't.)					
Schneller Fuss u Pfeilmädchen 1935 Erz	34A'40 Franckh	4A'35			
Tecumseh, der Berglöwe 1932 Erz	29T'40	9A'35			
Der strahlende Stern 1934 Erz	23T'40	6A'35			
STIEHLER, Arthur (1864-)					
Goldene Berge 1918 R	--	--	29T'30	--	10T'18
STILGEBAUER, Eduard (1868-1936)					
Götz Krafft. D Gesch e Jugend, 4 Bde 1904f					
1. Mit tausend Masten	--	--	80T'30	ni'21	--
2. Im Strom der Welt	--	--	64T'30	ni'21	--
3. Im engen Kreis	--	--	55T'30	ni'21	--
4. Des Lebens Krone	--	--	48T'30	ni'21	--
STOCKHAUSEN, Juliane (1899-)					
Die Soldaten d Kaiserin 1924 R	s 31/35	58T'32	39T'28	24T'25	
STRAADEN, Andries van (ie Johann Kaltenboeck, Ps: Max Felde, 1853-)					
Der Depeschenreiter 1901 Erz	37A'36 Union	--	35A'29	30A'24	21A'19
STRATZ, Rudolf (1864-1936)					
Schloss Vogelöd 1921 Gesch	--	--	113T'29		

TABLE B (con't.)

NAME	36/40	31/35	26/30	21/25	15/20
STRATZ, Rudolf (con't.)					
Das deutsche Wunder 1916 R	--	--	103T'30	--	
Seine englische Frau 1913 R	--	--	101T'28	95T'22	66A'20
Der weisse Tod 1897 R	76T'36	71T'35	66T'28	60T'22	40A'20
Du Schwert an meiner Linken 1912 R	--	--	74T'28	68T'23	50A'17
Für dich 1909 R	--	66T'30	63T'27	61T'24	43A'20
Herzblut 1909 R	--	--	66T'28	60T'23	31A'20
Alt-Heidelberg, du Feine... 1902 R	--	66T'32	63T'28	60T'25	20A'17
Stark wie die Mark 1913 R	--	--	53T'28	50T'23	40T'20
Liebestrank 1911 R	--	--	49T'28	47T'24	26A'20
Das freie Meer 1918 R	nAg'40	--	--	--	40T'18
König und Kärrner 1914 R	--	--	--	40T'21	--
Gib mir die Hand 1904 R	--	--	36T'28	30T'23	19A'20
Du bist die Ruh' 1905 R	--	--	33T'28	27T'22	12A'17
Das Licht vom Osten 1919 R	--	--	--	--	30T'19
Montblanc 1899 R	--	--	27T'29	25T'24	15A'20
Der du von dem Himmel bist 1906 R	--	--	25T'28	22T'23	12A'19
Vorbei. E Gesch aus Heidelberg 1904	--	--	--	--	21T'20
STRAUSS, Emil (1866-1960)					
Der Schleier 1920 Nov	170T'40+	ni'35	--		
Der Engelwirt 1900 Gesch	81T'40	75T'34	s 21/25	63A'22	--

TABLE B (con't.)

NAME	36/40	31/35	26/30	21/25	15/20
STRAUSS, Emil (con't.)					
Kreuzungen 1904 R	--	--	s 21/25	62A'25 S Fischer	--
Lebenstanz 1940 R	60T'40				
Freund Hein 1902 Lebensgesch	41T'36	--	s 21/25	36A'25+	24A'17
Der Laufen 1926 Erz	35T'40	--			
Prinz Wieduwitt 1939 Erz	30T'40				
Lorenz Lammerdien 1917 Erz	30T'40	15T'35	--	--	ni'17
Der Schleier 1930 Geschn	25T'39	--			
STRAUSS UND TORNEY, Lulu von (1873-1956)					
Bauernstolz 1901 Novn	100T'38	ni'32	85T'30++	--	--
Auge um Auge 1933 Nov	40T'39				
Der Hof am Brink 1906 Erz	30T'40	ni'35	--	5T'25	--
Der jüngste Tag 1922 R	26T'40	--	--	6T'24	
Der Judashof (Judas) 1911 R	24T'40	9T'33	--	5T'22	--
STROBL, Karl Hans (1877-1946)					
Der wilde Bismarck (Bismarck, Bd I) 1915 R	ni'40	48T'32	38T'27	35T'22	30T'19
D vier Ehen d Matthias Merenus 1913 R	--	--	c 41T'29	21T'22	--
Die Flamänder von Prag (D Schipkapass) 1908 R	39T'40	nAg'32	--	--	--
Mächte u Menschen (Bismarck, Bd II) 1917 R	ni'40	--	--	31T'23	23T'20

TABLE B (con't.)

NAME	36/40	31/35	26/30	21/25	15/20
STROBL, Karl Hans (con't.)					
D Runen Gottes (Bismarck, Bd III) 1919 R	ni'40	--	23T'28	20T'22	15T'19
STUTZER, Gustav (1839-1921)					
Meine Therese. Aus d Leben e Frau 1916	50T'36	nAg'32	27A'27 Wollermann	16A'22	2A'17
In Deutschland u Brazilien. Lebenserinn 1913	23A'37	--	17A'27	--	11A'21
SUDERMANN, Hermann (1857-1928)					
Frau Sorge 1887 R	350T'40	335T'36+	310T'31	280T'25	210A'20
Der Katzensteg 1880 R	255T'40	230T'36	220T'30	195T'25	150A'20
Das hohe Lied 1908 R	115T'39	s 26/30	113T'31	105T'24	77A'20
Es war 1894 R	111T'40	s 26/30	109T'30	103T'24	75A'20
Litauische Geschichten 1917	81T'40	--	75T'28	70T'22	60A'18
Geschwister 1888 Zwei Novn	--	--	--	51T'24	40A'19
Im Zwielicht. Zwanglose Geschn 1886	--	s 26/30	48T'28	46T'21	41A'18
Jolanthes Hochzeit 1892 Erz	--	s 26/30	43T'28	41T'21	36A'19
Das Bilderbuch meiner Jugend 1922	--	s 26/30	42T'30	40T'22	
Die indische Lilie 1911 Novn	--	s 26/30	42T'29	40T'23	28A'19
Der tolle Professor 1926 R	--	s 26/30	40T'26		
Purzelchen 1928 R	--	s 26/30	35T'29		
D Frau des Steffen Tromholt 1928 R	--	s 26/30	30T'29		

TABLE B (con't.)

NAME	36/40	31/35	26/30	21/25	15/20
SÜNDER, Artur (ie Hans Reimann, 1889-)					
Die Dinte wider das Blut after 1917 R	--	--	--	693T'22	--
SUPPER, Auguste (née Schmitz, 1867-1951)					
Das Mädchen Peter u der Fremde 1936 R	42T'39				
D grosse Kraft der Eva Auerstein (Das hölzerne Schifflein) 1937 R	31T'39				
Ausgewählte Erzählungen 1918	29T'39	--	27T'26	--	25T'19
Der Herrensohn 1916 R	--	--	25T'28	24T'24	22A'20
SVENSSON, Jon (Nonni)(ie Jón Stefán Sveinsson, 1857-1944)					
Nonni. Erle e jungen Isländers 1913	c 98T'39 (49A)	45A'35 Herder	35A'29	32T'23 (20A)	17T'19 (10A)
Nonni u Manni. Zwei isländ Knaben 1914	--	--	75T'27	ni'22	4A'20
Sonnentage. Nonnis Jugenderle... 1914	c 72T'39 (36A)	34A'35	30A'30	26T'24	13T'19 (7A)
Die Stadt am Meer. Nonnis neue Erle 1922	c 42T'40 (21A)	19A'32	14A'29	14T'25 (7A)	8T'22 (4A)
Aus Island 1918	37T'39	32T'35	27T'30	--	
Auf Skípolón. Neue Islandgeschn 1928	32T'40	27T'35	21T'29		
Wie Nonni das Glück fand 1934	25T'39	19T'35			
Die Feuerinsel im Nordmeer 1933	21T'40	17T'35			
SWANTENIUS, Swaantje (ie Fräulein Hanna Fuess, 1886-)					
Hermann Löns und die Swaantje 1921	--	125T'36	19A'27	105T'25	

TABLE B (con't.)

NAME	36/40	31/35	26/30	21/25	15/20
TAVEL, Rudolf von (1866-1934)					
Jä gäll, so geit's. Ei lustigi Gschicht... 1902	23T'39	19T'34	--	--	--
Teufelsmauer, Die. Heitere Geschn v Hans Hoffmann, O. Ernst, M. Eyth, H. Böhlau (Dt Humoristen, Bd 3) 1904	--	s 26/30	90T'27	--	--
THEDEN, Dietrich (1857-1909)					
Menschenhasser 1904 Krim-R	--	--	--	46T'25	30A'19
THIESS, Frank (1890-)					
Die Verdammten 1930 R	--	--	90T'30		
Frauenraub 1927 R	--	65T'33	15T'27		
Der Weg zu Isabelle 1934 R	38T'40				
Der Leibhaftige 1924 R	--	36T'33	--	15T'25	
Das Tor zur Welt 1926 R	--	--	30T'29		
Tsushima 1936 R	28T'38				
THOMA, Ludwig (1867-1921)					
Lausbubengeschn. Aus meiner Jugendzeit (with drawings by O. Gulbransson) 1935	240T'40	155T'35			
Jozef Filsers gesammelter Briefwexel, Tl 1 1912	135T'40	s 26/30	--	--	--
Lausbubengeschn 1905	--	120T'33	115T'28	--	--

TABLE B (con't.)

NAME	36/40	31/35	26/30	21/25	15/20
THOMA, Ludwig (con't.)					
Tante Frieda. Neue Lausbubengeschn 1907	115T'40	80T'33	--	70T'24	53T'18
Altaich 1918 Erz	100T'40	70T'34	--	53T'23	20T'18
Jozef Filsers gesammelter Briefwexel, Tl 2 1912	91T'40	48T'35	--	--	--
Das lustige Geschichtenbüchlein 1936	90T'40				
Geschichten. Eine Auswahl 1917	55T'39	50T'34	--	--	10T'17
Andreas Vöst 1905 R	49T'37	--	--	--	29T'20
Der Wittiber 1911 R	42T'39	32T'35	--	24T'23	--
Der Jägerloisl 1921 Gesch	40T'39	--	--	--	20T'21
Das Kälbchen, Der ungewendete Dichter u a Novn 1916	--	--	--	--	39A'20
Kleinstadtgeschichten 1908	--	--	39T'28	--	--
Meine Bauern. Sämtliche Bauerngeschn 1937	35T'40				
Gesammelte Werke in 7 Bdn 1922	35T'38	30T'33	--	6T'22	
Nachbarsleute. Sämtliche Kleinstadtgeschn 1938	30T'40				
Der Ruepp 1922 R	26T'37	--	--	20T'22	
Der Ruepp. Der Jägerloisl. Zwei Geschn	ni'40	ni'31			
Kaspar Lorinser 1937	25T'40				
Erinnerungen 1919	--	25T'31+	--	--	20T'19

TABLE B (con't.)

NAME	36/40	31/35	26/30	21/25	15/20
TOVOTE, Heinz (1864-1946) Also see APPENDIX A					
Im Liebesrausch 1890	--	--	--	49A'21 Eysler	34A'19
Heisses Blut 1895 Nov	--	--	--	30A'21	--
Der Erbe 1891 R	--	--	--	21A'21	--
TRELLER, Franz (1843-1908)					
Der Letzte vom "Admiral" 1899	55T'39	--	45A'27 Union	37A'23	27A'19
Der Sohn des Gaucho 1901 Erz	51T'39	42A'31	40A'28	33A'23	22A'19
Der Enkel der Königin 1904 Erz	37A'38	35A'32	32A'27	26A'22	21A'20
Der Gefangene der Aimaras Erz	32A'37	--	30A'28	24A'23	18A'20
Verwehte Spuren 1896 Erz	31A'28	24A'31	s 21/25	19A'23	13A'19
Das Kind der Prärie 1901 Erz	--	30T'32	20T'29	--	--
Unter dem Römerhelm 1909 Erz	--	--	--	24A'23	--
TREMEL-EGGERT, Kuni (ie Kunigunde Tremel, 1889-1957)					
Barb 1934 R	46A'40 Eher	15A'35+			
TRENKER, Luis (1892-)					
Der verlorene Sohn 1934 R	58T'38+				
Kameraden der Berge 1932	--	32T'35			

TABLE B (con't.)

NAME	36/40	31/35	26/30	21/25	15/20
TUCHOLSKY, Kurt (1890-1935)					
Rheinsberg. E Bilderbuch für Verliebte 1912	--	--	90T'28	50T'21	20T'17
Schloss Gripsholm 1931 Sommergesch	--	50T'32			
TÜGEL, Ludwig (1889-)					
Sankt Blehk od Die grosse Veränderung 1934 R	--	30T'35			
UDET, Ernst (1896-1941)					
Mein Fliegerleben 1935	150T'38				
UNGER, Hellmuth (1891-1953)					
Robert Koch (Helfer der Menschheit) 1929 R	100T'40	3A'32			
Germanien 1938 Gesch	25T'40				
UNRUH, Fritz von (1885-)					
Der Opfergang - Vor der Entscheidung 1916 Erz	--	30T'31	--	20T'25	10A'19
UTSCH, Rudolf (1903-1960)					
Herrin und Knecht 1936 R	77T'40				
VELMEDE, August Friedrich (nd)					
Kriegsdichter erzählen 1937	25T'40				
VERSHOFEN, Wilhelm (1878-1960)					
Der Fenriswolf 1914 R	31T'39	2A'31+	--	8T'22	5T'19

TABLE B (con't.)

NAME	36/40	31/35	26/30	21/25	15/20
VESPER, Will (1882-1962)					
Tristan und Isolde 1911 R	195T'40	191T'34	188T'29+	185T'22	--
Das harte Geschlecht 1931 R	120T'40	65T'35			
VIEBIG, Clara (ie Frau Clara Cohn, 1860-1952)					
Am Totenmaar. Margrets Wallfahrt. Das Miserabelchen. D Osterquell 1901 Erzn	--	--	120T'28	--	--
Einer Mutter Sohn 1906 R	s 26/30	s 21/25	57T'29	40T'22	28A'17
Töchter der Hekuba 1917 R	--	--	ni'30	47T'24	45A'20
Das schlafende Heer 1904 R	s 31/35	ni'33	46T'30	42T'22	32A'18
Das tägliche Brot 1901 R	--	--	46T'30	40T'22	36A'20
Das Weiberdorf 1900 R	--	--	46T'28+	44A'22	32A'18
Die Wacht am Rhein 1902 R	s 31/35	ni'33	44T'29	40T'22	36A'20
Vom Müller-Hannes 1903 Gesch	--	--	--	43T'25	ni'16
Das Kreuz im Venn 1908 R	ni'38	--	39T'29	34A'22	29A'20
Rheinlandtöchter 1897 R	--	--	37T'30	32A'22	29A'20
Kinder der Eifel 1897 Novn	--	--	32T'30	30T'25	21T'19
Die vor den Toren 1910 R	--	--	31T'30	27A'22	--
Eine Handvoll Erde 1915 R	--	--	29T'29+	27A'22	23A'20
Absolvo te 1907 R	--	--	28T'28	26A'22	20A'19
Eifelgeschn: Kinder d Eifel. Vom Müller-Hannes 1897, 1903 Novn	--	--	--	28A'23 Dt V-Anst	23A'20

TABLE B (con't.)

NAME	36/40	31/35	26/30	21/25	15/20
VIEBIG, Clara (con't.)					
Das rote Meer 1920 R	--	26T'31	--	--	10A'20
Die goldenen Berge 1927 R	--	--	22T'30		
Elisabeth Reinharz' Ehe. Es lebe die Kunst! 1899 R	--	ni'33	22A'29	14A'23+	11A'11
Das Eisen im Feuer R	--	--	--	22T'25	--
VIESÈR, Dolores (ie Wilhelmine Aichbichler, 1904-)					
Das Singerlein 1928 Gesch	70T'39	52T'32	33T'30		
VIETOR, Cornelius Rudolf (1863-1932?)					
Die letzte Königin von Neapel 1920 R	--	--	26T'30	--	
VILLINGER, Hermine (1849-1917)					
Die Rebächle 1910 R	--	--	27T'28	25T'22	22A'20
VOIGT-DIEDERICHS, Helene (1875-1961)					
Auf Marienhoff. D Leben e dt Mutter 1925	100T'40	50T'35	--	8T'26	
Luise 1916 Erz	40T'39	ni'35	--	--	2A'20
Aber der Wald lebt 1935 Erz	30T'40				
VOLCK, Herbert (1894-)					
D Wölfe. E dt Flucht durch Siberien 1918	161T'40	--	--	--	
VOLLMER, Walter (1903-)					
Die Schenke zur ewigen Liebe 1935 R	34T'38				

TABLE B (con't.)

NAME	36/40	31/35	26/30	21/25	15/20
VOSS, Richard (1851-1918)					
Zwei Menschen 1911 R	--	6A'35+ Engelhorn	620T'29	540T'25	300T'20
Der heilige Hass 1915 R	--	--	184T'27+	--	ni'19
Die Erlösung 1918 R	--	--	80T'25	68T'22	47T'20
Alpentragödie 1909 R	51T'40	--	44T'28+	36T'25	17A'20
Bergasyl 1881 Erz	48A'37 Keyser	--	32A'31 A Bonz	12A'23	--
Hassende Liebe 1915 R	--	--	30T'25	--	
VRING, Georg von der (1889-)					
Die Spur im Hafen 1936 Krim-R	45T'40+				
WAGGERL, Karl Heinrich (1897-)					
Das Wiesenbuch 1932	--	75T'34			
Brot 1930 R	58T'40	23T'35			
Das Jahr des Herrn 1933 R	30T'40	15T'35			
Mütter 1935 R	27T'40				
Wagreiner Tagebuch 1936	26T'38				
WALTER, Robert (1883-)					
Der Krippenschnitzer 1919 Erz	--	--	ni'28	30T'25	

TABLE B (con't.)

NAME	36/40	31/35	26/30	21/25	15/20
WASER, Frau Maria (1878-1939)					
D Geschichte d Anna Waser 1913 R	41T'39	37T'34	30T'29	26T'26	16A'20
Wir Narren von gestern 1922 R	--	--	21T'30	17T'24	
WASSERMANN, Jakob (1873-1934)					
Das Gänsemännchen 1915 R	--	291A'31 S Fischer	241A'30	82A'24	66T'20
Der Fall Mauritius 1928 R	--	112A'33	100A'29		
Christian Wahnschaffe 1919 R	--	107A'33	59A'28	51A'25	28A'19
Der niegeküsste Mund 1903 Drei Erzn	--	s 26/30	82A'28	77A'25	--
Etzel Andergast 1931 R	--	57A'34			
Laudin und die Seinen 1925	--	--	51A'28	30A'25	
Caspar Hauser od Die Trägheit d Herzens 1908 R	--	--	38A'29	29A'24	12A'16
D Wendekreis, 4. Faber od Die verlorenen Jahre 1924 R	--	--	37A'20	20A'25	
Christoph Columbus... 1929 E Porträt	--	s 26/30	35A'30		
D Wendekreis, 1. Der unbekannte Gast 1920 R	--	--	--	34A'25	10A'20
D Gesch des jungen Renate Fuchs 1900	--	--	34A'30	31A'25	--
Der Geist des Pilgers 1923 Drei Erzn	--	--	26T'30		
Der Aufruhr um den Junker Ernst 1926 Erz	--	s 26/30	25A'26		
Die Lebensalter Erwin Reiner (Die Masken Erwin Reiners) 1910 R	--	--	24A'29	18A'23	--

TABLE B (con't.)

NAME	36/40	31/35	26/30	21/25	15/20
WASSERMANN, Jakob (con't.)					
Der goldene Spiegel 1911 Erzn	--	--	24A'27	20A'22	10A'16
D Wendekreis, 3. Ulrike Woytich 1923 R	--	--	23A'27	11A'23	
D Wendekreis, 2. Oberlins drei Stufen und Sturreganz 1922 R	--	--	23A'28	20A'23	
Der Mann von vierzig Jahren 1913 R	--	--	23A'29	17A'22	--
WEBER, Alexander Otto (1868-)					
Mixed Pickles 1904	--	--	--	97T'24	71T'20
Ohne Maulkorb 1904	--	--	--	91T'24	70T'20
Satyr lacht - - 1904	--	--	--	67T'24	40T'18
Durch die Lupe 1905	--	--	--	53T'24	43T'20
Mehr Licht 1908	--	--	--	44T'24	34T'20
Der gefesselte Spötter 1911	--	--	--	41T'24	20T'20
Frech und Froh 1905	--	--	--	--	40T'20
Berlin und der Berliner 1905	--	--	--	--	36T'20
Ohne Feigenblatt 1909 Satn	--	--	--	--	33T'20
Das Salz der Erde 1906	--	--	--	--	30T'20
Nur nicht heiraten 1907	--	--	--	--	25T'20
Indiskretionen. Erlebtes u Erlauschtes I 1914	--	--	--	--	25T'20
Indiskretionen. Erlebtes u Erlauschtes II 1914	--	--	--	--	21T'20

TABLE B (con't.)

NAME	36/40	31/35	26/30	21/25	15/20
WEBER, Marianne (1870-1954)					
Die Frauen und die Liebe 1935	40T'38	20T'35			
WEGENER, Paul (nd)					
Der Galeerensträfling (nach d Film-R von P. W., bearbeitet v Erich Effler) 1920 R	--	--	--	--	25T'20
WEHNER, Josef Magnus (1891-)					
Sieben vor Verdun 1930 R	130T'40	60T'35			
Albert Leo Schlageter 1934	49T'40	10T'34			
WEISER, Franz Xaver (1901-)					
Das Licht der Berge 1931 R	35T'40				
WEISMANTEL, Leo (1888-)					
Das unheilige Haus 1922 R	s 31/35	50T'34	--	ni'25	
WEISS, Ernst (1884-1940)					
Tiere in Ketten 1918 R	--	s 26/30	ni'30	21T'22	10A'18
WENGER, Lisa (née Ruutz, 1858-1941)					
Der Rosenhof 1915 R	--	--	--	22T'21	17T'18
WERDER, Hans (ie Anna Adelheid von Bonin, 1856-1933)					
Tiefer als der Tag gedacht 1907 R	--	--	--	50A'25 0 Janke	--

TABLE B (con't.)

NAME	36/40	31/35	26/30	21/25	15/20
WERDER, Hans (con't.)					
Junker Jürgen 1889 R	--	42T'33	11A'26	--	--
Im Burgfrieden 1905 R	--	--	35T'29	5A'21	--
Der wilde Reutlingen 1891 R	--	--	--	30T'25	--
Schwertklingen 1896 R	--	--	--	25T'25	--
WERFEL, Franz (1890-1945)					
Barbara od Die Frommigkeit 1929 R	--	65T'30+	50T'29		
Verdi 1924 R d Oper	--	--	65T'28	50T'25	
Der Abituriententag 1928 Gesch	--	--	35T'28		
Die Geschwister von Neapel 1931 R	--	30T'31			
Geheimnis eines Menschen 1927 Novn	--	--	25T'27		
WERNER, Johannes (1864-1937)					
Franziska von Altenhausen 1927 R	16A'38 Hase & Koehler	100T'34	70T'30		
Boelcke der Mensch, der Flieger, der Führer d dt Jagdfliegerei... 1932	50T'40				
WIDMANN, Ines (1907-)					
Die Schwabenmargret 1936 R	21T'40				
WIECHERT, Ernst (1887-1950)					
Hirtennovellen 1935	190T'40+	40T'35			

TABLE B (con't.)

NAME	36/40	31/35	26/30	21/25	15/20
WIECHERT, Ernst (con't.)					
Der Todeskandidat. La Ferme Morte. Der Vater 1934 Drei Erzn	120T'39	40T'35			
Die Majorin 1934 Erz	115T'38	65T'35			
Wälder und Menschen 1936 Erinn	110T'38				
Die Magd der Jürgen Doskocil 1932 R	105T'39+	60T'35			
Das heilige Jahr 1936 Fünf Novn	64T'40				
Der Kinderkreuzzug 1935 Nov	58T'39	9T'36			
Der Totenwolf 1924 R	23T'40	20T'35			
WILAMOWITZ-MOELLENDORFF, Fanny Gräfin zur (née Baronin von Fock, 1882-)					
Carin Göring 1933	550T'40	300T'35			
WILDA, Johannes (1852- after 1934)					
Im Kurs der Leidenschaft 1914 R	--	--	--	nA'24	22T'20
WILDENBRUCH, Ernst von (1845-1909)					
Das edle Blut 1892 Erz	229T'39	--	209T'29+	189T'25	159T'19
dass - Schulausgabe	13A'39 G Grote	--	10A'29	8A'24	nn'19?
Kindertränen 1884 Erz	--	--	175T'29	158T'25	129T'19
dass - Schulausgabe	--	--	4A'30	3a'24	
Claudias Garten 1895 Leg	--	70T'35	23A'26	--	21A'20
Neid 1900 Erz	60T'39	--	52T'28	49T'22	46T'20

TABLE B (con't.)

NAME	36/40	31/35	26/30	21/25	15/20
WILDENBRUCH, Ernst von (con't.)					
Vice-Mama 1902 Erz	--	--	--	37T'23	36T'20
Schwester-Seele 1893 R	--	--	37T'31	36A'23	31A'20
Eifernde Liebe 1893 R	--	--	--	24T'23	21T'19
Lukrezia 1907 R	--	--	--	22T'25	19T'20
WILDUNG, Heinrich (nd)					
Das Pfahldorf c 1926 Erz	42A'39 J Beltz	29A'35	9A'30		
WILKE, Karl (nd)					
Prisonnier Halm... 1929 Gesch	s 26/30	22T'35	22T'29		
WILLE, Bruno (1860-1928)					
Die Abendburg 1909 Abenteuer	--	--	--	38T'23	33T'20
WINCKLER, Josef (1881-)					
Der tolle Bomberg 1924 R	230T'40	200T'32+	145T'30	110T'25+	
Pumpernickel. Menschen u Geschn um Haus Nyland 1926 Erzn	--	100T'33	--		
WINNIG, August (1878-1956)					
Heimkehr 1935 Erinn	90T'40	2A'35			
Der weite Weg 1932	85T'40				
Die Hand Gottes 1938	50T'40				

TABLE B (con't.)

NAME	36/40	31/35	26/30	21/25	15/20
WINNIG, August (con't.)					
D ewig grünende Tanne 1927 Zehn Geschn	40T'40	2A'33+			
Frührot. E Buch v Heimat u Jugend 1924	35T'40	20T'35	11T'26	5T'24	
Wunderbare Welt 1938 R	30T'38				
WINTERFELD-PLATEN, Leontine (nd)					
O Fraue, wundersüsse 1912 R	35A'36 F Bahn	34A'31	33A'28	30A'26	24A'18
Herzeleide 1917 R	--	29A'35	--	28A'22	18A'20
WISPLER, Leo (1890-1958)					
Spiel im Sommerwind 1937 Erz	68T'40				
WITTBER, Margarete (1898-)					
Len weiss nicht, was sie will 1932 Erz	30T'40				
Len weiss nun, was sie will 1933 Erz	23T'40				
WITTEK, Erhart (see also Ps: Fritz Steuben, 1898-)					
Männer. E Buch d Stolzes 1936 Anekn	112T'40				
Durchbruch anno achtzehn 1933 Erl	49T'40				
Bewahrung der Herzen 1937 Nov	30T'40				
WITTMAACK, Adolf (1878-1957)					
Konsul Möllers Erben 1914 R	--	s 21/25	--	31A'25 S Fischer	ni'16?

TABLE B (con't.)

NAME	36/40	31/35	26/30	21/25	15/20
WOHLBRÜCK, Olga (ie Frau Olga Wendland, 1867-1943)					
Die goldene Krone 1917 R	--	--	--	40T'21	30T'20
Der grosse Rachen 1915 R	--	--	--	23T'22	
WOLF, Friedrich (1888-1953)					
Kreatur 1925 R	--	--	55T'27		
WOLFF, Johanna (1858-1943)					
Das Hanneken. E Buch v Arbeit u Aufstieg 1913 Erz	35T'40	23T'33	13T'29	9A'21	--
WOLFF, Julius (1834-1910)					
Der wilde Jäger 1877 Mär	s 26/30	--	--	116T'22	114T'20
Der Raubgraf 1884 Gesch	ni'36	--	109T'29	99T'24	81T'20
Der Sülfmeister 1883 Gesch	ni'36	100T'30	99T'30	89T'25	68T'20
Lurlei 1886 Rom	s 26/30	--	80T'30	77T'23	74T'20
D Rattenfänger v Hameln 1876 Aventiure	s 26/30	--	--	--	78T'19
Das Recht der Hagestolze 1888 Gesch	s 26/30	--	55T'29	52T'24	47T'20
Tannhäuser. E Minnesang 1888	s 26/30	--	--	--	45T'20
Die Hohkönigsburg 1902 Gesch	s 26/30	--	44T'26	41T'22	36T'20
Der fliegende Holländer 1892 Sage	s 26/30	42T'31	--	39T'22	37T'19
Renata 1891 Dtg	s 26/30	--	--	36T'22	34T'19
Das schwarze Weib 1894 R	ni'36	--	--	29T'21	26T'18

TABLE B (con't.)

NAME	36/40	31/35	26/30	21/25	15/20
WOLFF, Julius (con't.)					
Der Landsknecht von Cochem 1898	s 26/30	--	--	26T'25	24T'20
Das Wildfangrecht 1907 Gesch	s 26/30	--	--	24T'23	20T'19
Der Sachsenspiegel 1909 Gesch	ni'36	--	--	23T'22	21T'20
Zweifel der Liebe 1904 R	s 26/30	--	23T'26	--	--
WOLFF, Ludwig (1876-)					
Garragan 1924 R	--	--	ni'28	25T'24	
WOLZOGEN, Ernst von (1855-1934)					
Das dritte Geschlecht 1899 R	--	--	ni'30	ni'21	125T'16
Die Gloriahose. 'S Meikatel u d Sexack 1897 Zwei Geschn	--	70T'32	--	65T'22	60T'19
WOTHE, Anny (ie Anny Mahn, 1858-1919)					
Aus dämmernden Nächten 1914 R	--	--	--	--	207T'19
Der Garten der Vergessenheit 1915 R	--	--	--	nA'24	112T'19
Die Vogesenwacht 1915 R	--	--	--	--	95T'19
Zauber-Runen 1919 R	--	--	--	c 87T'22 (5A)	70T'19 (4A)
Drei graue Reiter 1919 R	--	--	nA'29	--	60T'19
Bob Heil! 1919 R	--	--	45T'30	--	
Haus der Väter 1907 R	--	--	45T'30	--	ni'18
Der Hof des Schweigens 1913 R	--	--	--	39T'22	ni'18

TABLE B (con't.)

NAME	36/40	31/25	26/30	21/25	15/20
WOTHE, Anny (con't.)					
Die den Weg bereiten 1916 R	--	--	--	34T'22	8T'16
Die Sonnenjungfer 1919 R	--	--	33T'28	28T'23	10T'19
Hallig Hooge 1918 R	--	--	33T'28	28T'25	6T'18
Am roten Kliff 1910 R	--	--	32T'28	27T'23	--
Von fremden Ufern 1919 R	s 21/25	--	--	nA'24	30T'19
Das Tor des Lebens 1910 R	--	--	ni'26	nA'25	30T'19
Die Polarhexe 1922 R	--	--	--	26T'22	
Die Lawine 1917 R	ni'37	--	ni'29	26T'24	10T'18
Versunkene Welten 1908 R	--	--	25T'30	--	20T'19
Seegespenster 1922 R	--	--	23T'28	17T'22	
WRIEDE, Paul (1870-1926)					
Hamburger Volkshumor in Redensarten... 1924	--	--	--	55T'25	
WUNDT, Theodor (1895-1929)					
Matterhorn 1915 R	--	s 26/30	42T'29	--	
ZABEL, Eugen (1851-1924)					
D Roman e Kaiserin. Katharine II. v Russland 1911	107T'40	--	--	ni'24	--
ZACCHI, Ferdinand (1884-)					
Freerk Frandsens Blut 1920 R	36T'36	s 21/25	--	21T'22	4T'20

TABLE B (con't.)

NAME	36/40	31/35	26/30	21/25	15/20
ZAHN, Ernst (1867-1952)					
Lukas Hochstrassers Haus 1907 R	235T'40	139T'34	137T'30	105T'25	82T'20
Frau Sixta 1926 R	141T'40	46T'31	44T'28	20T'26	
Das zweite Leben 1918 Erz	s 26/30	--	111T'27	108T'22	100T'20
Herrgottsfäden 1901 R	106T'36	--	74T'27	49T'23	37A'20
Vier Erzn aus Helden d Alltags 1907	--	93T'34	91T'30	79T'25	70T'20
Lotte Esslingers Wille und Weg 1919 Erz	s 26/30	--	84T'26	81T'22	70T'20
Helden des Alltags 1905 Novn	84T'39	82T'33	80T'29	52T'22	41T'19
Die Clari-Marie 1904 R	84T'39	72T'33	49T'26	46T'22	41T'20
Nacht 1917 Erz	s 26/30	--	83T'26	81T'22	76T'20
Einsamkeit 1909 R	80T'39	--	ni'25	75T'23	61T'20
Jonas Truttmann 1921 R	s 26/30	--	72T'30	70T'22	
Firnwind 1906 Neue Erzn	s 26/30	--	67T'30	43T'22	35T'20
Die Liebe des Severin Imboden 1916 R	--	66T'33	64T'26	61T'23	50T'19
Albin Indergand 1900 R	--	--	63A'28 Huber	--	45A'18
Die Frauen von Tannò 1911 R	s 21/25	--	ni'25	58T'25	44T'19
Erni Behaim 1898 R	--	58T'31	--	34T'24	28T'20
Die da kommen und gehen! 1908	s 21/25	--	ni'25	56T'23	50T'20
Menschen 1900 Neue Erzn	s 26/30	--	55T'29	31T'22	25A'19
D Apotheker von Klein-Weltwil 1913 R	s 26/30	--	53T'26	50T'23	41T'20

TABLE B (con't.)

NAME	36/40	31/35	26/30	21/25	15/20
ZAHN, Ernst (con't.)					
Was das Leben zerbricht 1912 Erzn	s 21/25	--	ni'25	53T'22	45T'19
Schattenhalb 1903 Drei Erzn	s 26/30	--	50T'29	23T'21	20T'20
Bergvolk 1896 Drei Novn	s 26/30	--	47T'29	23T'22	17T'20
Erzn aus den Bergen 1912	s 26/30	--	43T'29	41T'25	38T'20
Der sinkende Tag 1920 Sechs Erzn	s 26/30	--	42T'20	--	
Uraltes Lied! 1914 Erzn	s 26/30	--	37T'27	34T'22	31T'20
Brettspiel des Lebens 1928 R	s 26/30	--	35T'28		
Die Hochzeit des Gandenz Orell 1927 R	s 26/30	--	35T'27		
Blancheflur 1924 Erz	--	32T'32	30T'28	28T'25	
Die tausendjährige Strasse 1939 R	26T'40				
Tochter Dodais 1928 R	s 26/30	--	25T'29		
Kämpfe 1902 Erz	s 21/25	--	--	22A'21 Dt V-Anst	19A'19
ZAPP, Arthur (Ps: V. E. Teranus, 1852-1925)					
Die Sünde wider das Weib 1918 R	--	--	43T'30	33T'22	9T'18
Was ist Liebe 1919 R	--	--	--	30T'23	23T'20
Wie Liebgard Stahl Mutter wurde 1919 R	--	--	--	22T'23	15T'20
Der Mann von fünfzig Jahren 1917 R	--	--	--	22T'23	8T'18
ZAUNERT, Paul (1879-)					
V Riesen u Zwergen u Waldgeistern 1937 Fünfzig Natursagen	65T'40				

TABLE B (con't.)

NAME	36/40	31/35	26/30	21/25	15/20
ZEDLITZ-TRÜTZSCHLER, Graf Robert (1863-)					
Zwölf Jahre am dt Kaiserhof 1923 Aufzn	--	--	40T'30	37T'25	
ZEIDLER, Paul Gerhard (Ps: C. F. Kerim, 1879-1947)					
Elisabeth von Platen 1921 R	s 21/25	--	25T'30	10T'21	
ZELLWEKER, Edith (ie Edith Godfroy-Zellweker, 1913-1938)					
Und seine Tochter ist der Peter 1935 R	23T'38				
ZERKAULEN, Heinrich (1892-1954)					
Anna und Sigrid 1931 R	234T'40	ni'34			
Rautenkranz und Schwerter 1927 R	23T'40	8T'35			
ZILLE, Heinrich (1859-1929)					
Das H. Zille-Werk, 1. Kinder der Strasse 1908	s 21/25	--	99T'25	84T'25	48T'18
Das H. Zille-Werk, 2. Mein Milljöh 1914	s 21/25	--	90T'25	74T'25	38T'18
Das H. Zille-Werk, 3. Rund ums Freibad 1926	s 26/30	--	25T'26		
Zille Vermächtnis (Hans Ostwald, ed) 1930	--	--	25T'30		
ZILLICH, Heinrich (1898-)					
Der Urlaub 1933 Nov	65T'40				
Zwischen Grenzen und Zeiten 1936 R	50T'40+				
Der Weizenstrauss 1938 R	45T'40				
Der baltische Graf 1937 Erz	40T'40				

TABLE B (con't.)

NAME	36/40	31/35	26/30	21/25	15/20
ZILLICH, Heinrich (con't.)					
Flausen u Flunkereien 1940 Geschn	25T'40				
ZÖBERLEIN, Hans (1895-1948?)					
D Glaube an Dtld. E Kriegserleben... 1931	38A'41+ Eher	17A'35+			
ZUR MEGEDE, Johannes Richard (1864-1906)					
Quitt! 1897 R	--	ni'32	46T'28	44T'23	38T'20
Der Ueberkater 1905 R	--	--	--	23T'22	20A'20
Modeste 1905 R	--	--	22T'24+	--	20T'20
ZWEIG, Arnold (1887-)					
Die Novellen um Claudia 1912 R	--	--	110T'30	73A'22+	18T'17
ZWEIG, Stefan (1881-1942)					
Sternstunden der Menschheit 1927	--	300T'31			
Brennendes Geheimnis 1931 Erz	--	170T'33			
Die Augen des ewigen Bruders 1922 Leg	--	170T'33			
Amok 1922 Novn e Leidenschaft	--	150T'31	70T'30	32T'24	
Verwirrung der Gefühle 1926 Drei Novn	--	90T'31	85T'30		
Joseph Fouché 1930 Bildnis	--	53T'32	40T'30		
Marie Antoinette 1932 Bildnis	--	50T'32+			
Die Kette. E Novellenkreis, 1. Erstes Erlebnis 1911 Vier Geschn	--	--	40T'28	15T'22	11T'20

TABLE B (con't.)

NAME	36/40	31/35	26/30	21/25	15/20
ZWEIG, Stefan (con't.)					
Die Baumeister d Welt, 1. Drei Meister: Balzac, Dickens, Dostojewski 1920	--	ni'36	30T'29	--	10T'21
Die Baumeister d Welt, 2. Der Kampf mit d Dämon... 1925	--	ni'36	--	22T'25	

APPENDIX A

In as much as it is impossible to prove the exact size of the editions of various publishers, I am adding this list of authors (fifty-eight) and titles (one hundred and sixty-six) for which no figures other than the number of Auflagen are found in the DBV. Many of these authors have already been included in TABLE B, but the works shown here were not sufficiently successful (i. e. had not been published in twenty-one or more Auflagen) to be included there. However, should the editions of the companies represented by these books have contained two or more thousand copies each, then these titles would also be worthy of inclusion in TABLE B. The publisher is indicated under the data as briefly as possible and one should read from left to right. If the name Reclam appears under a listing in the column for 1936/40 and no other publisher is found in the data of that title, Reclam published all the editions. If a publishing house is indicated but once in all the works of an author, this one firm is the source of all the Auflagen given. The format and abbreviations are those of TABLE B.

APPENDIX A

NAME	36/40	31/35	26/30	21/25	15/20
ADLERSFELD-BALLESTREM, Euphemia von (1854-1941)					
Heideröslein R	--	--	17A'29 Maschler	9A'22	7A'15 Schl V-Anst
Palazzo Iran 1909 R	16A'38 Reclam	14A'33	11A'30	9A'24	7A'18
Maria Schnee 1907 R	--	--	--	16A'24 M Seyfert	13A'20
Diplomaten 1907 R	15A'37 Reclam	14A'33	11A'28	10A'25	5A'20
Der Amönenhof 1918 R	--	--	13A'27 M Seyfert	--	4A'18
Die Dame im Monde 1915 R	--	--	12A'23	--	
Ave 1917 R	--	--	11A'30	8A'22	
Der Jungferturm 1909 Gesch	10A ?	--	--	--	--
Die Fliege im Bernstein 1919 R	--	--	nA ?	--	6A'19
ARNAU, Frank (ie Heinrich Schmitt, 1894-)					
Die grosse Mauer 1931 R	--	7A'31 Goldmann			
BAHR, Hermann (1863-1934)					
Himmelfahrt 1916 R	--	--	16A'28 Borgmeyer	--	8A'16 S Fischer

APPENDIX A (con't.)

NAME	36/40	31/35	26/30	21/25	15/20
BLANCKENBURG, Clara von (née von Bülow, nd)					
Ganz einfach Luise 1913 Nov	--	--	13A'30 F Bahn	12A'22	--
Der werfe den ersten Stein 1909 Gesch	--	--	13A'26	12A'25	10A'16
BOCK, Alfred (1859-1932)					
Der Flurschütz 1901 R	--	--	nd'29 Reclam U-B	12A'24 Dt V-Anst	11A'19
BOSSE, Alexandra von (nd)					
Rose Breiten 1913 R	--	--	--	6A'21 Reclam	2A'18
BREY, Henriette (1875-1953)					
Es fiel ein Reif 1912 R	--	12A'32 Bergland	3A'26	2A'24	
Joseph Ben David 1923 R	--	12A'32 Bachem	--	4A'23	
Der Heidevikar 1924 R	--	--	12A'29	4A'24	
DILL, Liesbet (ie Liesbet v Drigalski, 1877-1962)					
Unverbrannte Briefe 1909 R	--	--	--	13A'25 Dt V-Anst	11A'20
DOSE, Johannes (1860-1933)					
Frau Treue 1901 Geschn	--	14A'31 F Bahn	--	13A'25	10A'20

APPENDIX A (con't.)

NAME	36/40	31/35	26/30	21/25	15/20
DOSE, Johannes (con't.)					
Der Kirchherr v Westerwohld 1900 Erz	11A'38 F Bahn	10A'32	9A'27	8A'20	7A'20
DROONBERG, Emil (ie Emil Muschik-Droonberg, 1864-1934)					
Das Gold der Nebelberge 1917 R	--	--	20A'27 Hesse/Becker	13A'25 Goldmann	
ELLERT, Gerhart (ie Gertrud Schmirger, 1900-)					
Attila 1934 R	20A'37 Speidel	15A'35			
ENGEL, Georg (1866-1931)					
Claus Störtebecker 1920 R	--	17A'33 Union	14A'28	12A'23	10T'20 Grethlein
Der Reiter auf dem Regenbogen 1908 R	--	--	s 21/25	14A'24 Union	--
Die verirrte Magd 1911 R	--	--	--	11A'22	--
Die Prinzessin u d Heilige 1922 R	--	--	--	10A'22	
Der verbotene Rausch 1910 R	--	--	--	10A'23	--
ESCHELBACH, Hans (1868-1948)					
Im Moor 1903 Nov	--	--	nl'28 St Josef	15A'22 Veritas	--

APPENDIX A (con't.)

NAME	36/40	31/35	26/30	21/25	15/20
FELDE, Max (ie Johann Kaltenboeck, 1853-)					
Der Sohn der Wälder 1907 Erz	--	--	19A'29 Union	17A'25	12A'20
Mit vereinten Kräften. Neue Heldenstricke... 1916	--	--	--	11A'22	6A'18
1914-15. Denkwürdige Kriegserle 1915	--	--	--	11A'22	6A'16
FELDEN, Emil (1874-)					
Menschen von Morgen 1918 R	--	--	--	19A'24 E Oldenburg	8A'18
GAGERN, Friedrich von (1882-1947)					
Das Geheimnis 1919 R	13A'38 Parey	12A'35	--	10A'22	6A'21
GANGHOFER, Ludwig (1855-1920)					
D Märchen vom Karlfunkelstein 1905	19A'37 Union	18A'32	--	14A'22	11A'20
GOTTBERG, Otto von (1867-1935)					
Liebesglut R	--	--	--	--	13A'18 Dt V-Anst
GRABEIN, Paul (1869-1945)					
In Jena ein Student 1908	--	--	s 15/20	--	14A'20 Union

APPENDIX A (con't.)

NAME	36/40	31/35	26/30	21/25	15/20
HARTWIG, Georg (ie Emmy Köppel, 1850-1916)					
Wär' ich geblieben doch! 1907 R	--	19A'32 Union	17A'30	14A'23	9A'20
Das Rätsel von Kornfeld 1911 R	13A'38	11A'33	--	6A'22	5A'19
Willst du dein Herz mir schenken? 1912 R	--	13A'32	--	9A'22	6A'20
Die Generalstochter c 1910 R	--	12A'34	--	7A'21	3A'19
Der blaue Diamant 1909 R	--	12A'32	s 11/14	--	8A'20
Wenn du mich liebst 1904 R	--	12A'32	9A'29	--	7A'20
Alpenrose c 1915 R	--	11A'33	--	6A'21	2A'19
Hans Bickenbach 1914 R	--	9A'32	--	7A'23	5A'19
Bleib dir treu! 1920 R	8A'36	7A'32	4A'26	--	3A'20
HEIMBURG, Wilhelmine (ie Berta Behrens, 1850-1912)					
Ihr einziger Bruder 1882 Nov	--	--	20A'26 J M Gebhardtz	19A'21	18A'19
Antons Erben 1898 R	--	19A'32 Union	16A'29	14A'24	13A'20
Um fremde Schuld 1895 R	--	--	19A'27	--	11A'20
Sette Oldenroths Liebe 1902 R	--	17A'32	15A'30	14A'23	5A'19
Eine unbedeutende Frau 1891 R	--	--	16A'26	15A'23	12A'20
Die Andere 1886 R	--	--	--	16A'23	12A'20
Die lustige Frau Regina 1910 Novn u Skn	--	--	--	15A'23	8A'19

APPENDIX A (con't.)

NAME	36/40	31/35	26/30	21/25	15/20
HEIMBURG, Wilhelmine (con't.)					
Doktor Dannz u seine Frau 1903 R	--	--	15A'26 Union	10A'22	9A'20
Haus Beetzen 1895 R	--	--	--	15A'25	7A'19
Unter der Linde 1888 R	--	12A'32	--	11A'23	7A'20
Sabinens Freier. Auf schwankendem Boden 1891 Zwei Novn	--	--	10A'26	--	8A'20
HEINZE-HOFERICHTER, Mara von (ie Margarete, 1887-)					
Zwei Menschen gehen ihren Weg 1930 R	15A'35 Ensslin/Laiblin	9T'32			
HOFFENSTHAL, Hans von (ie Hans v Hepperger, 1877-1914)					
Marion Flora 1914 R	--	--	--	16A'25 Dt V-Anst	10A'19
HUCH, Rudolf (1862-1943)					
Die Familie Hellmann 1909 R	--	20A'32 P List	--	17T'21 Bücherlese-V	ni'17
HÜLSEN, Hans von (1890-)					
Der Kelch und die Brüder 1925 R	13A'39 Reclam	11A'33	7A'30		
KÄNEL, Rösy von (1895-1953)					
Jahrmarkt des Lebens 1933 Erz	17A'40 Buchhandlung d Evang Gesellschaft	11A'34			

APPENDIX A (con't.)

NAME	36/40	31/35	26/30	21/25	15/20
KÄNEL, Rösy von (con't.)					
Direktor Hansen u v Menschen hinter Gefängnismauern c 1928 Erz	14A'39	10A'33	5A'30		
	Buchhandlung d Evang Gesellschaft				
D Wahrsagerin 1930 E Bild aus d Volksleben	--	11A'34			
Spittelweibchen 1928 Gesch	--	11A'33	6A'30		
KAISER, Isabelle (1866-1925)					
Der wandernde See 1910 R	--	--	--	16A'24 Bachem	10T'18
Vater unser... 1906 R	--	15A'32	--	--	14T'20
Von ewiger Liebe 1914 Novn u Skn	--	--	--	12A'24	6T'19
KEMPIN, Lely (1878- before 1958)					
Die heilige Insel 1917 Gesch	--	16A'31	15A'27	13A'25	8A'21
		Velhagen/Klasing			
KENNICOTT, Mervyn Brian (ie Gertrud Hamer, née v Sanden, 1881-1940)					
Die Gesch v Tilmansöhne 1937 R	18A'37 Wunderlich				
KERN, Maximilian (1877-)					
Das Auge des Fo 1905 Erz	20A'38 Union	18A'31	--	15A'24	9A'19
Unter d Klaue d Drachen 1909 Gesch	15A'38	--	--	12A'25	9A'20

APPENDIX A (con't.)

NAME	36/40	31/35	26/30	21/25	15/20
KUHNERT, Adolf-Artur (1905-1958)					
Kriegsfron der Frauen 1929 R	--	--	6A'29 Reclam		
Karjane, Geliebte unseres Sommers 1933 R	5A'37	4A'34			
Paganini 1929 R	5A'38	--	3A'29		
LÖSCHER, Hans (1881-1946)					
Alles Getrennte findet sich wider 1937	nA'40 12A'37 Wunderlich				
Das befreite Herz 1939 R	6A'40				
MALTZAHN, Elisabeth (ie Frau Elisabeth Wengel, née Maltzahn, 1868-)					
Der Hofprediger Ihrer Durchlaucht 1899 Erz	--	--	18A'26 F Bahn	17A'24	14A'19
Ilsabe c 1898 Erz	--	--	17A'27	16A'26	11A'20
E Königin v Frankreich u Navarra 1903 Erz	--	--	15A'29	--	12A'20
Das heilige Blut 1901 Erz	--	--	13A'26	12A'21	9A'20
Dr. Bernhardus 1900 Erz	--	12A'35	11A'30	10A'21	8A'20
Der Gottesschatz 1921 R	--	--	11A'28	10A'22	
Der heilige Damm 1909 Erz	--	--	--	11A'24	8A'19
Die weisse Frau 1908 R	--	--	11A'26	10A'25	6A'12

APPENDIX A (con't.)

NAME	36/40	31/35	26/30	21/25	15/20
MORAHT, Robert (1884-)					
Werwolf d Meere. "U 64" jagt d Feind 1933	18A'40 Vorhut-V				
MÜHLE, Wilhelm von (ie Frau Sophie Kloerss, née Kessler, 1866-1927)					
Oll Priem u seine Jungens 1916	--	19A'34 Union	16A'26	11A'21	7A'19
Jan Feuerkopf 1920	--	--	14A'28	7A'22	
POSSENDORF, Hans (ie Hans Mahner-Mons, 1883-1956)					
Bux 1930 Zirkus-R	--	5A'35 O Janke	3A'30 Knorr/Hirth		
PRESBER, Rudolf (1868-1935)					
Der Tisch des Kapitäns 1926	--	--	17A'26 Eysler		
ROEHLE, Reinhard (1876-1938)					
Das Geheimnis von Ragpura 1919 Erz	--	--	17A'28 Union	14A'25	6A'20
Unter Bullerdieks Teerjacken 1915 Erz	--	--	--	17A'25	11A'20
Durch Urwald und Gertao 1916 Erz	--	--	--	16A'22	11A'20
Als Flüchtling um den halben Erdball 1917 Erz	--	--	--	11A'23	6A'19

APPENDIX A (con't.)

NAME	36/40	31/35	26/30	21/25	15/20
ROSEN, Erwin (ie Erwin Carlé, 1876-1923)					
Alle Gewalten zum Trotz. Lebenskämpfe... 1922	18A'40 Schramm	15A'35 R Lutz	--	9A'24 R Lutz	
ROTHMUND, Toni (1877-1956)					
Glas. E Buch dt Sehnsucht 1930 R	10A'38 Reclam	9A'34	4A'30		
Streit im Haus Iring 1934 R	7A'39	5A'35			
Gold? 1932 R	7A'38	5A'33			
Das Haus zum kleinen Sündenfall 1919 R	--	--	--	5A'23	
RUEDIGER, Minna (1841-1920)					
Waldtraut 1891 Erz	--	--	23A'29 F Bahn	21A'22	19A'20
Durch tiefe Wasser 1901 R	--	13A'32	12A'29	11A'24	8A'13
Harte Wege 1910 Erz	--	--	--	11A'22	8A'20
Um des Glaubens Willen 1894 Vier Geschn	--	--	--	11A'23	8A'16
Barbara 1893 R	--	--	11A'26	10A'24	9A'13
Stilles Heldentum 1913 Gesch	--	10A'32	--	--	5A'14
RUNKEL, Ferdinand (1864-)					
Der Schild des Rekkared Det-R	--	--	--	s 15/20	13A'18 Eysler

APPENDIX A (con't.)

NAME	36/40	31/35	26/30	21/25	15/20
SCHRÖER, Gustav (1876-1949)					
Der Freibauer 1913 R	--	13A'32 Hesse/Becker	8A'30	4A'23	3A'20
SCHULZE-SMIDT, Berhardine (1846-1920)					
Das Hansefeldt 1909 Erz	--	--	19A'27 Union	14A'21	11A'19
SELL, Sophie Charlotte von (1864-1943)					
Unterirdische Wasser 1912 R	--	7A'31 Steinkopf	--	6A'23	3A'20
SONNLECHNER, Oskar (1868-)					
D vorletzte Liebe d schönen Frau Erzsébet 1929 R	s 26/30	8A'35 Reclam	6A'30		
SPRINGENSCHMID, Karl (1897-)					
Da lacht Tirol 1935 Geschn	18A'40 Franckh	4A'35			
SUPPER, Auguste (1867-1951)					
Da hinten bei uns Erzn	--	--	--	14A'23 Salzer	--
TOVOTE, Heinz (1864-1946)					
Susi Gaudi 1923 R	--	--	--	20A'23 Eysler	

APPENDIX A (con't.)

NAME	36/40	31/35	26/30	21/25	15/20
TOVOTE, Heinz (con't.)					
Frau Agna 1901 R	--	--	--	18A'21 Eysler	--
Fräulein Griesbach 1909 R	--	--	--	--	17A'19
Sonnemanns 1904 R	--	--	--	16A'21	--
Die Scheu vor der Liebe 1921 R	--	--	--	15A'21	
Durchs Ziel 1914 R	--	--	--	--	14A'19
Um Evelin 1924 Gesch	s 31/35	13A'25 Zander	--	10A'24 Eysler	
In der Irre. D Leichenmarie u a Novn 1903	--	--	--	--	13A'19
Nimm mich hin! 1916 Novn	--	--	--	--	12A'17
Brautfahrt 1923 Nov	--	--	--	10A'23	
TRENKER, Luis (1892-)					
Leuchtendes Land 1937 R	7A'40 Eher				
VILLINGER, Hermine (1849-1917)					
Ein Lebensbuch 1911 R	--	--	--	8A'23 Reclam	6A'20
WEISS, Ernst (1884-1940)					
Nahar 1922 R	--	--	12A'30 Euphorion	10T'22 Rowohlt	

APPENDIX A (con't.)

NAME	36/40	31/35	26/30	21/25	15/20
WELLER, Tüdel (ie Anton, 1902-)					
Peter Mönkemann. Freikorpskämpfer an d Ruhr 1936 R	8A'40 Eher				
WERNER, Elisabeth (ie Elisabeth Bürstenbinder, 1838-1918)					
Am Altar before 1887 R	--	36A'32 Union	35A'30+	22A'22	19A'20
Glück auf! 1887 R	--	27A'33	21A'30+	19A'25	14A'20
Gesprengte Fesseln before 1887 R	--	26A'32	20A'30+	19A'23	12A'19
Vineta 1896 R	--	24A'32	18A'30+	17A'23	14A'20
Sankt Michael 1887 R	--	23A'32	16A'26+	14A'23	9A'20
Wege des Schicksals 1912 R	--	22A'33	19A'30	17A'22	10A'20
Fata Morgana 1896 R	--	18A'32	14A'29	13A'23	10A'20
Die Alpenfee 1889 R	--	17A'32	14A'26	12A'23	9A'20
Um hohen Preis 1887 R	--	--	17A'30	15A'25	8A'19
Gebannt u erlöst 1894 R	--	16A'33	14A'26	13A'23	8A'20
Flammenzeichen 1901 R	--	--	14A'30	13A'23	10A'20
Frühlingsboten 1894 R	14A'36	13A'32	--	11A'23	5A'19
Runen 1903 R	--	--	13A'26	11A'22	9A'19
Hexengold 1900 R	--	--	13A'26	10A'22	7A'20
Freie Bahn 1893 R	--	13A'32	--	12A'23	8A'20
Ein Held der Feder before 1887 R	--	--	--	13A'25	10A'20

APPENDIX A (con't.)

NAME	36/40	31/35	26/30	21/25	15/20
WESTKIRCH, Luise (1858-1941)					
Das Licht im Sumpf 1919 R	--	--	--	13A'23 Reclam	9A'20
Der Staatsanwalt 1907 R	12A'37 Union	9A'33	--	6A'22	3A'19
Im Teufelsmoor 1901 R	11A'38	--	--	10A'23	5A'19
Das Gespensterschloss 1920 R	9A'38	6A'33	--	--	3A'20
Die vom Rosenhof 1920 R	--	--	8A'27 Reclam	7A'21	4A'20
Der verlorene Sohn 1927 R	s 26/30	7A ?	5A'30		
Jenseits von Gut und Böse 1902 R	--	--	6A'27	5A'24	--
Auf der Menschheit Höhen	--	--	--	5A'23	2A'20
WILDUNG, Heinrich (nd)					
Im Grenzland Erz	19A'39 J Beltz	--	--	--	--
Der Spielmann c 1926 Erz	17A'39	9A'35	4A'30		
Die Kreuzfahrer 1930 Erz	11A'38	9A'35	2A'30		
WINTERFELD-PLATEN, Leontine von (nd)					
Das grosse Ja 1920 R	--	19A'30 F Bahn	18A'29	16A'21	10A'20
Vom wundersamen Wanderweg der Lori Reck 1916 R	--	19A'32	--	18A'24	12A'19

APPENDIX A (con't.)

NAME	36/40	31/35	26/30	21/25	15/20
WINTERFELD-PLATEN, Leontine von (con't.)					
Königin Not 1914 R	--	19A'35 F Bahn	18A'26	17A'25	12A'20
Das Lied von der blauen Blume 1913 R	--	17A'32	16A'26	15A'25	10A'19
Kreuzwege 1918 R	--	15A'34	14A'29	13A'19	11A'19
Das Schwert von Thule 1919 R	--	14A'33	13A'28	12A'19	10A'19
Eisenmutters Nestlinge 1916 Erz	--	--	--	--	14A'18
Lies Rainer 1921 Gesch	--	12A'31	--	11A'24	3A'21
Der Mann in Erz 1915 R	--	11A'31	--	10A'24	7A'15
ZOBELTITZ, Fedor von (1857-1934)					
Das nette Mädel 1909 R	--	ni'32	--	s 1920	11A'20 Dt V-Anst
Höhenluft 1906 R	--	--	--	10A'21 Reclam	9A'20
ZÖBERLEIN, Hans (1895-)					
Der Befehl des Gewissens 1937 R	12A'40 Eher				

BIBLIOGRAPHY

Arens, Hanns. "Bestseller, die keiner mehr lesen will," Die Welt der Literatur, Nr. 21 (24. Dezember 1964), 716.

Beer, Johannes (ed.). Der Romanführer. Der Inhalt der deutschen Romane und Novellen der Gegenwart. Teil I: Alverdes - Gurk. Teil II: Haensel - Musil. Teil III: Nabl - Zweig. Stuttgart: Hiersemann Verlags-G. m. b. H., 1952, 1953, 1954.

Bertkau, Dr. Friedrich (ed.). Kürschners deutscher Literatur-Kalender 1949. Berlin: Walter de Gruyter & Co., 1949.

________. Kürschners deutscher Literatur-Kalender 1952. Berlin: Walter de Gruyter & co., 1952.

Bonsels, Waldemar. Indienfahrt. Frankfurt a. M.: Rütten & Loening, 1922.

When individual novels such as this one are listed, they were used for the advertising material found in them. Refer to Chapter II.

Brockhaus, Der Grosse. Wiesbaden: Eberhard Brockhaus, 1952.

Brockhaus, Der Grose. Handbuch des Wissens in zwanzig Bänden. Leipzig: F. A. Brockhaus, 1928.

Conrad, Heinrich (ed.). Christian Gottlob Kayser's vollständiges Bücher-Lexikon. 31. Band: 1899 - 1902, A - K. Leipzig: Chr. Herm. Tauchnitz, 1903.

________. Christian Gottlob Kayser's vollständiges Bücher-Lexikon. 32. Band: 1899 - 1902, L - Z. Leipzig: Chr. Herm. Tauchnitz, 1904.

________. Christian Gottlob Kayser's vollständiges Bücher-Lexikon. 33. Band: 1903 - 1906, A - K. Leipzig: Chr. Herm. Tauchnitz, 1907.

________. Christian Gottlob Kayser's vollständiges Bücher-Lexikon. 34. Band: 1903 - 1906, L - Z. Leipzig: Chr. Herm. Tauchnitz, 1908.

________. Christian Gottlob Kayser's vollständiges Bücher-Lexikon. 35. Band: 1907 - 1910, A - K. Leipzig: Chr. Herm. Tauchnitz, 1911.

_______. Christian Gottlob Kayser's vollständiges Bücher-Lexikon. 36. Band: 1907 - 1910. L - Z. Leipzig: Chr. Herm. Tauchnitz, 1911.

Degener, Herrmann A. L. (ed.). Wer ist's? Leipzig: Verlag von H. A. Ludwig Degener, 1922.

_______. Wer ist's? Berlin: Verlag Herrmann Degener, 1928

_______. Degeners Wer ist's? Berlin: Verlag Herrmann Degener, 1935.

Deutsches Bücherverzeichnis. Erster Band: 1911 - 1914. A bis K. Leipzig: Verlag des Börsenvereins der deutschen Buchhändler, 1916.

Deutsches Bücherverzeichnis. Zweiter Band: 1911 - 1914. L bis Z. Leipzig: Verlag des Börsenvereins der deutschen Buchhandler, 1916.

Deutsches Bücherverzeichnis. Vierter Band: 1915 - 1920. A bis K. Leipzig: Verlag des Börsenvereins der deutschen Buchhändler, 1922.

Deutsches Bücherverzeichnis. Fünfter Band: 1915 - 1920. L bis Z. Leipzig: Verlag des Börsenvereins der deutschen Buchhändler, 1922.

Deutsches Bücherverzeichnis. Siebter Band: 1921 - 1925. A bis G. Leipzig: Verlag des Börsenvereins der deutschen Buchhandler, 1926.

Deutsches Bücherverzeichnis. Achter Band: 1921 - 1925. H bis O. Leipzig: Verlag des Börsenvereins der deutschen Buchhändler, 1927.

Deutsches Bücherverzeichnis. Neunter Band: 1921 - 1925. P bis Z. Leipzig: Verlag des Börsenvereins der deutschen Buchhandler, 1927.

Deutsches Bücherverzeichnis. Zwölfter Band: 1926 - 1930. A bis G. Leipzig: Verlag des Börsenvereins der deutschen Buchhandler, 1931.

Deutsches Bücherverzeichnis. Dreizehnter Band: 1926 - 1930. H bis O. Leipzig: Verlag des Börsenvereins der deutschen Buchhandler, 1932.

Deutsches Bücherverzeichnis. Vierzehnter Band: 1926 - 1930. P bis Z. Leipzig: Verlag des Börsenvereins der deutschen Buchhandler, 1932.

Deutsches Bücherverzeichnis. Siebzehnter Band: 1931 - 1935. A bis K. Leipzig: Verlag des Börsenvereins der deutschen Buchhändler, 1936.

Deutsches Bücherverzeichnis. Achtzehnter Band: 1931 - 1935. L bis Z. Leipzig: Verlag des Börsenvereins der deutschen Buchhändler, 1937.

Deutsches Bücherverzeichnis. Zwanzigster Band: 1936 - 1940. A bis K. Leipzig: Verlag des Börsenvereins der deutschen Buchhändler, 1942.

Deutsches Bücherverzeichnis. Einundzwanzigster Band: 1936 - 1940. L bis Z. Leipzig: Verlag des Börsenvereins der deutschen Buchhändler, 1943.

Diederichs, Eugen (ed.). Das deutsche Gesicht. Ein Weg zur Zukunft. Zum XXX. Jahr des Verlags Eugen Diederichs in Jena. Jena: Eugen Diederichs Verlag, 1926.

Federer, Heinrich. Berge und Menschen. Berlin: G. Grote'sche Verlagsbuchhandlung, 1920

Festschrift der Deutschen Dichter-Gedächtnis-Stiftung zum 10jährigen Bestehen 1901 - 1911. Hamburg-Grossborstel: Verlag der Deutschen Dichter-Gedächtnis-Stiftung, 1912.

Frenssen, Gustav. Jörn Uhl. Berlin: G. Grote'sche Verlagsbuchhandlung, 1919.

Greiner, Martin. Die Entstehung der modernen Unterhaltungsliteratur: Studien zum Trivialroman des 18. Jahrhunderts. Edited by Therese Posen. Reinbek bei Hamburg: Rowohlt Verlag, 1964.

Grimm, Hans. Volk ohne Raum. München: Albert Langen/Georg Müller, 1933.

Heer, J. C. An heiligen Wassern. Stuttgart/Berlin: J. G. Cotta'sche Buchhandlung Nachf., 1910.

Herzog, Rudolf. Das Lebenslied. Stuttgart/Berlin: J. G. Cotta'sche Buchhandlung Nachf., 1912.

_______. Der alten Sehnsucht Lied. Stuttgart/Berlin: J. G. Cotta'sche Buchhandlung Nachf., 1923.

_______. Die vom Niederrhein. Stuttgart/Berlin: J. G. Cotta'sche Buchhandlung Nachf., 1921.

Hinrichs' Katalog 1910 - 1912. Dreizehnter Band. 1. Teil. 1. Hälfte: Titelverzeichnis A - K. Leipzig: J. C. Hinrichs'sche Buchhandlung, 1913.

Hinrichs' Katalog 1910 - 1912. Dreizehnter Band. 1. Teil. 2. Hälfte: Titelverzeichnis L - Z. Leipzig: J. C. Hinrichs'sche Buchhandlung, 1913.

Keller, Paul. Ferien vom Ich. Breslau: Bergstadtverlag Wilh. Gottl. Korn, 1920.
The date of this publication is not shown in the book, but has been derived from the information found in the advertising and the data of this paper.

Koehler und Volckmar Barsortimentslagerkatalog 1924. Leipzig und Stuttgart: Koehler und Volckmar, 1924.

Koehler und Volckmar, Koch, Neff & Oetinger Barsortimentslagerkatalog 1941-42. Leipzig und Stuttgart: Koehler und Volckmar, Koch, Neff & Oetinger, 1942.

Kosch, Wilhelm. Deutsches Literatur-Lexikon, Biographisches und bibliographisches Handbuch in zwei Banden. Halle (Saale): Max Niemeyer Verlag, 1928.

________. Deutsches Literatur-Lexikon. Biographisches und bibliographisches Handbuch in vier Banden. Bern: A. Francke A.-G. Verlag, 1949.

Kunisch, Hermann. Handbuch der deutschen Gegenwartsliteratur. München: Nymphenburger Verlagshandlung G. m. b. H., 1965.

Kunze, Horst (ed.). Gelesen und Geliebt. Aus erfolgreichen Büchern 1750-1850. Berlin: Rütten & Loening, 1959.

Langenbucher, Wolfgang. Der aktuelle Unterhaltungsroman. Beiträge zu Geschichte und Theorie der massenhaft verbreiteten Literatur. Bonn: H. Bouvier und Co. Verlag, 1964.

Langenscheidt, Paul. Diplomatie der Ehe. Berlin: Dr. P. Langenscheidt, 1919.

________. Prinzessin Thea. Berlin: Dr. P. Langenscheidt, 1925.

Lee, Charles. The Hidden Public: The Story of the Book-Of-The-Month Club. Garden City: Doubleday & Company, Inc., 1958.

Lennartz, Franz. Deutsche Dichter und Schriftsteller unserer Zeit. Stuttgart: Alfred Kroner Verlag, 1959.

_______. Die Dichter unserer Zeit. Stuttgart: Alfred Kröner Verlag, 1938.

Lexikon der Frau in zwei Bänden. Zürich: Encyclios Verlag A.-G., 1953.

Löns, Hermann. Das zweite Gesicht. Jena: Eugen Diederichs Verlag, 1921.

Lüdtke, Dr. Gerhard (ed.). Kürschners deutscher Literatur-Kalender auf das Jahr 1925. Berlin und Leipzig: Walter de Gruyter & Co., 1925.

_______. Kürschners deutscher Literatur-Kalender auf das Jahr 1926. Berlin und Leipzig: Walter de Gruyter & Co., 1926.

_______. Kürschners deutscher Literatur-Kalender auf das Jahr 1930. Berlin und Leipzig: Walter de Gruyter & Co., 1930.

_______. Kürschners deutscher Literatur-Kalender auf das Jahr 1932. Berlin und Leipzig: Walter de Gruyter & Co., 1932.

_______. Kürschners deutscher Literatur-Kalender auf das Jahr 1934. Berlin und Leipzig: Walter de Gruyter & Co., 1934.

_______. Kürschners deutscher Literatur-Kalender 1937/38. Berlin und Leipzig: Walter de Gruyter & Co., 1937.

_______. Nekrolog zu Kürschners Literatur-Kalender 1901 - 1935. Berlin und Leipzig: Walter de Gruyter & Co., 1936.

Lüdtke, Gerhard and Metzner, Kurt (ed.). Kürschners deutscher Literatur-Kalender 1939. Berlin: Walter de Gruyter & Co., 1939.

Mann, Thomas. Das Gesamtwerk im Bermann-Fischer Verlag. October, 1936.
This is an advertising flier of four pages which bears the date of issue on the border.

Meiner, Dr. Annemarie. Reclam. Eine Geschichte der Universal-Bibliothek zu ihrem 75jährigen Bestehen. Leipzig: Verlag von Philipp Reclam Jun., 1942.

Menz, Dr. Gerhard (ed.). Der deutsche Buchhandel der Gegenwart in Selbstdarstellungen. Leipzig: Verlag von Felix Meiner, 1925.

Meyer, Heinrich. "Grundlagen der Literatursoziologie," Studium Generale, Jahrg. 17, Heft 1, 1964, 1-33.

Meyers Handbuch über die Literatur. Mannheim: Bibliographisches Institut - Allgemeiner Verlag, 1964.

Othmer, G. Othmers Vademecum des Buchhändlers und Bücherfreundes: Die wichtigsten Erscheinungen der schönwissenschaftlichen Literatur Deutschlands und des Auslandes mit biographischen und anderen Vermerken. Leipzig: J. C. Hinrichs'sche Buchhandlung, 1904.

Otto, August. Volksschriftsteller und Hauspoeten. Ein Beitrag zur Geschichte der volkstümlichen deutschen Literatur des 19. Jahrhunderts. 1. Heft. Soest: Rittersche Buchhandlung P. G. Cappell, 1907.

Pataky, Sophie (ed.). Lexikon deutscher Frauen der Feder. Berlin: Verlagsbuchhandlung von Carl Pataky, 1898.

Riess, Curt. Bestseller. Wie Bücher zu Welterfolgen wurden. München: Wilhelm Heyne Verlag, 1964.

Rötzer, H. G. "Die Antwort der gefallenen Dichter," Rheinischer Merkur, Nr. 47 (20. November 1964), 15.

Die Neue Rundschau. Stockholm: Bermann-Fischer Verlag, 1945.
This was a special edition published to commemorate Thomas Mann's seventieth birthday.

Schieber, Anna. Alle guten Geister... Heilbronn: Verlag von Eugen Salzer, 1920.

Schmitt, Fritz and Fricke, Gerhard. Deutsche Literaturgeschichte in Tabellen. Teil III: 1770 bis zur Gegenwart. Bonn: Athenäum-Verlag, 1952.

Schuder, Werner (ed.). Kürschners deutscher Literatur-Kalender 1958. Berlin: Walter de Gruyter & Co., 1958.

________. Kürschners deutscher Literatur-Kalender 1963. Berlin: Walter de Gruyter & Co., 1963.

Skowronnek, Richard. Morgenrot. Berlin und Wien: Verlag Ullstein & Co., 1916.

Spemann, Adolf. Wilhelm Spemann. Ein Baumeister unter den Verlegern. Stuttgart: J. Engelhorns Nachf. Adolf Spemann, 1943.

Stein, Werner. Kulturfahrplan. Berlin-Grunewald: F. A. Herbig Verlagsbuchhandlung (Walter Kahnert), 1954.

Türck, Hermann. Der geniale Mensch. Berlin: Wilhelm Borngräber Verlag, 1917.

Vollständiges Verzeichnis aller Werke, Buchserien und Gesamtausgaben mit Anmerkungen zur Verlagsgeschichte 1886 - 1956. Frankfurt am Main: S. Fischer Verlag, 1956.

Weise, Gerhard. "Die Flut der Groschen Romane. Konsumliteratur für Millionen," *Die Woche*, Freitag, den 30. Juli 1956, 3 (in the section "Kulturpolitik").

Wer ist Wer? Berlin-Grunewald: Arani Verlags-G. m. b. H., 1948.

Westermanns Monatshefte. 106. Jahrgang, Heft 12 (Dezember, 1965), 124.

Wolff, Julius. *Der Sülfmeister*. Berlin: G. Grote'sche Verlagsbuchhandlung, 1922.

Zahn, Ernst. *Das zweite Leben*. Stuttgart & Berlin: Deutsche Verlags-Anstalt, 1918.